OF SPINS, SIXES AND SURPRISES

Soumyadipta 'Shom' Biswas is a senior sales executive, a newspaper columnist, a short-story writer and a dabbler in sundry other things.

He used to write a weekly column on books in *The New Indian Express*, and his short stories have been published in literary magazines in India and Singapore, notably the *Quarterly Literary Review Singapore*, *Out of Print*, *The Bombay Review* and *Spark*. A regular quizzer, he was a semi-finalist at the University Challenge Quiz (2003–04) televised on BBC World. He is a collector of antique sports books, especially *Wisden*s, and is an active member of the Bangalore Writers Workshop (BWW).

Quizmaster, entrepreneur and a true knowledge seeker, **Titash Banerjea** has been actively involved with the world of quizzing for more than 10 years. He has hosted many events, including the Starmark Open Sports Quiz, the Cycle Heritage Quiz on Indian Heritage for schools, the Nairobi Rotary Quiz Night, and many more. He has been a champion quizzer, with victories in the Karnataka Quiz Association (KQA) Annual Sports Quiz, the KQA Cricket Quiz and Prahelika (organized by the ISI Kolkata) to name a few. After working with two multinational companies, he started his own knowledge services venture, Gyaanspace, which had been the primary content providers for CricIQ, the biggest ever online cricket quiz organized by ESPNcricinfo. He is currently based in Bengaluru.

Praise for the book

A thrilling ride through the history of Indian cricket, zooming in on moments that shaped the game and the personalities who raised its stature.

—Siddhartha Vaidyanathan
Writer and Author of *What's Wrong with You, Karthik*

OF SPINS, SIXES AND SURPRISES

---

50 Defining Moments in
INDIAN CRICKET

SHOM BISWAS and
TITASH BANERJEA

Published by
Rupa Publications India Pvt. Ltd 2023
7/16, Ansari Road, Daryaganj
New Delhi 110002

Sales centres:
Bengaluru Chennai
Hyderabad Jaipur Kathmandu
Kolkata Mumbai Prayagraj

Copyright © Shom Biswas and Titash Banerjea 2023
Illustrations by Arun Ramkumar

The views and opinions expressed in this book are the authors'
own and the facts are as reported by them which have been
verified to the extent possible, and the publishers are not in
any way liable for the same.

All rights reserved.
No part of this publication may be reproduced, transmitted,
or stored in a retrieval system, in any form or by any means,
electronic, mechanical, photocopying, recording or otherwise,
without the prior permission of the publisher.

P-ISBN: 978-93-5702-629-1
E-ISBN: 978-93-5702-850-9

First impression 2023

10 9 8 7 6 5 4 3 2 1

The moral right of the authors has been asserted.

Printed in India

This book is sold subject to the condition that it shall not,
by way of trade or otherwise, be lent, resold, hired out, or otherwise
circulated, without the publisher's prior consent, in any form of binding or
cover other than that in which it is published.

CONTENTS

Foreword	*vii*
Introduction	*ix*

1. The Ranji Wizardry — 1
2. Baloo's Moment — 7
3. Nayudu's Fireworks — 12
4. The Amar–Nissar Express — 17
5. Merchant of Excellence — 23
6. Hazare's Fightback — 28
7. A Test Win, st Last! — 32
8. The Great Sibling Rivalry — 37
9. Pataudi Eyes Greatness — 41
10. The Spin Quartet Arrives — 46
11. Sunny Days Have Come — 51
12. Others, Plus Chandra — 57
13. Sensation At Home too — 63
14. Kapil's Lazarus Moment — 67
15. The Golden Day — 73
16. Champions, Once Again — 80
17. The Six That Sunk India — 85
18. Power Play — 91
19. Then Came a New God — 97
20. The Domestic Cliffhanger — 104
21. Tigers at Home — 109
22. Darkness under Floodlights — 115
23. The Lord's Play — 120

24.	An Unexpected Collapse	125
25.	Desert Storm!	130
26.	Magic in Kotla	136
27.	A Very Very Special Miracle	142
28.	The Young Lords Rise	153
29.	Murder in the Dark	159
30.	Cutting a Path to Immortality	165
31.	The Wall and V.V.S.	172
32.	The Sultan of Multan	179
33.	Overpromised, Under-Delivered	185
34.	Dhoni's Devils	190
35.	A Monkey (Gate) off India's back	197
36.	A New World Order	204
37.	Chasing Away Nightmares	209
38.	Chin Music, Desi Style	214
39.	The Shot Heard around the World	219
40.	Father Time Comes Knocking	228
41.	New India, Old Captain	235
42.	'Do Not Go Gentle into That Good Night'	240
43.	A New Face of India Takes Centre Stage	247
44.	Mithali and Jhulan	253
45.	Performance of a Lifetime	258
46.	A Tryst with Destiny	262
47.	The Last Frontier	267
48.	A New Decade, a New Era	273
49.	Lambs to the Slaughter, No More	279
50.	Only the Beginning	285

Afterword	291
Acknowledgements	297

FOREWORD

It's not easy to be in love with cricket. The demands on one's time are truly endless. Once you're done with the live sport and the analysis for the day, there are reams and reams of wonderful matches to be relived and explored again. And then the debates, always the debates. Who was better, Mankad or Gavaskar or Tendulkar, Nissar or Bumrah, Bedi or Ashwin? There are so many conflicting and passionate views.

And now, Soumyadipta Biswas and Titash Banerjea have added one more wrinkle to those endless discussions with their *Of Spins, Sixes and Surprises*, talking about the matches that, in their opinion, had the maximum influence on the game in India.

There are many interesting and eclectic choices in the provided list that starts well before Independence, includes the likes of Palwankar Baloo and K.S. Ranjitsinhji, and does not forget to recount some of the great domestic Ranji matches that are sadly mostly forgotten. And I totally agree with their choice of the greatest-ever limited-over innings in the history of Indian cricket. Go on, read the book and find out for yourself!

To truly set the cat among the pigeons, the authors have decided to end with a set of All Time Indian XIs in all three formats. They have given their teams for different eras and have also come up with their All Time XIs in different formats inclusive of all eras.

I don't expect you to agree with all their choices, but I do think you will have a wonderful time going through the book and reliving some of the most iconic matches of our storied cricket history.

—Joy Bhattacharjya
Sports analyst, author and quizmaster

INTRODUCTION

The initial cricket matches one remembers watching were 30-minute highlight packages of the World Championship of Cricket in 1985, and one remembers the refrain of a neighbourhood uncle about India's young leg-spinner, that his full name contains the names of four gods! The players wore coloured clothes, but the television at our homes was black-and-white, so one saw different shades of grey.

One of the first cricket books one could remember reading was a small one (less than a hundred pages) about 15 great Test matches. It was easy to read and comprehend—three or four pages describing the action, a page of photographs and a full-page scorecard, that's all. There wasn't much in the way of context-setting, or any pretence of literary aspirations or profound research. This was cricket at its truest—talking about the match, the protagonists and what they did. Wasn't that fun?

It was! One could imagine Gordon Greenidge flaying the English attack for a rasping fourth-innings 214 not out at Lord's, or Joe Solomon hitting bullseye from square leg to run-out Ian Meckiff at the Gabba, or perhaps that day in Headingley, when Ian Botham decided that the word 'impossible' had no place in his dictionary.

One doesn't find such books these days. If you visit the cricket or sports section in bookshops, you will find either glossy coffee-table books, ghostwritten biographies of cricketers, or scholarly tomes on the history of the game. We, the co-writers, are the worst kind of cricket tragics—we are cricket-book tragics. And our type invariably tends to find others of the ilk. We have seen hagiographies of all kinds of cricketers in a cricket-book tragic's house, dog-eared at page 43. When asked how the book has been so far, a wry 'hmph...' comes our way. But we know that when the next hagiography lands up in the bookstore, they, and we, would end up buying copies nevertheless.

Then there are the delicious tomes, which we love to bits. We hunt for them in bookshops and online marketplaces, we read them like thrillers and we discuss the living daylights out of them. How could we not? Duncan Hamilton, Gideon Haigh, Ramachandra Guha are our heroes! But we also know that our 10-year-old selves would perhaps not have been able to sink our teeth into their works.

The inspiration behind this book came from a cousin's visit to Shom's house in early 2019. He is younger to Shom, and is a cricket tragic of a different variety. He is a television-cricket tragic. Not a run is scored in international cricket or in the Indian Premier League (IPL), which he has not watched on his television, or at least on the live-scores window in his mobile phone. He came by for a visit and looked over the shelves of the cricket books in Shom's house. 'Give me a book,' he requested. 'A book on cricket matches, a lot of cricket matches that I can read about.'

Shom could not think of a single book on his shelves that could fit the criteria. On Titash's recommendation, he eventually settled on *It Never Rains* by Peter Roebuck, one of our favourite cricket writers. The cousin did like the book, but we realized that it was not a perfect fit. There aren't many books that speak of the joy of simply reading about one excellent game of cricket after another. If they add up to tell a story, then that's great.

There is a big population of cricket fans, like this cousin, who love and follow the game with passion, who visit cricketing websites regularly, but who are not interested in reading a history book. They would rather read about the matches themselves, and even an illustrated biography of the next shiny superstar would not satiate their deep interest in the game.

What does one do if there aren't many books that tell the stories of matches? Well, one can certainly ask their cousin to go look for match reports on the Internet. But then there are fools like us who decide, with no prior experience of writing books, to, ahem, fill the gap in their bookshelves—and write that book themselves. Well, this is that book. *Of Spins, Sixes and Surprises* tracks the history of the game as it has been played in India, not in terms of an anthropological study but instead through matches. We present the 50 matches that, in our opinion, shaped the history of cricket in India.

You would notice that there is a bit of a bias towards more recent matches—but that is only natural, we feel. There was much about Indian cricket before 1983, but there has been even more since, in terms of impact. Debate is always welcome—is there any greater pleasure in life than debating to learn rather than to win?

1

THE RANJI WIZARDRY

He would later become Colonel His Highness Shri Sir Ranjitsinhji Vibhaji II, Jam Saheb of Nawanagar. At the turn of the twentieth century though, he was the ruler of the hearts and minds of a far greater reach. He was the most famous purveyor of the game that defined the Empire. Ranji, as he was more popularly known, never played for India, but cricket for India started with Ranji.

Ranji was 'the first Indian of any kind to become universally known and popular', as John Lord remarked in *The Maharajahs*. 'Universally known' obviously meant 'known to the Western world'. He was the first export to the West that had a 'Made in India' mark.

The Arrival of Ranji

It was serendipity that made this supple-wristed, keen-eyed young man land up in England. Ranji was not born a prince; he was a distant relative of the Jam Saheb of Nawanagar, a princely state in Gujarat. The king did not have an heir and thus decided to adopt Ranji in his youth. An actual heir arrived a few years later, and this prompted Ranji to be schooled away from the courts, in Rajkot. And from there, he was sent to England in 1888. Ranji was not yet 16.

K.S. Ranjitsinhji

In England, he joined the St Faith's College, where his cricketing skills were honed. He then moved to Cambridge University, where he made it to the university's cricket team (and was a Cambridge Blue[1]) in his final year. After that, he joined the county cricket team of Sussex, in 1895. In his first season with Sussex, he averaged 50 runs an innings, and came to be regarded as one of the best batter in the English county circuit. Within a year, he was playing for England.

While in Cambridge, Ranji faced many discriminations—he only became a Blue in his final year—before he got a chance to play for England. Lord Harris, the head of the selectors, ruled against his playing for England in the first Test at Lord's in the 1896 series for the reason that he was not born in England. The reason was flimsy—Lord Harris himself was born in West Indies. Again, fortune intervened; as per the laws of the game during those days, the selection of the Marylebone Cricket Club (MCC) team rested with the local cricket boards. The second Test being in Old Trafford, Manchester, the Lancashire Cricket board decided to field Ranji.

England had taken a 1-0 lead in the series, having won the first Test at Lord's. Australia, the visiting team, had the fantastic Clem Hill and George Giffen. Both could lay claim

---

[1]The colour commonly used by sports teams of the University of Cambridge.

to being at the top of the world—Hill as a batter and Giffen as an all-rounder. There was also Syd Gregory, the stylish, middle-order, attacking batter; Hugh Trumble, the off-spinning devil of the sticky wicket; and, Ernie Jones, then the quickest bowler in the world.

England was similarly blessed. Its team was captained by the Grand Old Man of Cricket, W.G. Grace, the predominant figure of cricket back then. Johnny Briggs was a reputed left-arm orthodox spinner of the day, and perhaps the most unfortunate of cricketers—he died in a mental asylum after having repeated bouts of epileptic seizures. John Thomas Hearne, or 'Old Jack' Hearne, was a fine medium-pace bowler. Stanley Jackson was a stylish middle-order batter. And in Tom Richardson, England had a fast bowler who was the equal of Australia's Ernie Jones. Among these greats of the era was Ranji.

England vs Australia, 2nd Test, Old Trafford, Manchester, 16-18 July 1896

George Henry Stevens 'Harry' Trott, the captain of Australia, won the toss and decided to bat on a fine, even-paced Old Trafford wicket. The decision was vindicated by opener Frank Iredale's 108 and Giffen's 80, which helped Australia post a healthy first innings total of 412. Australia's score could have been higher had it not been for a monster effort by Richardson, who sent down 68 overs to pick up 7 wickets for 168.

England fared much worse when it was their time to bat. Apart from Ranji's 62 and a rearguard undefeated 65 by wicketkeeper Arthur Frederick Augustus 'Dick' Lilley, nobody else in the vaunted English batting line-up could stand up to the Australian bowlers. England was bowled out for 231; and, 181 runs behind Australia's score, it was asked to follow-on, as per the prevailing rules of the match.

England's second innings started on a shaky note. Wickets fell at a steady rate, and at the close of play on Day 2, the team was 6 wickets down for 109—still 72 runs in arrears. Ranji was at the crease, with 41 to his name.

18 July 1896 was a defining day, for it was the first day in the history of cricket when an Indian man was the star of the game. The pages of the *Wisden Cricketers' Almanack* 1896 read: 'Much depended upon Ranjitsinhji, and the famous Indian fairly rose to the occasion, playing an innings that could, without exaggeration, be fairly described as marvellous. He... punished the Australian bowlers in a style that...no other English batter has approached.'[2]

The rest of the English batters could not support Ranji, and the England innings folded at 305. Ranji, having scored more than half of England's runs, remained unbeaten at 154. Incidentally, his entire score for the day was achieved before lunch; thus, he had scored 113 runs before lunch, making it the first instance of a 100 being scored by a batter before lunch.

Australia had 125 to chase—not a particularly easy task against the English bowlers, even if the target seemed small. Richardson tore into the Australians, bowling with fire and venom. Runs came at a trickle. Sydney (Syd) Edward Gregory curtailed his natural fluency to produce a 33 and that was worth more than the score board reflected.

At the drop of the seventh wicket though, the Australians were still 25 runs short. Trumble and James Joseph 'Stumper' Kelly, the wicketkeeper, got about producing a memorable last few hours of Test cricket. With only 9 runs to win, Kelly edged

---

[2]"Match Reports|England v Australia 1896', *ESPNcricinfo*, 15 March 1897, https://es.pn/3G3MV3q. Accessed on 31 March 2023.

a chance to his counterpart, Lilley—a chance that was spilled. And with it, so was the match. Trumble and Kelly got the remaining 9 runs, and won the match to square the series. Richardson's 13 wickets failed to get their reward.

But Indian cricket had won. Ranji had arrived.

Ranji continued his domination over the bowlers right until 1904. From 1895 to 1904, he scored more than 1,000 runs in each of the seasons. He was arguably the best and the most well-liked of all players, across the cricket-playing world. In 1904, he returned to Kathiawar to take over as the Jam Saheb of Nawanagar, and was regarded by most as a just and well-liked ruler. He died of a heart attack in 1933.

Noted writer and critic, Sir Neville Cardus, once wrote, 'When Ranji passed out of cricket, a wonder and a glory departed from the game forever.'[3] It was a deep sentiment but probably misplaced. The memory of the wonder and the glory gave rise to a cricketing nation, one of the world's most influential. What would have happened if instead of a prince from Kathiawar, an Indian boy would have reached Preston or Newcastle, Liverpool or London, and won their club sides a Football Association Challenge Cup? Would India have been a footballing nation then?

---

[3]'Oldest Surviving Cricket Film Featuring K.S. Ranjitsinhji', *Sportstar*, 22 June 2016, https://bit.ly/3YL1Ztr. Accessed on 13 March 2023.

> **SCORECARD**
>
> **Australia:** 412 all out (Iredale-108, Giffen-80; Richardson-7/168, Briggs-2/99) and 125/7 (Gregory-33, Trumble-17*; Richardson-6/76, Briggs-1/24)
>
> **England:** 231 all out (Lilley-65, Ranji-62; McKibbin-3/45, Trott-2/46) and following on 305 all out (Ranji-154*, Stoddart-41; McKibbin-3/61, Giffen-3/65)
>
> **Result:** Australia beat England by 3 wickets

2

BALOO'S MOMENT

When Ranji returned to India to lay claim to becoming the Jam Saheb of Nawanagar, he did not engage himself with Indian cricket, even after being approached by the Indian cricket administrators multiple times to help bolster the game in India. Though he was an Indian prince, he was strictly a cricketer of the British Empire.

Beginning of Organized Cricket in India

The roots of organized cricket in India can be traced back to the Parsis. One of the first organized cricket matches in India was the annual game played between the European members of the Bombay Gymkhana and the Zoroastrian Cricket Club in Bombay. This was christened the Presidency Match. The first of these games was played in 1877, and matches from 1892 onwards were given a first-class status. The Hindu Gymkhana and the Muslim Gymkhana developed good teams of their own, and by 1907, the Presidency Match became the Bombay Triangular, with the addition of the Hindus, and the Bombay Quadrangular with the Muslims in 1912. In 1937, a fifth team (after Hindus, Muslims, Europeans and Parsees), 'The Rest', comprising Buddhists, Jains and Indian Christians, was added. By the time of India's independence in 1947, this communal set-up was changed to the state-wise Ranji Trophy tournament, after a period of the previous uneasy coexistence, with both the tournaments (Ranji Trophy and Bombay Pentangular) being played in parallel and jostling for supremacy.

The first Indian cricket team to tour the British Isles was led by the Maharaja of Patiala, Bhupinder Singh. An administrator of repute and a great patron of cricket, albeit a player of little merit, his first-class batting average was an unimpressive 17.37. Among his other claims to fame was the donation to the Ranji Trophy, and an estimated 88 children that he fathered.

The Indian team was quite special, though. In tune with the times, it consisted of a fixed number of players from each religious community. Some were stalwarts from the local Indian tournaments, others patrons of the game (along with the Patiala ruler, there was Maharajkumar Shivajirao Gaekwad of Baroda), and a few were Indian students residing in England. The team comprised Hormasji Dorabji Kanga, an opening batter who was the first Indian to score a double-century in first-class cricket and later an administrator for Mumbai cricket. The Kanga League, which famously drenched the annual Mumbai tournament, where a 30 is supposed to be the equivalent of a century anywhere else, is named after him. Khershedji Rustomji Meherhomji, his opening partner, had a few memorable innings on that tour. Manek Pallon Bajana scored a century against Somerset, and later settled in England to play the rest of his cricket for that county. Bangalore Jayaram, the oldest in the team, was regarded as a hero by the last Governor-General of India, C. Rajagopalachari. Salamuddin, a student at the Muhammadan Anglo-Oriental College in Aligarh, had an excellent series with the ball. But the best players of the Indian team were the Palwankar brothers. There was Palwankar Shivram, an off-spinning all-rounder of repute. And there was Palwankar Baloo, that near-mythical genius of left-arm spin and India's first great bowler; he was the star of the team, and the hallowed English grounds was the canvas for his art.

Breaking the Barrier

It is important at this point to talk about Palwankar Baloo. He was a Dalit as per the Indian caste system. He came to cricket by happenstance, as part of the ground-staff at the Poona club. The English cricketer J.G. Greig once asked Baloo to throw some balls at him, so that he could practise his batting. The observant Baloo had picked the art of left-arm orthodox spin bowling during his groundskeeping chores, and Greig was impressed by his skills. Practising alongside Greig, Baloo honed his exceptional natural talent to become a seriously good left-arm spinner—perhaps the best in the world.

Eventually, the 'Hindus' team selectors for the Triangulars were forced to take notice of this Dalit. But there was strong objection to his selection. However, Baloo's talent was unmistakable, and eventually a place was made for him in the team. On the field, he was superior to any other player, but in the lunch break, he was not allowed to enter the players' pavilion. He would sit outside the pavilion steps, eating out of a separate plate and even washing it before going back to the field to play. Such was the humiliation faced by the greatest Indian cricketer of his time.

The performance of the Indian cricket team in that 1911 season was not memorable, if one goes just by the records. The team played 23 matches, of which 14 were given first-class status. They won two, drew two and lost 10 of those 14. But the fact that the team won two matches against county sides and became consistently competitive by the end of the tour went a long way in establishing the credibility of Indian cricket in the international cricketing arena. The first Indian win was against Leicestershire, and it was the second match that shaped Indian cricket.

Leicestershire vs Indians, Aylestone Road, Leicester, 13-15 July 1911

The Indians had lost every previous first-class match they had played, and there was not much hope for them against Leicestershire, although they were considered a quality team. Kanga and Meherhomji started off with an opening partnership of 178 runs, the Indians having chosen to bat first. Kanga, who captained this match in the Maharaja of Patiala's absence, scored 163; Meherhomji scored 86; and, with a stellar middle-order contribution from Shivram (85) and lower-order resistance from Salamuddin (43), the Indians scored a respectable 481 in the first innings.

The innings saw the main Indian bowlers, Baloo and Salamuddin, come to the fore. Sharing the bulk of the bowling, both had 5-wicket hauls. Despite an opening partnership of 116—with Wood scoring 43 and Knight, 62, Leicestershire folded for 283—both were asked to follow-on.

Baloo's magical left arm rose to the occasion again in the second innings, and he snared 6 Leicestershire wickets this time, to bowl them out for 248. His match haul was an impressive 11/185. With able support from Salamuddin, he was able to decimate the Leicestershire innings. The Indians' victory target was only 51, and the Indian batters achieved the target with minimum fuss, getting to 53 with the loss of 3 wickets.

Palwankar Baloo's journey in cricket and later political life was riddled with hardships, none of which were of his making. He had to face rejections and difficulties every step of the way. This, though, was his and his brother Shivram's moment under the sun. They had given Indian cricket its first true moment to savour. We owe it to ourselves to acknowledge this exceptional cricketer, this exceptional man.

SCORECARD

Indians: 481 all out (Kanga-163, Homji-86; Shipman-3/133, Brown-2/70) and 53/3 (Shivram-12*, Kanga-11*; Shipman-3/35)

Leicestershire: 283 all out (Knight-62, Wood-46; Salamuddin-5/79, Baloo-5/92) and following on 248 all out (Sharp-54*, Zsturman-46; Baloo-6/93, Warden-2/44)

Result: Indians beat Leicestershire by 7 wickets

3

NAYUDU'S FIREWORKS

When people are asked to put together a list of India's greatest ever batters, the name of Colonel Cottari Kanakaiya (C.K.) Nayudu might not feature on the list of a casual Indian cricket fan. He does not have the sheer volume of runs of the likes of Sachin Tendulkar, Rahul Dravid or Sunil Gavaskar. He does not even have the eye-popping statistics of a Vijay Merchant or a Vijay Hazare. However, to the diehard follower of Indian cricket and the ones who saw him play, the Colonel remains an icon. A pathbreaker, he set the platform for India's emergence on the world stage.

C.K. Nayudu was, in our opinion, without a shadow of a doubt, Indian cricket's first superstar, one who could take on the best that England and the world had to offer, and dominate. So, it was only fitting that it would be Nayudu who would play what can well be described as the most important innings in the history of Indian cricket—not one that propelled India to a great Test win, not one that sealed a series, but one that gave birth to the idea of India as a cricketing nation, even before the nation itself existed as a sovereign entity. One man stood up on 1 December 1926 and showed that India was now ready to challenge the world.

A Brief Background

The 1926–27 tour of the MCC to India was led by Arthur Gilligan, a former England captain. His country captaincy career started with hauls of 6 for 7 and 5 for 83 against South Africa.[4] Gilligan's career soon faced a major roadblock with a blow to the heart while batting during a Gentlemen versus Players game. He would never be the same bowler again, playing his last Test in 1925. However, his standing in the English game still remained strong, as he became a selector. The 1926–27 tour was his last tour abroad as a player.

C.K. Nayudu

The MCC team of 1926–27, although not a full England national team, was a formidable unit in its own right. It featured several players who had either represented the country or would represent the country in the near future. Prominent among those was the redoubtable seam bowler, Maurice Tate, the first triple centurion in Test cricket, Andrew Sandham, and England's future captain, Robert Elliott Storey 'Bob' Wyatt. This side was expected to steamroll its opponents on this tour.

The tour seemed to be following a predictable script as the MCC arrived in Bombay (now Mumbai) undefeated, having dominated teams from Sindh, Rajputana and Punjab. Except for an encounter against the Hindus and The Rest, the MCC held enormous first innings leads in all matches. No player or

---

[4]'Result | 1st Test, Birmingham', *ESPNcricinfo*, 14–17 June 1924, https://tinyurl.com/pmz83bme. Accessed on 31 August 2023.

team had looked like they could dominate the visitors or even pose a significant challenge. It was all about to change soon.

On 30 November 1926, the MCC faced its first opposition on the Bombay leg of the tour—the Hindus. The Hindus was easily the most formidable team that the MCC had faced so far. Captain Vithal Palwankar (younger brother of the famous spinner, Palwankar Baloo) was quietly confident. 'Let the MCC team come, and we will take care of the rest,' he told the Marathi newspaper, *Navakal*.[5] The Hindus line-up had some formidable stars: the Grand Old Man of Indian cricket D.B. Deodhar and future India internationals Janardan Navle, Ladha Ramji, Cotah Ramaswami and C.K. Nayudu.

Hindus vs MCC, Gymkhana Ground, Bombay, 30 November–1 December 1926

The Bombay Gymkhana played host to this encounter. The MCC won the toss and chose to bat. Day 1 brought loads of action, as the Somerset all-rounder Guy Fife Earle raced to a century, batting at number 6. His 130 was studded with eight sixes. The MCC's bowling mainstay, Tate, starred with the bat, making a vital 50. Shankarrao Godambe was the Hindus' main contributor with the ball, taking 4 wickets. The MCC team was bowled out for 363 in 87.1 overs. The Hindus came out to bat towards the end of Day 1, and lost a wicket before stumps, closing the day on 16 for 1.

On Day 2, the fall of the second wicket brought Nayudu at the crease. What followed was a remarkable exhibition of stroke play, the likes of which had seldom been seen in this

---

[5]Guha, Ramachandra, *Corner of a Foreign Field: The Indian History of a British Sport*, Penguin Random House, New Delhi, 2016, p. 194.

country. With Laxmidas Purshottamdas Jai proving an able ally and holding fort, Nayudu launched into a breathtaking attack. He picked Stuart Boyes out for special treatment, hitting him for sixes in consecutive overs. The crowd erupted with joy. Wyatt and all the English bowlers were attacked with the same ferocious intent. By the time Nayudu reached 50, he had already hit four sixes. The word of something special happening spread throughout the city. Soon, the crowd had grown manifold, with spectators climbing trees and occupying rooftops to catch a glimpse of the exploits. Nayudu's innings ended when he was caught by Boyes off George Geary having scored a sensational 153, which included a record 11 sixes. Each stroke seemed to be a statement that India was ready to make its presence felt in the world of cricket and had a player whose talents could rival any in the cricketing world. Godambe, India's hero with the ball, contributed some handy late order runs, making a crucial 58. The Hindus ended their innings just 7 runs short of the MCC total. With not too many overs remaining, a draw was a foregone conclusion. The MCC ended its second innings on 74 for 1.

The result, though, seemed inconsequential. The abiding memory of this match would be Nayudu's brilliance. A colossus had arrived in Indian cricket and we finally had our first home-grown superstar. Deodhar carried on Nayudu's good work by scoring a superb 148 in a match that followed.

Gilligan's Support to India's Test Status

Gilligan went back to England, suitably impressed. He was a fairly influential figure in the world of cricket, and his support to India's ascent to Test status set in motion a chain of events. The Board of Control for Cricket in India (BCCI) was formed in December 1928, with R.E. Grant Govan as president and Anthony de Mello as secretary. Soon, India was accepted into the Imperial Cricket Conference (the forerunner of the current governing body of cricket, the International Cricket Council).

Finally on 25 June 1932, it was time for India to play its first ever Test, against England at Lord's. It was fitting that the man to lead India out on the field was Colonel C.K. Nayudu. A new era had begun.

SCORECARD

MCC: 363 all out (Earle-130, Sandham-52; Godambe-4/80, Ramji-3/105) and 74/1 (Boyes-38*, Brown-16; Ramaswamy-1/26)

Hindus: 356 (Nayudu-153, Godambe-58; Astill-5/75, Geary-2/27)

Result: Match drawn

4

THE AMAR-NISSAR EXPRESS

The great Walter Hammond once said about the Indian Test captain Amar Singh, 'He came off the pitch like a crack of doom.'[6] If India's readiness for the big stage was exhibited by the exuberant stroke-play of C.K. Nayudu against Arthur Gilligan's MCC in 1926, India's presence at the grandest stage of all, the Mecca of Cricket, Lord's, was established through devastating pace. Indian cricket's first day in Tests, 25 June 1932, will forever be remembered for the memorable opening burst by arguably India's quickest opening bowling attack (till Jasprit Bumrah and Mohammad Shami started to operate in tandem). Mohammad Nissar and Amar Singh ensured that the cricketing world would not take its newest entrant lightly. This is the story of the first Test India played.

Post India's induction into the Imperial Cricket Conference, a tour by the MCC to India in 1930–31 and a return tour by an Indian team in the summer of 1931 was agreed upon. However, cricket could not remain insulated from the political and social climate prevailing in India at that time. The nation was rising against the British, and the clamour for independence had begun to get stronger. With the Indian National Congress

---

[6]Menon, Suresh, 'He Came off the Pitch Like the Crack of Doom', *Bangalore Mirror*, 21 June 2010, https://bit.ly/3yFdIiF. Accessed on 14 March 2023.

(INC) giving the clarion call for Purna Swaraj and the launch of the Civil Disobedience Movement by Mahatma Gandhi, the MCC tour to India was cancelled. Even the Bombay Quadrangular was called off. After a period of upheaval, for around two years, a decision was finally taken to go ahead with a tour of the Indian team to England in the summer of 1932.

Ranjitsinhji was the chairman of the selection committee to choose the Indian cricket team. One of his greatest contributions as a selector was spotting the talent of Amar Singh and handpicking him for the 1932 tour. Amar Singh made a lasting impact, and became India's highest wicket taker on the tour.

When it came to selecting the captain of India's team to England in 1932, it wasn't just cricketing logic that was at play. Indian cricket still heavily relied on the patronage of the princes. The Maharaja of Patiala and the Maharaja of Vizianagram or 'Vizzy' intensely lobbied for the captaincy. The Maharaja of Patiala was initially appointed the captain. However, soon, both Vizzy and he withdrew from the tour and the captaincy went in the hands of the Maharaja of Porbandar. It was famously pointed out that the Maharaja collected more Rolls Royces on the tour (three) than runs (a grand total of two in three first class matches). The side that the Maharaja was scheduled to lead was an eclectic mix of caste, creed and religion. They spoke 8–10 languages among them; and had Hindus, Muslims, Parsees and Sikhs. It was truly an All-India Team, which was what it was called officially. On 2 April 1932, the crew of India's cricketing elite set sail aboard the *RMS Strathnaver*, travelling from Bombay for the historic tour.

Apart from the lone Test, the Indian team played several first-class matches. One of the first examples of the class possessed by this Indian team was in its first encounter at

Lord's. C.K. Nayudu, now 36 years and six months old, gave the British public a glimpse of what Arthur Gilligan's team had experienced in 1926 at the Bombay Gymkhana, as he batted his way to a superb 118 not out against the MCC.

Before the first Test was scheduled to begin on 25 June, the Maharaja of Porbandar stepped down from captaincy in favour of Nayudu.[7] Even K.S. Ghanshyamsinhji of Limbdi, the vice-captain of the squad, did not play the Test match. England selected a formidable XI for the game, led by its tough-as-nails captain, Douglas Jardine. On a tricky pitch, Jardine won the toss and chose to bat.

England vs India, Only Test, Lord's Cricket Ground, London, 25-28 June 1932

A tidy number of 24,000 spectators gathered for the historic encounter at Lord's, and all of them must have gasped in awe at the sheer pace and quality of the Indian new ball attack. Nissar and Amar Singh were both 22 at the time, and they stormed in with gusto. The crowd was stunned when the great Herbert Sutcliffe was bowled by Nissar in just the third over, playing the ball on to his wicket. It was Percy Holmes' turn next, as he was bowled neck and crop by Nissar. 11 for 2. A third wicket followed soon, as Frank Woolley was run out. 19 for 3. A team of 11 debutants driven by two young bowlers with pace and skill was making life very uncomfortable for England. Amar Singh deservingly got his name on the scoreboard as he took the prized wicket of Wally Hammond, who had been bowled. Jardine and Les Ames engineered a strong comeback

---

[7]"The First Captain of Indian Cricket Team: C.K. Nayudu", *Sportsadda*, 13 February 2021, https://bit.ly/3K08bbD. Accessed on 31 March 2023.

with innings of 79 and 65, respectively. However, it was the exploits of the Indian new ball pair that the crowd, which was witness to the opening day at Lord's, talked about for years to come. England was bowled out for 259. Nissar got on the honours board at Lord's in his very first attempt, taking a memorable haul of 5 for 93. Amar Singh may have picked up just 2 wickets, conceding 75 runs, but his figures did not do justice to the quality of bowling he exhibited.

According to cricketer and author Charles Burgess (C.B.) Fry, Nissar was quicker than Harold Larwood—the same man who terrorized Australia in the infamous 1932–33 Bodyline series. The legendary cricket writer Sujit Mukherjee wrote, 'From the first ball he strained nerve and tendon and sinew to achieve his sole purpose—that of bowling fast.' As for Amar Singh, who ended the tour with 111 wickets, *Wisden* read, 'Amar Singh was the best bowler seen in England since the war.'[8]

Coming back to the Test, as expected, India's batters found the quality of the English bowling led by the formidable opening pair of Bill Bowes and Bill Voce a tough challenge. Naoomal Jeoomal Makhija, S. Wazir Ali and C.K. Nayudu put up creditable performances but could not mount a significant enough resistance against the English attack. India was bowled out for 189, and trailed by 70 runs.

In the second innings, the Indian bowlers once again made early inroads, reducing the English to 67 for 4. This time, it was Jahangir Khan, Vizzy's replacement in the Indian squad, who made the biggest impact. Jahangir Khan, whose son Majid Khan went on to become a star for the Pakistan team, took 4 wickets—his list of wickets reads like a who's who of English

---

[8] Menon, Suresh, 'He Came Off the Pitch Like the Crack of Doom', *Bangalore Mirror*, 21 June 2010, https://bit.ly/40PNR3C. Accessed on 31 March 2023.

victims—Percy Holmes, Frank Woolley, Wally Hammond and Eddie Paynter. For England, it was once again Jardine who stood tall, adding a resolute 85. Making a steady recovery after the early setbacks, England declared their second innings at 275 for 8, setting India a formidable target of 346 runs.

In the fourth innings, England clinically scythed their way through the Indian batting line-up, reducing it to 108 for 7. It was then that Amar Singh stepped up to give the Lord's faithful another reason to remember him by. He batted his way to score an impressive half-century, the first ever by an Indian in a Test match, that too in India's very first Test match. The Indian innings ended on a score of 187—it lost the match by 158 runs. The last batter dismissed was Amar Singh.

He continued to be a thorn in England's flesh for the next few years, as he took a haul of 7 for 86 against England at Chennai in 1934; it remained the best bowling spell by an Indian until Vinoo Mankad's wizardry at the same venue 18 years later. Nissar and Amar Singh repeated their heroics at Lord's in 1936, bowling England out for 134 in the host country's first innings in a Test. This time, it was Amar Singh who played the star role, with a remarkable figure of 6 for 35.

Amar Singh tragically died of pneumonia when he was just entering his cricketing prime, at the age of 29 years and 169 days. The Indian cricket fan ought to be forever grateful to Amar Singh and Mohammad Nissar for letting the world know that Indian cricket was here to stay. India can proudly claim to have one of the best collections of fast bowlers in the world today, but let them all remember that it all started with a crack of doom.

SCORECARD

England: 259 all out (Jardine-79, Ames-65; Nissar-5/93, Nayudu-2/40) and 275/8 declared (Jardine-85*, Paynter-54; Jahangir Khan-4/60, Amar Singh-2/84)

India: 189 all out (Nayudu-40, Jaoomal-33; Bowes-4/49, Voce-3/23) and 187 all out (Amar Singh-51, S. Wazir Ali-39; Hammond-3/9, Voce-2/28)

Result: England beat India by 158 runs

5

MERCHANT OF EXCELLENCE

While India had begun playing Test cricket abroad, the national cricket scene was in need of a structure. The Bombay Quadrangular was in the national consciousness, and there were other tournaments in cricketing centres across India. This was also the time of the country coming together and unshackling itself from the British rule. Mahatma Gandhi's Salt Satyagraha had got the country together, and a tournament that pitted communities against one another naturally seemed at odds with the nation's direction. As a result, the Bombay Quadrangular was paused between 1930 and 1934, and the time seemed perfect for an all-India state-wise cricket tournament, which was in line with a united India.

However, it was not a smooth sail. The Quadrangular was extremely popular, a lot more popular in the minds of the national cricket enthusiasts than the new, state-wise tournament, and its return was eagerly awaited. J.C. Maitra, sports editor of the *Bombay Chronicle* and a proponent of the national zonal cricket tournament (as opposed to a communal one) had to agree.

But it would be unfair to blame the common cricket fan. The Quadrangular was a popular, long-standing tournament, and the anticipation during the four-year gap had made it even more so. On the other hand, state boundaries had only recently been drawn in many cases, and several of the teams in this nationwide cricket tournament were aggregated teams from multiple states. Take the example of a few teams in the tournament: United Provinces, Northern India, Central Provinces and Berar, and Central India. These are not teams with a commonality or drawn out of a common entity, be it linguistic or cultural. On the other hand, the Parsees, Europeans, Hindus and Muslims can very easily be identified with, and supported by, the members of those communities. However, as the Quadrangular lost importance and the inter-state competition expanded to include most states, the latter became immensely popular.

Some excellent books have been written on the competition between the two tournaments. For now, it's enough to say that some of the most influential administrators of the times were involved in the fracas. Ranji got involved. Even the Mahatma's opinion was sought.[9] The winning team of the tournament was almost given the Lord Willingdon Trophy instead of the Ranji Trophy! In the two competing factions were the Maharaja of Patiala and the Maharajkumar of Vizianagram —both of whom offered to present the trophy given to the winner. Maharaja of Patiala won in the end, and his trophy, named the Ranji Trophy, was eventually the one that was presented, and not the one from Vizianagram, which was the one named after Lord Willingdon.

The inter-zonal tournament eventually started in 1934. This first edition included 15 teams. South Zone was represented by Madras, Mysore and Hyderabad; West by Gujarat, Maharashtra,

---

[9]Ganguly, Arghya, 'The Link between Cricket and Mahatma Gandhi', *The Times of India*, 30 January 2010, https://bit.ly/3KnlEf9. Accessed on 31 March 2023.

Bombay, Sind and Western India; North by United Provinces, Northern India, Delhi, Southern Punjab and the Army; East by Central Provinces and Berar and Central India.

The first match of the competition was played on 4 November 1934, between Madras and Mysore. It still holds a unique record in the annals of Indian cricket—it was completed in one day! Mysore, batting first, were dismissed for 48. Madras then batted, and was all out for 130. Mysore then proceeded to get all out for 59, thus handing out an innings-and-23-run victory to Madras, all on Day 1 of the match.[10]

Brilliant performances littered the tournament. S.M. Hadi of Hyderabad was the first man to score a century in the tournament, with an unbeaten 132 against Madras. George Abell of Northern India scored the tournament's first double-hundred—201 in his match against the Army. Baqa Jilani, who later gained infamy over a fracas with Nayudu on the England tour of 1936, took a hat-trick in the semi-final, playing for Northern India against Southern Punjab. A.G. Ram Singh of Madras, the patriarch of a family that had seen first-class cricketers for three generations, took the most wickets in the tournament, scalping 22 batters.

Bombay vs Northern India, Ranji Trophy Final, Gymkhana Ground, Bombay, 9–12 March 1935

The tournament eventually reached its finals on 9 March, at the Gymkhana Ground was meeting Northern India in the finals. Kanga might lay claim to being the first batter of the 'Bombay School' of batting, but the first true great of that pedigree was

---

[10]'Ranji Trophy, 1934/35', *CrincinfoIndia*, https://bit.ly/3yB3JdZ. Accessed on 14 March 2023.

indubitably Vijaysingh Madhavji Merchant. This tournament saw the establishment of the legend Vijay Merchant.

The two teams were almost equally strong on paper. Bombay had, along with Merchant, present and future India players in wicketkeeper Dattaram Hindlekar and captain L.P. Jai. Northern India had Baqa Jilani, fresh from his hat-trick in the semi-final; George Abell of the double hundred fame; Amir Elahi who went on to become a dual-international for India and Pakistan; quick bowler Devraj Puri; and the father of the voice of sports on Doordarshan in the '80s and the '90s, Narottam Puri.

Bombay batted first. The Northern India bowlers breathed fire, with Puri, Saeed Ahmed and Mubarak Ali taking wickets (Jilani had an off day) to dismiss Bombay for 266. Merchant was run-out for 9 runs. Even that score would have been difficult to reach had it not been for a rearguard 54 by the No. 8 batter Padmakar Chury.

In reply, Northern India could not build up substantial partnerships either and collapsed for 219, giving Bombay an unexpected first-innings lead. The chief wicket-taker for Bombay was Merchant, who took three wickets with his medium-pacers.

Bombay's second innings saw Merchant excel again, this time displaying full batting pomp. After 5 wickets had fallen for 70, with Bombay teetering on the edge, Merchant had a scintillating 135-run partnership with experienced quick-bowling all-rounder Hormasji Vajifdar. Merchant scored a brilliant 120, Vajifdar had 71, and Bombay crept up to a respectable round 300 all out, leaving Northern India with the daunting task of scoring 348 runs to win the final.

Vajifdar was an equal hero of the finals, along with Merchant, as he got his best first-class performance of 8/40, leaving the Northern India team all out for 139 runs—a full 208 runs short.

Bombay had won the tournament, the first of many, helped by a scintillating innings by their star player Merchant, and a once-in-a-lifetime performance by Vajifdar.

Vijay Merchant with the Ranji Trophy

SCORECARD

Bombay: 266 all out (Chury-54, Jai-41; Mubarak Ali-4/71, Puri-2/44) and 300 all out (Merchant-120, Vajifdar-71; Puri-6/101, Jilani-3/58)

Northern India: 219 all out (Ahmed Raza-50, Abell-43; Merchant-3/53, Wadkar-2/26) and 139 all out (Ahmed Raza-62*, Hussain-19; Vajifdar-8/40, Havewala-2/43)

Result: Bombay beat Northern India by 208 runs

6

HAZARE'S FIGHTBACK

Vijay Hazare was the other half of the great Indian batting duo of the '30s and the '40s. Merchant's and Hazare's careers coincided, and the two were constantly pitted against each other: Hindus (Merchant) versus The Rest (Hazare), at the Pentangular; and Bombay (Merchant) versus Baroda or Maharashtra (Hazare) for the Ranji Trophy. 'Merchant or Hazare—who is better?' was the question that created many a storm in cricketing circles in those days.

Unlike Merchant's correct, classical technique and feline grace, Hazare's stance and technique appeared stodgier and more homespun. Author and cricket commentator John Arlott described it as following: '…one hand at the extreme top of his bat handle, the other at the extreme bottom pressing against the blade, the bat between the pads, so that it cannot be moved straight forward or straight back, the batter's entire weight thrown down upon it, right shoulder pulling around to set him foursquare to the bowler'.[11]

Merchant and Hazare were unfortunate that the Second World War coincided with the zenith of their careers. Merchant only played 10 Test matches, and Hazare, the slightly younger man, played 30. Hazare was also stuck with weaker teams

---

[11]Arlott, Johnm, 'A Man with "No Nerves at All"', *Rediff.com*, 21 December 2004, https://bit.ly/3TkXeph. Accessed on 15 March 2023.

compared to Merchant in the domestic tournaments. The Rest was no match for Merchant's 'Hindus' at the Pentangular, and Bombay was the predominant team in the Ranji Trophy.

That didn't stop Hazare from producing some amazing rearguards, often going toe-to-toe with Merchant, perhaps the premier Indian batter of his era. He scored two triple-hundreds, one for Maharashtra against Poona in 1939–40, and the other in a memorable match for The Rest against Hindus in the finals of the Pentangular of 1943–44. He scored 309 in a completed innings of 387 by The Rest, compiling nearly 80 per cent of the team's total. The Rest, however, lost to the Hindus by an innings. Such were the life and times of Vijay Samuel Hazare.

Playing these boy-on-the-burning-deck innings so often, Hazare was more prepared than most to play a memorable hand in a Test match at Australia, one of the best teams the world has seen. This was at the Adelaide Oval in 1948, against Sir Donald Bradman's rampaging team, which went on to be termed the Invincibles. Sid Barnes and Arthur Robert Morris as openers; Arthur Lindsay Hassett and the precocious Neil Harvey in the middle-order; Don Tallon as the wicketkeeper; one of the premier fast-bowling combinations the world has ever seen in Ray Lindwall and Keith Miller; and above all else, Bradman himself—this was a formidable team, with claims to be considered the greatest of all time. It was against them that Hazare's best was crafted.

Australia vs India, 4th Test, Adelaide Oval, Adelaide, 23-28 January 1948

Bradman won the toss and elected to bat. This proved to be a prudent decision. Morris fell early, but Barnes and Bradman piled up runs. After a 236-run partnership, Barnes returned to the pavilion after a workman-like 112. Hassett joined Bradman, and the runs continued. Bradman completed the most predictable of double-hundreds, and got out to Hazare's medium pace soon after, for 201. The third consecutive century-partnership followed, this time between Hassett and the debonair all-rounder Miller, before the latter departed for a well-made 67. The rest of the team continued to keep the scoreboard ticking, and the total score eventually stood at 674. Hassett was stranded not out, although he fell 2 runs short of his double hundred.

India, batting next, was immediately in trouble, losing its opener Chandu Sarwate and makeshift No. 3, wicketkeeper Probir Sen with 6 runs on the board. Captain Lala Amarnath and the other opener, Mankad, steadied the innings somewhat. Amarnath scored a quick-fire 46 before getting caught by Bradman off the spinner Ian Johnson. Hazare walked in, and batted carefully, along with Mankad, to take the team score beyond a hundred. Mankad lost his wicket a little while later, and Gul Mohammad departed next. Hazare was steady at the other end. He was joined by Dattu Phadkar, and they forged a solid partnership. Both played carefully but with little flourish. However, the runs followed. Hazare got a deserved hundred, but was dismissed soon after, leg before wicket (LBW) to Johnson for a well-made 116. The Indian innings finished within 60 runs of Hazare's dismissal, but not before Phadkar managed to complete his century as well and finished on 123. Despite the bravery and concentration of Hazare and Phadkar, India were nearly 300 runs behind in the first innings and had to follow-on.

India's second outing followed similar patterns. However, this time there was no Phadkar to provide support to Hazare. The latter stepped in to bat with the scorecard at 0/2. He was in the zone during the first innings, and never did he get out of the zone in the second innings. Support was meagre—Colonel Hemchandra 'Hemu' Adhikari scored 51 and Gul Mohammed 34, but there was no other to provide company. He played an innings of rare restraint, determination and focus, and was seventh out for a sparkling 145. India was all out at 277, still 16 runs short of the runs required to make Australia bat again.

Vijay Hazare

This was the apogee of Hazare, the batter. It was unfortunate that Hazare, as well as Merchant, had lost more than six years of their cricketing prime to the Second World War, but their international records are still formidable, with near-50-run averages. The gentlest and most retiring of Indian batters, for all his efforts, could not quite make Australia bat again.

SCORECARD

Australia: 674 all out (Bradman-201, Hassett-198*; Rangachari-4/141, Phadkar-2/74)

India: 381 all out (Phadkar-123, Hazare-116; Johnson-4/64, Miller-2/39) and following on 277 all out (Hazare-145, Adhikari-51; Lindwall-7/38, Miller-1/13)

Result: Australia beat India by an innings and 16 runs

7

A TEST WIN, AT LAST!

With the batting prowess of Merchant and Hazare ably backed by Pahlan Ratanji 'Polly' Umrigar, and with all-rounders of the pedigree of Amarnath, Mankad and Phadkar, it would have been fair to say that the Indian Test team had started progressing from the 'minnows' stage to the 'competitive' stage. But to establish themselves as the team of a serious cricketing nation, the Indians had to start winning. But they hadn't yet, not until the middle of the last century. That changed during the 1951–52 tour of the English cricket team to India. And fittingly, the often-unlucky last-man-standing of Indian cricket, Vijay Hazare, became the man to lead India to that cherished moment.

English cricket was going through its own winds of changes. Cricket in England was in the early 1950s, still in the thralls of the aristocracy—only an amateur could be the captain of the English side. Most English counties would also enlist only an amateur as their captain. Perfectly deserving candidates, with astute cricketing brains, would never get to captain England because they were not born with the kind of privileged backgrounds to take cricket as a pastime and not a profession. Thus, undeserving players would get a chance to not just play for, but even lead the team, solely for being amateurs. However, there were murmurs of dissent among the ranks. During that time, Frederick Richard 'Freddie' Brown, an amateur and an adequate cricketer at the highest level, was the captain of the English team. But he refused to take the long tour to India, and the MCC was left to find an alternative to Brown. The selectors opted for Nigel Howard, a distinctly average cricketer—nowhere close to being good enough to represent England solely as a player—as perhaps the best amateur player available in the counties, to lead the English. Another amateur, Donald Carr, became the vice-captain.

Also, as Stephen Lynch says in an article in 2015 in ESPNcricinfo, the English perhaps did not consider the Indian team seriously enough to take a full-strength squad on tour.[12] Len Hutton and Denis Compton did not tour, and neither did Jim Laker and Alec Bedser. This wasn't some kind of a Sunday League side, though; there were all-time greats in Tom Graveney and Brian Statham in the English ranks, and other useful players in off-spinner Roy Tattersall, and all-rounders Allan Watkins and Jack Robertson. And anyway, one can only beat the team that's in front of oneself!

This series also saw India's ranks being bolstered by the addition of youngsters Vijay Manjrekar and Pankaj Roy, and the precocious leg-spinner Subhash Gupte—the three players who served Indian cricket with distinction in the years to come.

India had the upper hand in the first Test of the series, played in Delhi. Merchant and Hazare both scored centuries, but England was saved in the second innings by a performance of great determination by the all-rounder Watkins. There was some bad news in store for India: Merchant had injured his shoulder heavily while fielding during England's second innings,

---

[12]Lynch, Stephen, 'The Forgotten English Captain', *ESPNcricinfo*, 11 May 2015, http://tinyurl.com/2wrn6bhr. Accessed on 4 September 2023.

Vinoo Mankad

and had no further part to play in the series. It indeed became the last Test Merchant played, and was a bittersweet ending for India's most complete batter in the initial cricketing years. The Test ended in a draw.

The second Test was a draw as well. Roy, the bespectacled Bengal opener, filled in well for Merchant, scoring a century, and Hazare too got a hundred. In reply, England posed a respectable total, largely due to Graveney's 175 and another stellar performance by Watkins. Mankad was having a good series with the ball, and in this match, he contributed with the bat as well. The third Test at the Eden Gardens, Calcutta (now Kolkata) saw another draw, only memorable for pitifully slow scoring rates.

India vs England, 4th Test, M.A. Chidambaram Stadium, Madras, 23-28 January 1952

The fourth Test in Kanpur saw a result that was not favourable for India. On a pitch that took turn from the first day, English spinners Tattersall, Robertson and left-armer Malcolm Hilton destroyed the Indian batting line-up for 121 and 157 in two innings, and the English side won by 8 wickets. Good bowling in the first innings by Mankad and off-spinner Ghulam Ahmed was not good enough for India.

After showing considerable promise throughout the series, the Indians were on the brink of another tame series defeat. The fifth and final Test, at the M.A. Chidambaram stadium in Madras (now Chennai), was a do-or-die contest for India.

Umrigar was having a poor series, and was considered for the sack. But the selectors decided to persist with him for one last time. And that eventually turned out to be a masterstroke.

England's captain Howard, who had been consistently poor in the series, had now contracted pleurisy and could not lead the team. Vice captain Carr, who had played only one match in the series previously, was asked to lead the team in his absence. He won the toss and elected to bat first.

England's first innings was all about the brilliant left-arm spin of Vinoo Mankad. England were all out for 266— Robertson and the wicketkeeper Dick Spooner put up some fight, but once Spooner was dismissed by Hazare, the rest of the England batting line-up collapsed under the turn and trickery of Mankad, who took 8 wickets.

India's first innings could be seen as a story of two halves. The first half was dominated by Roy. In an innings of control, discipline and some crisp strokes square of the wicket, Roy scored 111 and laid the platform for the rest of the innings. The others in the top order got starts but failed to capitalize, and by the time Amarnath was dismissed, India were 216/5, still 50 runs short of England's first innings total.

But then came the second half of the innings, starting with a partnership of brave stroke play from Umrigar and all-rounder Phadkar. The two put on a century-partnership, and after Phadkar was for 61, Umrigar continued to score at a fast clip with the next man in, quick bowler C.D. Gopinath.

This partnership yielded nearly a 100 runs. Eventually, Hazare declared the innings at 457/9, with Umrigar not out on 130. India had a near-200 run lead.

In England's second innings, on a pitch offering some turn, Mankad again got about to work on the English batters, and in this innings, he was ably assisted by off-spinner Ghulam Ahmed. Despite a hint of resistance by the all-rounders Robertson and Watkins, England finished their second innings at 183, to hand India an easy innings-and-8-run victory. Both Mankad and Ghulam Ahmed ended with 4 wickets.

Mankad finished with a match-haul of 12/108. Umrigar and Roy had scored hundreds, and Hazare had led the Indian team to the holy grail—a Test victory.

On a side note, the return series, when India toured England in 1952, saw England fielding its full-strength team! And this was also the series when, for the first time, a professional, Sir Leonard Hutton, was asked to captain England.

SCORECARD

England: 266 all out (Robertson-77, Spooner-66; Mankad-8/55, Hazare-1/15) and 183 all out (Robertson-56, Watkins-48; Mankad-4/53, Ahmed-4/77)

India: 457/9 declared (Umrigar-130*, Roy-111; Carr-2/84, Tattersall-2/94)

Result: India beat England by an innings and 8 runs

8

THE GREAT SIBLING RIVALRY

We have stayed away from the politics of India's struggle for independence, and the subsequent pain of Partition. But what is cricket if not a reflection of real life? And this is the point we are trying to make in the book when Partition and geopolitics seep into our game... Let us now delve deeper into the beginning of the great cricketing rivalry between India and Pakistan, a rivalry which could lay legitimate claim to being the biggest rivalry in the cricketing world. Pakistan toured India in 1952 to play five Test matches. It had been five years since Partition.

Lala Amarnath, who was India's captain, was born in Lahore and had played with many of the Pakistan players in Ranji Trophy. Abdul Hafeez Kardar, an Oxford Blue, had played three Tests for India before Partition, and had appeared for Northern India in Ranji Trophy and for the Muslims in the Bombay Pentangular. Amir Elahi was another Pakistani who had played Test cricket for India previously. Gul Mohammad played for India in this match, and went on to play for Pakistan in 1955. It was truly a sibling rivalry. Those were simpler times, when competitiveness on the field did not extend outside the playing arena.

The first Test was played in Delhi, and India's then President Rajendra Prasad was in attendance. It was a four-day Test. India fielded a strong batting line-up, with Mankad, Roy, Hazare, Manjrekar, Umrigar and Gul Mohammed, along with captain Amarnath. Pakistan had the better quick bowling attack, with Fazal Mahmood and Khan Mohammad; and in Amir Elahi and Abdul Hafeez Kardar, a very competitive spin attack. Indian batting versus Pakistani bowling, which became the bedrock of the rivalry, was apparently in place right from day one. However, Pakistan had in its ranks the original subcontinental Little Master, Hanif Mohammad, then a 17-year-old schoolboy.

India vs Pakistan, 1st Test, Feroz Shah Kotla, Delhi, 16–18 October 1952

India won the toss and elected to bat. Khan Mohammad was a canny medium-fast bowler, perhaps not as feted as his long-time fast bowling companion, Fazal Mahmood, but this was his moment to give the debutantes a quick breakthrough. He dislodged the stumps of Mankad and Roy in quick succession, and by the end of his first spell, India was two down for 26. The stage was set for an all-hands-on-deck Hazare innings, and he did not disappoint. While wickets kept falling at the other end—Fazal Mahmood, Kardar and Elahi got on the act as well—Hazare continued to provide stability to the innings. He was the sixth out at 76, with the team score at 180. And with Gul Mohammad soon to follow, India was precariously placed at seven-down for less than 200.

It was time for another rearguard recovery from India. Adhikari came to the fore now, initially with important short partnerships with medium-pacer G.S. Ramchand and wicketkeeper Probir Sen, and then with a near-miraculous 109-run partnership for the last wicket with off-spinner Ghulam

Ahmed. Ahmed got a half century, Adhikari remained not out on 81, and India managed to score a respectable 372 in the first innings.

Pakistan opened its innings with Nazar Mohammad and Hanif Mohammad. It is interesting to note that their respective sons, Mudassar Nazar and Shoaib Mohammad, also played together for Pakistan in the future. Coming back to the match, they made a sedate, solid start. The score inched up to 64, when Nazar Mohammad was run out. This was the trigger for India's premier left-arm spinner Mankad to cast a web around the Pakistani batters. Young Hanif held up one end, while wickets kept falling from the other. Eventually, Hanif was out to the wily Mankad for 51, with the team total at 112. Fazal Mahmood entertained the crowd for a little while, hitting out against the Indian bowling, but eventually Pakistan was all out for 150 and asked to follow on. Mankad had a memorable bowling figure of 47 overs, 27 maidens, 52 runs and 8 wickets.

Pakistan's second innings did not begin as well as the first one did. Hanif got out quickly, bowled by India's captain Amarnath. The familiar pattern of the first innings followed, with Mankad tightening his grip around the Pakistani batters. In the second innings, he was ably supported by Ghulam Ahmed in a near-repeat of India's first Test win against England. Imtiaz Ahmed and Pakistani captain Kardar offered brave resistance, and Fazal Mahmood employed the long handle yet again. However, Pakistan was dismissed for 152. India got home comfortably, winning by an innings and 70 runs.

The Pakistanis, though, were not disheartened, and came storming back in the second Test in Lucknow to secure an innings victory. Fazal Mahmood's 12 wickets and Nazar Mohammad's hundred were the notable performances. India won the third Test at Brabourne Stadium, Bombay, through performances by Hazare and Mankad. The two other Tests were drawn, thus giving India a series victory. It was, however, a creditable performance by Pakistan, and the cricketing world was in little doubt that this would be a significant cricketing rivalry in the future, and Hanif Mohammad and Fazal Mahmood were players who would be at the helm of Pakistani cricket's future development.

SCORECARD

India: 372 all out (Adhikari-81*, Hazare-76; Elahi-4/134, Khan Mohammad-2/52)

Pakistan: 150 all out (Hanif Mohammad-51, Nazar Mohammad-27; Mankad-8/52, Ghulam Ahmed-1/51) and following on 152 all out (Kardar-43*, Imtiaz-41, Mankad-5/79, Ghulam Ahmed-4/35)

Result: India beat Pakistan by an innings and 70 runs

9

PATAUDI EYES GREATNESS

'Someone opened a dressing room window at that instant and there was a black hole behind the bowler's arm.'[13] This was Nariman Jamshedji 'Nari' Contractor describing the moment just before getting struck by a brutal delivery from West Indies fast bowler Charlie Griffith, which lead to a deep fracture and unfortunately ended his career. It was perhaps the most visceral, sickening moment in the history of Indian Test match cricket in 1962. Thankfully, with the efforts of the general physicians and a neurosurgeon who flew in from Trinidad, Contractor's life was saved. However, his Test career was over.

The catastrophic injury led to Mansoor Ali Khan Pataudi, the Nawab of Pataudi (Jr), taking over as the captain of India. At the time, he was the youngest captain in the history of Test cricket. In 2004, Zimbabwe's Tatenda Taibu surpassed his record, which in turn was later broken by Rashid Khan of Afghanistan. Pataudi's performances for Oxford are still part of folklore. His brilliance was there for all to see, as he scored a century against Cambridge in his university debut. He soon became the first Indian to lead Oxford, assuming the captaincy in 1961. He was on course to a record-breaking season, having

---

[13]Majumdar, Boria, *The Illustrated History of Indian Cricket*, Lustre Press, 2009.

scored 1,216 runs by the end of June.

However, disaster struck on 1 July. Pataudi was returning to the hotel, where they were staying, with his teammate Robin Waters, when a Humber crashed into Robin Waters' Mini. Pataudi, or Tiger as he was known, lost most of his sight in his right eye.

But it was only a matter of a few weeks before he returned to the field, with only one properly functioning eye. He worked out a method for being able to bat with his impediment. As per *Wisden*, his method involved 'pulling his cap down over his right eye to reduce the double vision and effecting a more open stance'.[14] The remarkable recovery led to his Test debut against England at Delhi at the age of just 20. India got a glimpse of his phenomenal talent when he scored a match-winning 103 in India's 128 run victory at Chepauk, Madras.

Awaiting a Trial by Pace

A trial by pace awaited the Indians as they made their way to the West Indies in February 1962. Wesley Hall was fast gaining a reputation as one of the most fearsome quick bowlers in the world. In Sven Conrad 'Charlie' Stayers and Chester Donald Watson, Hall had strong support. The West Indies also had exceptional talent in the spin bowling and batting department.

The first two Tests ended in comfortable victories for the hosts. The Indians seemed clueless against the West Indies pace attack, especially Hall. The Kensington Oval at Bridgetown, Barbados, the fastest pitch in the West Indies, was the venue

---

[14]'Wisden Obituary, Mansur Ali Khan Pataudi', *ESPNcricinfo*, https://es.pn/400BAs1. Accessed on 10 April 2023.

for the next Test, but before that there was the small matter of a four-day encounter against Charles Christopher 'Charlie' Griffith and the Barbados side.

The Barbados side for that match would have given any Test side of the day a run for their money. Hall had arguably an even more dangerous new ball partner in this match, and it was Griffith. The events after lunch on Day 2 shook both Indian and world cricket.

Mansoor Ali Khan Pataudi

The first three balls of Griffith's first over after lunch were all unnervingly quick bouncers. Rusi Surti, who was at the crease with captain Nari Contractor pointed out that Griffith was chucking. But disaster struck on the fourth ball.

India vs West Indies, 3rd Test, Kensington Oval, Bridgetown, Barbados, 23-28 March 1962

For the third Test, the mantle of captaincy fell on the 21-year-old Nawab of Pataudi, who had not played the first two Test matches. Pataudi had Contractor's vote of confidence. Pataudi's communication skill and personality also gave him an edge. In famed wicketkeeper Farokh Engineer's words: 'He commanded respect, because he was a prince and he held himself like royalty.'[15] As Pataudi walked up for the toss at

---

[15]'Tiger Pataudi: Extraordinary Resolve, Princely Demeanour, India's Great Captain–Almanack', *Wisden India*, 22 September 2020, https://tinyurl.com/2p8z7j2x. Accessed on 14 September 2023.

Kensington Oval alongside Frank Worrell, Test cricket had found its youngest-ever captain. The West Indies won the toss and elected to field on a pitch that had plenty of life for fast bowlers.

The Indian opening partnership of M.L. Jaisimha and Vijay Sardesai put together a partnership of 56, and it ended with Sardesai being dismissed by Lance Gibbs. Things were soon about to go downhill for India, as Worrell got Surti's wicket and then Hall tore into the core of India's batting with 3 quick wickets of Jaisimha, Manjrekar and Umrigar. The newly appointed Indian captain, playing his first Test of the series acquitted himself bravely, as he fought his way to score 48 runs before being caught and bowled by Alf Valentine. Some quick lower order runs by Salim Durani followed, and India posted a decent total of 258.

The West Indies batting was in magnificent form. Joe Solomon, Rohan Kanhai, Frank Worrell and Conrad Hunte all scored half centuries as the West Indies posted an imposing 475.

In the Indian second innings, a superb partnership between Sardesai and Manjrekar guided India to 158 for 2, before Worrell threw the ball to Gibbs who had gone 30-plus overs without taking a wicket. In the next 15 overs Gibbs bowled, there were 14 maidens and 8 wickets (for just 6 runs). He ended with remarkable figures of 8 for 38. India was bowled out for 187. The match ended with an innings and 30-run win for the hosts.

Even though the Test and the series was lost, for the Indians it was a new beginning under a leader who would bring about a major transformation in India's approach to Test cricket. In legendary leg-spinner Bishan Singh Bedi's words, 'He [Pataudi] was the first leader of Indian cricket who told everybody in the dressing room, "Look, you are not playing for Delhi, Punjab, Madras, Calcutta or Bombay, you are playing for India. You are Indian."[16] He also recognized India's inherent strength in spin and became the mastermind of the formation of arguably the world's greatest ever spin quartet of Bedi, E.A.S. Prasanna, B.S. Chandrasekhar and S. Venkataraghavan. Under him, the Indian team was no longer content to play for creditable draws but went for victories given the slightest opportunity.

What heights Pataudi could have achieved as a batter with two healthy eyes can only be speculated. A total of 2,793 runs at an average of 34.91 did no justice to the immense promise he showed in his years in England. It was Pataudi's leadership during a pivotal time in Indian cricket that ensured his place as a legend of the game.

SCORECARD

India: 258 all out (Pataudi-48, Durani-48; Hall-3/64, Worrell-2/12) and 187 all out (Sardesai-60, Manjrekar-51; Gibbs-8/38, Stayers-2/24)

West Indies: 475 all out (Solomon-96, Kanhai-89; Umrigar-2/48, Borde-2/89)

Result: West Indies beat India by an innings and 30 runs

---

[16]"The Most Charismatic Cricketer of His Generation", *ESPNcricinfo*, 22 September 2011, https://tinyurl.com/4xcs79ks. Accessed on 14 September 2023.

10

THE SPIN QUARTET ARRIVES

'...while bowling into the wind with a lot of spin, the ball climbs up. That is the time the batsman feels he can reach out and he comes out, commits himself, but the ball drops and that is the instant when the batsman invariably and inadvertently reaches out. That's when it looks like someone is flying a kite—controlling the string.'

—Erapalli Prasanna[17]

It was with this control and deception that Prasanna engineered India's first ever overseas Test win at New Zealand's Carisbrook in Dunedin.

The social and economic realities for cricketers in those times were drastically different from what they are today. After his first two Tests in 1962, Prasanna had to fulfil a promise he had made to his father—that of completing his engineering degree and getting a job. A wait of almost half a decade followed before Prasanna made his comeback into Test cricket.

With Prasanna's return to the side against the West Indies in January 1967, the grand scheme of Pataudi in reshaping India's bowling attack and moulding them into a potent force

---

[17]Ramnarayan, V., 'The Science of Deception', *The Cricket Monthly*, 2 October 2014, https://bit.ly/3Fo5FKR. Accessed on 15 March 2023.

The Spin Quartet Arrives

(Clockwise from top left) E.A.S. Prasanna, Bishan Singh Bedi, B.S. Chandrasekhar and S. Venkataraghavan

was finally coming to fruition. The spin quartet that went on to mesmerize batters all over the world for the next decade was finally complete.

What made them special was that they all had different strengths. If Prasanna and Bedi deceived the batters with flight and guile, Chandrasekhar bamboozled them with wickedly turning deliveries at high pace. Venkataraghavan, on the other hand, tested the batter's patience as he bowled ball after ball with unerring accuracy. The Indian team also had the left-arm spinner Rameshchandra Gangaram 'Bapu' Nadkarni to call upon when needed; he was miserly in giving runs.

Prasanna's first few series after his comeback ended in disappointment for India. After a series defeat to the West Indies at home in 1966–67, India was routed 3-0 and 4-0 in consecutive overseas trips to England and Australia. One of the few redeeming factors was Prasanna's impressive haul of 25 wickets in four Tests on the tour to Australia.

India had proved itself capable of challenging almost any opposition at home, but overseas Tests had been an altogether different task. Sceptics doubted India's prospects even as the team travelled to New Zealand in February 1968 to take on one of international cricket's more non-fancied sides. New Zealand, which had played its first Test match way back in 1930, had won only three Test matches in almost four decades, without a single series victory.

India vs New Zealand, 1st Test, Carisbrook, Dunedin, 15-20 February 1967

In the first Test at Carisbrook, Dunedin, Barry Sinclair, the New Zealand captain, won the toss and elected to bat. After the early dismissal of Bruce Murray, Graham Dowling and Bevan

Congdon put together a partnership of 145, which steered New Zealand towards a comfortable position. Nadkarni made the crucial breakthrough by dismissing Congdon, opening the floodgates for the Indian bowlers. With Nadkarni stifling the New Zealand batters at one end, Syed Abid Ali made significant inroads into the New Zealand batting. Abid Ali ended with superb figures of 4 for 26. New Zealand managed a total of 350—Dowling scoring the highest with 143.

In reply, the highest score of the Indian innings was an 80 made by the left-handed batter Ajit Wadekar. Although not considered the most gifted player by many, his tour of New Zealand turned out to be his finest series as a Test batter, as he ended up scoring 328 runs. After Wadekar's dismissal, the Indians lost wickets regularly. Right-arm seamer Dick Motz was the wrecker-in-chief, taking 5 wickets in the innings. However, India managed to eke out a 9-run lead, after an invaluable and unexpected last wicket partnership of 57 between Bedi and Ramakant Desai.

In the second innings, Prasanna showed his wizardry. His well-flighted off-breaks and deceptive straighter ones were too much for the inexperienced New Zealand batters to handle. Bruce Murray, Bevan Congdon, Bryan Yuile, Dick Motz, Bruce Taylor, Roy Harford—all perished to his skills. New Zealand made 208 in its second innings, with Prasanna taking 6 for 94. So, a target of 200 runs lay between India and a historic first overseas victory.

In the run chase, Wadekar scored another half century. He forged an important 103-run third wicket partnership with Rusi Surti, and got India within 39 runs of the target by the close of Day Four.

Wadekar was dismissed on Day Five with the Indian score on 163. Pataudi soon followed Wadekar to the pavilion, with

India still 31 runs short of the target. The experienced duo of M.L. Jaisimha and Chandu Borde allayed any fears that the Indian cricketers or supporters would have had, as they comfortably made the remaining runs. In their 30-second attempt, India had finally won away from home. Prior to this match, it had lost 21 matches and drawn 10, playing overseas.

India went on to win the series 3-1. Wadekar continued with his fine form, making a superb 143 in the crucial third Test at Wellington. With the ball, Prasanna was the hero, picking up 24 wickets in the series at an average of 18.79. Prasanna revelled under the attacking captaincy of Pataudi. In 23 Tests under Pataudi, Prasanna picked up 116 wickets at an average of 27.42.

The win at Dunedin and the eventual series win heralded possibly India's greatest-ever run of performances on foreign soil. Wadekar inherited a very strong team built by Pataudi, with several magicians with the ball. A golden period was about to begin for Indian cricket, and the keys to success lay in the fingers of Bedi, Prasanna, Chandrasekhar and Venkataraghavan.

SCORECARD

New Zealand: 350 all out (Dowling-143, Congdon-58; Abid Ali-4/26, Nadkarni-2/31) and 208 all out (Murray-54, Burgess-39; Prasanna-6/94, Nadkarni-1/13)

India: 359 all out (Wadekar-80, Engineer-63; Motz-5/86, Alabaster-3/66) and 200/5 (Wadekar-71, Surti-44; Alabaster-3/48, Taylor-1/51)

Result: India beat New Zealand by 5 wickets

11

SUNNY DAYS HAVE COME

Indian cricket got its first truly Indian superstar during its tour of the West Indies in 1971—arguably only the second Indian batter who could credibly be called the best batter in the world, after Ranji. Indian cricket had Sunil Manohar Gavaskar. And Gavaskar, known as Sunny to the cricketing fraternity, by sheer force of will, made Indian cricket take its first step towards modernity.

This journey to modernity began with the tour of the West Indies in 1970–71. There was controversy even before the start of the series. Vijay Merchant, through his casting vote as the chief of selectors, ensured that Indian cricket had a new captain in Ajit Wadekar. One of the two other contenders for the captaincy, Chandu Borde, was not selected; he retired without playing another Test. The other, the Nawab of Pataudi, declined to tour. Wadekar wanted middle-order batter Dilip Sardesai and wicketkeeper Farokh Engineer included in the touring party, but only got his wish granted for the first of the two.[18]

The West Indies was captained by Sir Garry Sobers, perhaps the greatest all-round cricketer the world has seen. He was the best batter in the West Indies team, perhaps its best

---

[18]Dhole, Pradip, 'Rusi Jeejeebhoy: India's Reserve Wicketkeeper on the 1971 West Indies Tour', *Cricket Country*, 26 October 2016, https://bit.ly/3JIQKgI. Accessed on 16 March 2023.

quick bowler, and also the best left-arm wrist spinner. He had, however, got into the team as a left-arm orthodox spinner. It was a good team, with Roy Fredericks, Clive Lloyd and Rohan Kanhai. There weren't many great quick bowlers in the West Indian ranks. West Indies' best spin bowler, Lance Gibbs, did not play due to the form of Jack Mollinson Noreiga—rumour had it that the Indians gave away their wickets to Noreiga in tour matches to trick the West Indies selectors to pick him ahead of Gibbs, whom the Indians feared more.

The first Test at Sabina Park, Kingston, Jamaica, ended in a draw. Sardesai scored 212 in India's first innings, and the West Indies could only score 217 in reply to India's 387. The wily Wadekar landed a blow to the West Indians' confidence by asking them to follow on. As it was a rain-affected match, the West Indies saved the match with ease, with Kanhai scoring an unbeaten 158 and Sobers 93. But India had landed the first psychological blow.

Gavaskar had not played the first Test, and debuted in the next one at Queen's Park Oval, at Port of Spain, Trinidad. India landed the first telling blow of the series in this Test. Its four-pronged spin attack of Bedi, Prasanna, Venkataraghavan and Durani restricted the rivals to less than 300 in both innings. India got to 352 in the first innings, thanks to another century by Sardesai, and Gavaskar and Eknath Solkar for scoring 50s, notwithstanding a 9/95 by Noreiga. In the second innings, the Indians got to the 125 they needed quite comfortably on the back of another 50 from Gavaskar—1-0 to the touring side.

The third and fourth Tests were draws. The third was a tedious affair, with the run rate barely inching above 2 per over, though Gavaskar got his first Test hundred in the first innings. The fourth was quite the opposite, with India clinging on to a draw in the fourth innings through a brave 117 not out by (who else but) Gavaskar.

India vs West Indies, 5th Test, Queen's Park Oval, Port of Spain, 13-19 April 1971

The fifth was a six-day Test, held at the same venue where India had played the second successful second Test—Queen's Park Oval. The West Indians had to fight back or be ready to face the embarrassment of losing a home series. Island pride was at stake.

India batted first, and Gavaskar continued his glittering form. He scored 124 in a show of supreme patience, and had a great partnership with Sardesai, who scored 75. The others in the top-order did not contribute much, barring a surprising 51 by Venkataraghavan, one of the only two 50s that he scored in his entire Test career.

The West Indies, in reply, batted with adventure. Sobers scored a sparkling 132; Charlie Davis, having a great series, scored 105; and Maurice Foster was unfortunate to be out for 99. The West Indies ended up with a lead of 166. India now had the daunting task of batting nearly three days to save the Test.

What came next was the innings that truly developed the legend of Gavaskar. With superhuman powers of concentration and an obsessive dedication to the task at hand, he batted for more than two days on a crumbling wicket, to score a towering 220. By the time the Indian innings was finished, the West Indies had an impossible target of 262 off 40 overs. Through a quick-fire 64 by Lloyd, it made a decent fist of it, but once the wickets started falling, the team decided to shut shop and save the Test. It was a draw, and India won the series.

Sunil Gavaskar

Willard C. Harris was a cricket-mad calypso musician, who went by the stage-name of Lord Relator. He was there for all six days of the fifth Test, and watched this 21-year-old, who was about the same age as Relator himself, with wonder. What powers of concentration! And Relator expressed his appreciation in the only way he knew, by writing and performing this lovely calypso song:

Erapalli Prasanna
Jeejebhoy and Wadekar
Krishnamurthy and Vishnoo [sic.] Mankad
Them boys could play real cricket
On any kind of wicket
They make the West Indies team look so bad
We was in all kinda trouble
Joey Carew pulled a muscle

> Clive Lloyd got 'bout three run out
> We was in trouble without a doubt
> It was Gavaskar
> De real master
> Just like a wall
> We couldn't out Gavaskar at all, not at all…
> You know the West Indies couldn't out Gavaskar at all.[19]

What is Gavaskar's contribution to Indian cricket? It is not a difficult question to answer. In our opinion, Gavaskar was the first true professional of Indian cricket. He was definitely in the conversation for being the best batter in the world at that point. He had every shot in the book, but was cautious in using them, knowing fully well that his was the first wicket that the opposition wanted. His technique was perfect, and was a true embodiment of the 'Bombay School' of batting. What started with Kanga and blossomed with Merchant had now reached its zenith with Sunny. A Sunil Gavaskar forward defence was the platform on which most Indian Test wins of the next decade and a half was built. He broke Sir Donald Bradman's record of the most Test hundreds, and became the first cricketer to score 10,000 Test runs.

Gavaskar, through the weight of a mountain of runs, led Indian cricket on to a path of greatness. It was also due to his efforts that Indian cricketers began to get paid better—something that they deserved.

---

[19] '"We Couldn't Out Gavaskar At All": The Calypso that Immortalised Indian Cricket's Famous Triumph of 1971', *Scroll.in*, 6 March 2016, https://bit.ly/3TiqIEq. Accessed on 16 March 2023.

SCORECARD

India: 360 all out (Gavaskar-124, Sardesai-75; Holford-3/68, Shepherd-3/78) and 427 all out (Gavaskar-220, Wadekar-54; Noreiga-5/129, Shepherd-2/45)

West Indies: 526 (Sobers-132, Davis-105; Venkataraghavan-4/100, Prasanna-3/146) and 165/8 (Lloyd-64, Kanhai-21; Abid Ali-3/73, Venkataraghavan-2/11)

Result: Match drawn

12

OTHERS, PLUS CHANDRA

'Mate, they want you on that balcony pronto, else we could have a ruddy riot on our hands.' This was Ken Barrington, the England manager, speaking with Ajit Wadekar, the Indian captain.[20] Wadekar had literally slept through arguably India's greatest cricketing moment till date. The riot being referred to was the bedlam that had resulted at the Oval, after Syed Abid Ali had struck the winning boundary. In fact, before the ball had touched the ropes, a large part of the euphoric Indian crowd had rushed towards the ground. Within moments, the Indian batters were being carried on the shoulders of the ecstatic Indian supporters.

One could not blame the Indians in the audience at the Oval that day, as India had claimed an epoch-making series victory. The team had overcome not only close to four decades of disappointment in Test matches in England but also the colonial hangover from years of being ruled by Britain. The Indian captain was nonchalant upon being woken up by Barrington. His first reaction was: 'I always knew we would win!'[21]

---

[20]Burton, Simon, 'A First Win in England: India and the Elephant Will Never Forget', *The Guardian*, 21 August 2018, https://bit.ly/3Jtc8Wc. Accessed on 16 March 2023.
[21]Choudhury, Angikaar, 'Remembering 1971: When Chandrasekhar Reigned and India Made History in England', *Scroll.in*, 28 July 2018, https://bit.ly/3zmCqoo. Accessed on 31 March 2023.

This is the story of the match where India not only conquered the old enemy but laid claim to being the best Test team in the world.

The confidence exuded by the Indian captain came in large part from the historic series win on foreign soil against the West Indies. The team had a squad of battle-hardened cricketers—an astute captain, a young batting superstar and the greatest collection of spinners ever assembled. The most unique of this group of spinners was a 26-year-old leggie from Karnataka, B.S. Chandrasekhar. It was on the shoulders of this unorthodox but brilliant bowler that India went on to claim the historic win at the Oval in 1971.

Diagnosed with poliomyelitis when he was only five, Chandrasekhar, also known as Chandra, had a right arm, which was uniquely flexible and allowed him to get a menacing bite off the wicket. Once he developed the ability to turn his leg breaks consistently and the intricacies of loop, he was almost unplayable on his day. In Bedi's words, 'When I saw Chandu walking on the field, trust me, I felt I saw God in him!'[22] Chandrasekhar was part of 14 wins, and in those matches, he had staggering numbers of 98 wickets at an average of 19.27, and a strike rate of 45.4. Some of his most lethal spells came on foreign soil, as his quick, high-arm action allowed him to generate bounce off faster tracks. England became one of his favourite hunting grounds.

India came into the Test series against England, having lost 15 of 19 Test matches in the country. England, at the time, could justifiably claim to be the best team in the world, having won five consecutive Test series. The Indian team, though, was

---

[22]Singh Bedi, Bishen, 'I Saw God in Chandu', *Rediff.com*, 19 May 2005, https://bit.ly/3mX0Rpq. Accessed on 16 March 2023.

brimming with self-belief after its victory in the Caribbean. The series was also a comeback for Chandra, who had been out of the side following a leg injury on the tour to Australia in 1967–68.

The first two Tests were rain-affected and ended in draws. The first match was a thriller, with India on 145 for 8, chasing 183 on the last day, before rain intervened. The second match was dominated by England, and rain saved India the blushes after it was reduced to 65 for 3, chasing an imposing 420.

Chandrasekhar had a relatively quiet series, going into the Oval Test, picking up only five wickets in the first and going wicketless in the second. Just prior to the third Test, he had got a morale-boosting 6 wicket haul against Nottinghamshire in the second innings. The next six-wicket haul of Chandra's career went down in history as the Indian bowling performance of the century, as per *Wisden*.

England vs India, 3rd Test, Oval, London, 19-24 August 1971

Electing to bat first on a pitch expected to aid the spinners towards the latter half of the game, John Jameson, Allan Knott and Richard Hutton chipped in with valuable half-centuries, as England notched up a competitive total of 355, before being bowled out in the final over of the first day. India's best bowler was the left-arm swinger Eknath Solkar, who had thrilled English cricket fans that season with his sensational close-in fielding.

After the second day was washed out due to rain, India ran into early trouble on Day 3, as both the openers, Gavaskar and Mankad were dismissed with the score on 21. Wadekar and Sardesai then arrested the slide with a valuable partnership of 93 runs. Ray Illingworth once again made a telling impact, picking up three quick wickets in the middle-order. India was reduced to 125 for 5, before Engineer and Solkar launched a strong recovery. India ended its innings on 284, though still trailing England by 71 runs.

Chandra made an early impact in England's second innings, running out John Jameson for 16. It was then time for the famed 'Mill Reef' remark. Sardesai and Chandra were both fond of horse racing, and Mill Reef was the Derby-winning horse of that season. As Chandra bounded in to bowl to John Edrich with the score on 24, Sardesai shouted, 'Mill Reef daalo'.[23]

Edrich was unable to get his bat down in time to a faster one by Chandra, and was clean bowled. Chandra's 'Mill Reef' remark terrorized batters for years to come. From then on, there was no stopping the Indian. Solkar picked up an astonishing catch off Chandra's bowling to dismiss Keith Fletcher, and England went into lunch on the fourth day, at 24 for 3.

The Test match coincided with the festival of Ganesh Chaturthi. A group of Indian supporters brought in an elephant named Bella, from the Chessington Zoo, to parade it on the ground during the lunch interval on the fourth day. After lunch, Venkat joined the party picking up Basil D'Oliveira and Knott. Solkar dived forward to take another brilliant catch to dismiss Knott. India's spin quartet will forever be indebted to Solkar for his stunning athleticism and courage, fielding so close in. The lower order had no answer to Chandra's skill and variety. A few English batters tried valiantly to counter attack but to

---

[23]Bhushan, Aditya, 'India-England 1971 Oval: 22 Tests for a Victory on the 22 Yards in Old Blighty', *Sportskeeda*, 26 August 2019, https://bit.ly/42S2OE2. Accessed on 31 March 2023.

no avail. Before the English team could fathom what had hit it, the innings was wrapped up for 101. Chandra had scalped 6 wickets for 38 runs. A target of 173 now stood between India and a historic victory.

The Indian innings got off to another poor start, as Gavaskar and Mankad were again dismissed early. Once again it was time for Wadekar and Sardesai to steady the ship. A resolute effort followed, as the fourth day's play ended with India on 76 for two—97 runs remaining to win.

Campbell Page from the *Observer* wrote that on the final day, 'Every Indian tourist, businessman, waiter and schoolboy in London seemed to be at the Oval.'[24] Wadekar was run out without adding to his overnight score, in the very first over of the day. G.R. Viswanath, the one with a magical wrist which he used with great style to execute the square cuts, joined Sardesai, and together they got India within 50 runs of the target. Sardesai and Solkar then fell in quick succession, as the deadly Derek Underwood struck twice. Enter Farokh Engineer. Mixing caution with aggression, Engineer made a crucial contribution of 28. Viswanath was dismissed with the score on 170.

It was then Abid Ali, who hit the winning runs—a square cut for 4 that never reached the boundary, as the partisan Indian crown rushed onto the field. India had beaten arguably the best team in the world in its own backyard.

When the Indian team returned home, there were spectacular celebrations. The team's flight was diverted to Delhi, so that the then Prime Minister (PM) Indira Gandhi

---

[24]Burnton, Simon, 'A First Win in England: India and the Elephant Will Never Forget', *The Guardian*, 21 August 2018, https://bit.ly/3LpzJtp. Accessed on 16 March 2023.

could greet them. When the team reached Bombay, a victory parade was organized as the players made their way to a reception at the Cricket Club of India. As many as 1.5 million people lined the streets and fans flung flowers in the path of their heroes. It was truly a landmark occasion. In Wadekar's words, the win tamed India's sense of inferiority. India was now ready to take its place as one of the major forces in world cricket. At the helm of affairs was an extraordinarily calm captain, who was so assured of his team's victory that he decided to take a nap and rest before the next day's trip to Sussex.

SCORECARD

England: 355 all out (Knott-90, Jameson-82; Solkar-3/28, Venkataraghavan-2/63) and 101 all out (Luckhurst-33, D'Oliveira-17; Chandrasekhar-6/38, Venkataraghavan-2/44)

India: 284 all out (Engineer-59, Sardesai-54; Illingworth-5/70, Snow-2/68) and 174/6 (Wadekar-45, Sardesai-40; Underwood 3/72, Luckhurst-1/9)

Result: India beat England by 4 wickets

13

SENSATION AT HOME TOO

Indian cricket was forging its path in international waters; it was but natural that our focus turned towards the world game. However, it was domestic cricket that gave the country some of its future greats. And it was in domestic cricket tournaments that some of the Indian greats played.

It was unfortunate that the Bombay Pentangular started losing popularity and was stopped after India gained independence. The Ranji Trophy was competed in with great gusto, and Bombay straddled the field like a behemoth. Readers might recall the exploits of Vijay Merchant, the first great Indian batter, in winning the Ranji Trophy in its first year, in 1934–35 for Bombay. Merchant, and Bombay, continued to win more often in the following years.

The trend continued even after Merchant's retirement. Even before the arrival of Sunil Gavaskar, there were other stalwarts from Bombay cricket that dominated India's domestic scene—batters such as S.M. Kadri, K.C. Ibrahim, L.P. Jai, Rustomji Sheriyar 'Rusi' Modi and Polly Umrigar; and bowlers like Bapu Nadkarni, Ramakant Desai, as well as brothers Subhash Gupte and Baloo Gupte.

Bombay was most dominant between 1958–59 and 1972–73 with 15 consecutive winning seasons. It seemed at one point that it would never let go of its grip on the trophy.

That was to change in a thrilling encounter, the story of which is narrated here.

Karnataka vs Bombay 1973-74, Ranji Trophy, Semi-Final, Chinnaswamy Stadium, Bangalore, 15-18 March 1974

The semi-final of the Ranji Trophy 1973–74 was played from 15–18 March 1974. Both Bombay and its opponent Karnataka sported strong teams. Bombay had Ramnath Parkar, captain Ajit Wadekar, Ashok Mankad (son of the legendary Vinoo Mankad), Sudhir Naik and the all-rounder Solkar. Bombay had Gavaskar too. The team's bowling was a who's who of those who had been unfortunate to miss out on an India cap: fast bowler Abdul Ismail, leg-spinner Rakesh Tandon and long-serving left-arm spinner Padmakar Shivalkar.

Karnataka had its answer to the surgical brilliance of Gavaskar in the magic of G.R. Viswanath. Supporting him were the precocious Brijesh Patel, Sudhakar Rao and the enterprising wicketkeeper–batter Syed Kirmani. The South Indian team's bowling was perhaps even better than Bombay's, with India's magician of the England tour of 1971, Chandrasekhar, and perhaps the greatest off-spinner ever to grace Indian cricket, Prasanna. Bombay was expected to win, but it was not a cakewalk.

Karnataka batted first. Ismail was all fire and brimstone, a genuine quickie on his day. He tore onto the Karnataka batters, and soon got opener Vijayakumar out. Viswanath came in at No. 3, and was deemed not out for a contentious leg-before appeal, against Ismail. Gavaskar thought that his brother-in-law, Viswanath, was plumb in front. As it stood, however, Viswanath survived.

And he thrived. He was soon in his bewitching groove, and was flaying the Bombay bowlers all about the park through his trademark drives, cuts and flicks. He crafted a dominant century stand for the second wicket with Sanjay Desai. This was followed by another big partnership with Brijesh Patel, who himself went on to make a century. Viswanath eventually got out to Tandon, caught by Gavaskar. Ismail had previously come back for his second spell to get Patel out. The rest of the innings folded within a hundred more runs to end with a respectable, but by no means impregnable, score of 385.

Bombay's innings started ominously for Karnataka—Gavaskar and Parkar settled down well. A batter of Gavaskar's pedigree had to be dismissed early for Karnataka to have a chance in this match. But that was not to happen here. The Little Master got to double figures, and then quickly got to 30. Bombay was inching towards 50.

But the wily old engineer, Prasanna, had one last trick up his sleeves. After bowling an array of spinning off-spinners to set Gavaskar up, he bowled a sudden, floaty arm-ball. Gavaskar played for the spin, was caught unawares and lost his off-stump. For once, at the most critical of stages, a bowler got the upper hand over Gavaskar—a rare phenomenon. It was also a testament to how good Prasanna was.

There was some life left in Bombay yet. Wadekar and Ashok Mankad were formidable players at this level. A solid century-partnership was built, and by the end of the second day, both of them were unbeaten, with less than 200 to get the first innings lead—which would win it the Ranji Trophy match in case the match ended in a draw.

Early on the third day, an unfortunate incident occurred. Turning to return to the crease, Wadekar slipped at the wicket, and was run out. Everything was over, bar the shouting. Sudhir

Naik and wicketkeeper Subhash Bandiwadekar resisted for a while. But it was just prolonging the inevitable. Prasanna and Chandrasekhar, two of the premier spinners in the world, had tasted blood. They would not relent. Bombay was bowled out for 307 runs. Prasanna took 5 wickets and Chandra, 4. Karnataka had the first-innings lead.

The rest of the match was played out with a few chances of an outright result. It was a predictable draw, but Karnataka was declared the winner on first-innings scores.

Aftermath: Karnataka won the 1973–74 Ranji Trophy, beating Rajasthan by 185 runs in the final. The following year, Bombay and Karnataka met again in the finals, in Bombay. This time though, notwithstanding a Viswanath century, and 6 wickets by Prasanna in the first Bombay innings, Bombay got their sweet revenge with a comfortable 7-wicket victory. Gavaskar scored a memorable 96 not out in the first innings to guide Bombay through. Bombay was back in the saddle.

SCORECARD

Karnataka: 385 all out (Viswanath-162, Patel-106; Shivalkar-4/94, Tandon-4/125) and 279/8 declared (Patel-62, Rao-53; Tandon-4/114, Rege-2/60)

Bombay: 307 all out (A. Mankad-84, Wadekar-62; Prasanna-5/117, Chandrasekhar-4/145) and 84/0 (Parkar-49)

Result: Karnataka beat Bombay on first innings lead

14

KAPIL'S LAZARUS MOMENT

A few years back, *Wisden* did a feature on Kapil Dev's greatest moments on the cricket field, in his own words. The moments were chosen by Kapil, the title captions by *Wisden*. His spell of 5 for 28 at the Melbourne Cricket Ground (MCG) in 1981 was justifiably called the Lazarus moment.[25] At this time, it seemed that Kapil's Test match career was over. Yet he rose, after battling a thigh injury, and propelled India to an incredible victory. He was the messiah that Indian cricket was looking for. He rejuvenated the Indian bowling department, which was trying to come to terms with the departure of its iconic spin quartet (Bedi, Prasanna, Chandra and Venkat). Kapil Dev Ramlal Nikhanj, also known as the Haryana Hurricane, heralded a new era in Indian cricket, and inspired generations of fast bowlers. This is the story of the match and the spell that set him on the path to greatness.

It started in Pakistan.

India's tour of Pakistan in 1978 was a watershed moment in Indian cricket. The 'Asian Bradman', Zaheer Abbas, put on a masterful performance, as the famed Indian spin attack—which had mesmerized batters for the best part of a decade

---

[25]Cowen, Henry, 'Kapil Dev Picks Eight Standout Moments from His Illustrious Career', *Wisden India*, 21 March 2020, https://bit.ly/40wV092. Accessed on 31 March 2023.

and a half—failed to bowl out the Pakistani team even once in the three Tests. Pakistan cruised to a 2-0 Test series win. The era of the legendary quartet of Bedi, Prasanna, Chandra and Venkat was effectively over. Amid the gloom, a strapping 19-year-old from Haryana provided the silver lining. Kapil made his debut in the first Test at Faisalabad.

India did not have a fast bowler who could genuinely push the batters on the back foot, since the days of Mohammad Nissar and Amar Singh. Kapil announced himself on the international arena with a delivery to Sadiq Mohammad in his second over. The ball ascended steeply and missed Sadiq's cap by inches. Sadiq called for a helmet, in the days where its use was very rare. This felt surreal for an Indian supporter, who had grown up listening to the radio, with news of the likes of Budhi Kunderan and Sunil Gavaskar opening the bowling!

From then on, Kapil quickly established himself as the leader of the Indian attack. When Pakistan came to India in 1979–80 for the return series, he put on a superb exhibition of swing bowling with pace, picking up 32 wickets as India went on to win the six Test match series 2-0. His feats with the bat were also impressive, as he became the youngest Test centurion for India when, at 20 years and 18 days, he scored 126 against a fiery West Indies attack in Delhi.

Soon, Kapil was regarded as one of the foremost all-rounders in the world, along with Richard Hadlee of New Zealand, Imran Khan of Pakistan and Ian Botham of England. The four achieved remarkable feats over the next decade. Dinner table debates on who was the best among them were commonplace.

Kapil ended his career as one of the most prolific cricketers, both in terms of runs and wickets. His longevity and fitness, while he carried the Indian attack for more than half a decade, was extraordinary. His courage and positivity in tough circumstances also made him stand out, and the match at the MCG in 1981 demonstrated that best.

India's series Down Under began with the traditional New Year's day Test at the Sydney Cricket Ground (SCG). India's batters had no answer to the speed and penetration of the Australian pace attack. Dennis Lillee and Leonard Stephen 'Len' Pascoe together accounted for 13 wickets and Chappell hit a magnificent 204, as Australia won the first Test by an innings and 4 runs.

In the second Test at Adelaide, Sandeep Patil played a memorable knock of 174, but the hosts dominated again. India was fortunate to escape with a draw as Day 5 ended, with Australia just 2 wickets away from sealing the series.

India vs Australia, 3rd Test, MCG, Melbourne, 7-11 February 1981

The scene now shifts to the iconic MCG for the final Test, and very few would have given the Indian team much of a chance to square the series.

On a green pitch, Australian captain Chappell won the toss and elected to field. Lillee and Pascoe threatened to dismantle the Indian batting yet again, as India fell to 115 for 6. Then, in the company of Kirmani, Viswanath went about the task of rebuilding the innings. His trademark square cut, square drives and cover drives were a joy to behold. Kirmani perished with the score at 164, and after that Viswanath went into an overdrive, and was particularly severe on leg spinner Jim Higgs. He handled the pacers with elan as well, as he made a brilliant 114, one that remains surely among the greatest knocks by an Indian on foreign soil. The Indian innings ended at 237.

Indian bowlers then made some early breakthroughs, reducing Australia to 81 for 3. India's joy was short-lived. Chappell and Allan Border, followed by Doug Walters, batted with great patience and ensured a big lead for the hosts. Australia scored 419, with Border making a resolute 124.

There was high drama in the second innings, when Indian captain Sunil Gavaskar threatened to stage a walkout, after what he felt was a poor LBW decision. After being given out, off a delivery from Lillee, an enraged Gavaskar asked his batting partner Chetan Chauhan to walk off with him. Chauhan had to oblige. Thankfully, cooler heads prevailed and the match continued.[26]

The opening partnership had put on 165 runs before the unfortunate incident. However, once Gavaskar was dismissed, the Indian innings lost momentum. Chauhan, clearly shaken by the incident, perished soon after for a valuable 85. The Indian innings folded for 324. Australia needed 143 to win, and was expected to reach the target with ease.

India was on the back foot even before Australia's chase started. Shivlal Yadav was ruled out from bowling due to an injury he suffered while batting in the first innings. Dilip Doshi was playing the match with a fractured instep, an injury he sustained in a tour match against Victoria before the MCG Test. India's main weapon Kapil had strained a thigh muscle, and was unable to take the field on the fourth day. Patil opened the bowling with Karsan Ghavri.

---

[26]'Sunil Gavaskar Finally Reveals Why He Walked off the Pitch at MCG in 1981', *Cricket Addictor*, 1 January 2021, https://tinyurl.com/27sum74v. Accessed on 19 September 2023.

It was Ghavri and Doshi who rose to the occasion, taking 3 Australian wickets before the close of play on Day 4. This included a first ball dismissal of Australia's batting mainstay, Greg Chappell, who was bowled by Ghavri. Australia ended Day 4 on 24 for 3. The team still had Kim Hughes on the crease, with the likes of Border and Walters to follow. The match was poised for an enthralling finish.

On the last day, India's talisman Kapil came on to bowl with his thigh strapped, having taken painkillers the night before. Doshi was the first to strike on the fifth morning, bowling Hughes, while the batter was trying to cut against the spin. Kapil, at the other end, had gone wicketless in his first five overs. Gavaskar, the captain, fully aware that his strike weapon could aggravate his injury, asked Kapil to take rest for a few overs. Kapil, ever the warrior, refused.

Kapil focussed on bowling straight, and let the pitch do the rest. Bruce Yardley was the first to go, clean bowled off a short of a good length delivery that came in sharply. Border was next, with Kirmani showing his famed footwork behind the stumps, catching the Australian down the leg side. Rodney Marsh and Dennis Lillee were soon bowled by the champion Indian fast bowler. Len Pascoe was then run out, with the score at 79.

Finally, with 83 on the board, Jim Higgs was trapped in front by another incoming delivery from the relentless Kapil. As the umpire raised his finger, a jubilant Kapil jumped up in joy. Inspired by the Wisden Indian Cricketer of the Century, India staged a remarkable turnaround. The epic comeback was aptly summarized by R. Mohan, who wrote in *Indian Cricket* in 1981: 'Instead of limping off like Napoleon from Moscow, the Indians could hold their heads aloft as they left Melbourne for New Zealand, having risen Lazarus-like from the depths of defeat to savour the aroma of victory that was indeed little short of a miracle.'[27]

> **SCORECARD**
>
> **India:** 237 all out (Viswanath-114, Kirmani-25; Lillee-4/65, Pascoe-3/29) and 324 all out (Chauhan-85, Gavaskar-70; Lillee 4/104, Yardley-2/65)
>
> **Australia:** 419 all out (Border-124, Walters-78; Doshi 3/109, Patil-2/28) and 83 all out (Walters-18, Hughes-16; Kapil 5/28, Ghavri-2/10)
>
> **Result:** India beat Australia by 59 runs

---

[27]Meher-Homji, Kersi, 'The MCG Thriller of 1981', *Roar*, 25 December 2018, https://bit.ly/40Z27XS. Accessed on 4 April 2023.

15

THE GOLDEN DAY

If one were to celebrate a foundation day for Indian cricket, 25 June would be the obvious choice. Not only did India make its Test debut on this day in 1932, it was also the day when 'Kapil's Devils' amazed the world by conquering the mighty West Indies in the 1983 World Cup finals, paving the way for the Indian team to become the towering presence in the world of cricket that it is today.

Incidentally, the theatre for both these memorable moments, spread 51 years apart, was the Mecca of cricket, Lord's. The 1983 World Cup win not only inspired a whole generation of cricketers but also awakened the Indian cricket fraternity to the enormous potential of the limited-overs game. The winds of change had come with the arrival of the young all-rounder from Haryana, who bowled fast and hit the ball with enormous power. This was a cricketer built for the new age of cricket, and it was only proper that under his leadership, an Indian team would change the course of cricket history.

The Road to the World Cup

India's performance in limited-overs cricket in the first eight years of play was abysmal. The format was, in fact, treated with disregard by the cricketers themselves. Images of a

Kapil Dev

fan rushing to the ground, questioning India's strategy as Gavaskar crawled his way to 36 off 174 balls, while India was chasing 335 against England in the first ever World Cup match are still etched in the memories of cricket followers. India claimed a solitary win in the first two World Cups, and that was against East Africa, a cobbled-up team of associate players. A shake-up was needed to awaken the Indian team from its limited-overs slumber.

After a brief brush with captaincy, in a home one-day international (ODI) series against Sri Lanka in Sunil Gavaskar's absence, Kapil was chosen by the selectors as the permanent captain for the tour to the West Indies in 1983. One incident in March in the same year, which filled the Indian team with massive confidence, was their shock win over the mighty two-time defending champion, the West Indies, in a bilateral one-day match in their home ground at Berbice, Guyana.

The initial goal was to make the semi-final. The Indians had a bowling attack, which was perfectly suited to the early English summer. Apart from the sheer class of their captain, they had multiple medium pace options, all capable of moving the ball. Spinning options such as Ravi Shastri and Kirti Azad added depth to the attack. The bookmakers did not share the same belief in the Indian team as the team went into the tournament as 66-1 outsiders.

India was drawn in a tough group that had defending champions, West Indies and Australia. The fourth team in the group was Zimbabwe.

In its first match of the tournament, the Indian team repeated its giant killing act of Berbice, beating the West Indies by 34 runs at Old Trafford, with Yashpal Sharma's dogged batting and Roger Binny's clever seam bowling being the key factors. The significance of this win can be gauged from the fact that this was India's first victory against a Test-playing nation at the World Cup.

A win against Zimbabwe followed. However, India's fairytale in the 1983 English summer was not without its share of ups and downs, as India suffered back-to-back defeats against Australia and the West Indies. It needed to win both the remaining group games to be certain of a semi-final berth. For a large part of the morning of 18 June 1983, at the Royal

Tunbridge Wells, it seemed India would be bidding goodbye to the World Cup at the group stage for the third consecutive time. That was until the Haryana Hurricane struck.

Kapil came into bat at 9/4, after the Zimbabwean seamers Peter Rawson and Kevin Curran had run through the Indian top- and middle-order. India was soon reduced to 17/5, a scoreline that has now become etched in the memory of almost every Indian cricket fan. Undaunted, Dev went on to play an astonishing innings, which remains a strong contender for being the greatest men's World Cup innings of all time. He scored 175 off 138 balls, with 16 fours and 6 sixes, as India posted 266 for 8, and then went on to win the match by 31 runs. The only apt word to describe this comeback was 'miracle'.

In India's final group match, both Madan Lal and Binny took 4 wickets each as India beat Australia by 118 runs. India was through to the semi-final of a World Cup for the very first time. At Old Trafford, Manchester, Bob Willis' England lay in wait.

The English media were uber confident of the home team's comfortable passage to the final, having avoided facing Australia. Phrases such as 'marvellous piece of luck' and 'virtual passport to the final' were used. The Indians had different ideas. An all-round effort by Mohinder Amarnath (2/27 in 12 overs with the ball and 46 with the bat), the class of Kapil with the ball (3/35), the resolute batting of Yashpal (61) and the belligerence of Patil (51 off 32 balls) carried India to a famous 6-wicket win.

India vs West Indies, World Cup Final, Lord's Cricket Ground, London, 25 June 1983

India's opponents in the 1983 World Cup final could stake a legitimate claim to being one of the greatest collections of cricketing talent ever assembled. Led by the redoubtable Clive Lloyd, the side featured one of the greatest batters ever to play the game—Sir Vivian Richards, along with possibly the greatest opening partnership of all time, Gordon Greenidge and Desmond Haynes. The fast-bowling line-up included: Andy Roberts, Joel Garner, Malcolm Marshall and Michael Holding. In 17 World Cup matches held in 1975, 1979 and 1983, the team had been beaten only once. The final was expected to be a cakewalk against the surprise finalists, India. However, what many experts missed out was that the Indian team had beaten the West Indies twice in the last four matches. This was a team that was not going to be intimidated.

On a greenish pitch, Lloyd won the toss and elected to bowl. The West Indies drew first blood with the score on just 2, as Gavaskar edged a Roberts delivery into the gloves of Jeffrey Dujon. Krishnamachari Srikkanth then put on a sparkling display of stroke-play. His chancy knock of 38 ended up as the highest score in the match. He also rode his luck at times, with edges falling between gaps. Srikkanth fell with the score at 59. After that, wickets kept falling in a heap. Amarnath (26) and Patil (27) attempted to arrest the slide but to no avail. The Indian innings folded for 183. Roberts led the way for the West Indies, taking 3 wickets.

The world champions needed 184 to seal their third consecutive World Cup, but something was different about 25 June 1983. Boria Majumdar's *Illustrated History of Indian Cricket* mentioned an interview the author once had with Jeffrey Dujon. The West Indies wicketkeeper had said that there was hardly any celebration in the West Indies' camp after his team had bowled India out for a paltry total. Dujon somehow knew in his heart that the West Indies would struggle, and he had mentioned the same to Roberts at the break; Roberts had agreed. Dujon's fear came true.[28]

The West Indies suffered an early setback as Greenidge shouldered arms to an incoming delivery from Balwinder Singh Sandhu. Out came Sir Isaac Vivian Alexander Richards. It seemed he had come out with the intention of showing the Indians their place in the cricketing hierarchy. He was smashing the Indian bowlers all over the park, before there was another moment of inspiration from captain Kapil. With the score on 57 for 2, Madan Lal bowled a short of a length delivery to Richards. The legend rocked back and pulled the ball, but slightly mistimed his shot. Up in the air, the ball seemed destined to fall in no man's land, till Indian supporters saw the Indian captain gallantly running towards the ball from deep mid-on. He had run backwards all the way to deep mid-wicket and taken a superbly judged catch.

The match then turned on its head. Madan Lal took his third wicket as Gavaskar snapped up Gomes in the slips. Lloyd followed soon after, driving the ball straight to Kapil off a delivery from Binny. Faoud Bacchus did not last long. There was chaos in the stands, the Indian fans were jubilant. Hopes of an unthinkable victory abounded. Dujon and Marshall then set about engineering a comeback and fought their way to a 43-run partnership.

It was Amarnath's turn to get into the act. Dujon edged a straight delivery from Amarnath on to his stumps. Marshall was dismissed by Amarnath as well, caught by Gavaskar. Amarnath was relentless in his accuracy that day, and got just the right movement off the seam: 124 for 8, 2 wickets remaining for a landmark victory for the Indians. The Indian captain finally got his first wicket when Roberts was adjudged LBW

---

[28]Majumdar, Boria, *Illustrated History of Indian Cricket*, Lustre Press, 2009.

off his bowling. Kapil's figures of 11 overs, 21 runs conceded and one wicket became a vital reason for the West Indies batting being stifled.

The final word, deservingly, belonged to Amarnath, who had batted with such courage and bowled with such discipline. Holding went to pull another straight one, and was caught plumb in front, with the West Indies 43 short of the Indian total. The ecstatic Indian supporters ran onto the field. India was the world champion. Back home, a whole country of almost a billion people was in delirium. Kapil's Devils would be legends forever.

The win made Indian cricketers superstars. Posters of the Indian cricketers started adorning households throughout the country. With a nation of one billion madly in love with the game, it was clear that India was cricket's greatest business opportunity. In four years, it was India's turn to host a World Cup final. A new powerhouse in world cricket had emerged, and India will forever be grateful to that XI of Kapil's Devil's that lorded over the best team in the world at the Mecca of cricket.

SCORECARD

India: 183 all out in 54.4 overs (Srikkanth-38, Patil-27, Amarnath-26; Roberts-3/32, Marshall-2/24)

West Indies: 140 all out in 52 overs (Richards-33, Dujon-25; Amarnath-3/12, Madan-Lal 3/31)

Result: India beat the West Indies by 43 runs

16

CHAMPIONS, ONCE AGAIN

India's World Cup victory was a momentous occasion and it changed the landscape of world cricket forever. However, at that point in time, the win was seen in the larger cricketing world as an off-day for the almighty West Indies against the plucky outsiders, India. This idea gained more ground in the light of the West Indies' tour of India soon after the World Cup, the so-called 'Revenge Tour', where the guests absolutely demolished India in both the Tests and the one-day matches.

The next major multinational one-day cricket tournament after the 1983 World Cup was the Benson and Hedges World Championship of Cricket, held in Australia in early 1985. The seven Test-playing nations at that point—Australia, England, the West Indies, New Zealand, India, Pakistan and Sri Lanka—were invited to participate. The West Indies was the overwhelming favourite. The Australians were strong contenders, and India and Pakistan were the outsiders.

India had had a change of the old guard: Viswanath was out of the squad, and so were Yashpal, Kirti and Patil; Sandhu's moment had passed and Kirmani was also ready to hand over the wicket keeping gloves. The team was infused with young blood. Young guns from the 1983 team, Ravi Shastri and K. Srikkanth, were permanent members of the team now. In came batters Mohammad Azharuddin and Ashok Malhotra, quick bowlers Chetan Sharma and Manoj Prabhakar, leg-spinner L. Sivaramakrishnan, and wicketkeeper Sadanand Viswanath. With the experience of captain Gavaskar, Kapil, Amarnath and Vengsarkar, and World Cup heroes Binny and Madan Lal, it was perhaps the strongest Indian ODI team of the time.

Group A, with Australia, England, India and Pakistan, was stronger than Group B, where the West Indies would have it easy, playing New Zealand and newly-admitted Sri Lanka, which was then weak and far from the world-conquering team it became in a decade. This was also one of the first international cricket tournaments to be played under floodlights, and with coloured clothing. The dazzling changes captured the imagination of cricket followers around the world.

India beat Pakistan comfortably in the first match, restricting the rivals to 183 through excellent seam bowling from Binny and Kapil, and fine leg spin from Sivaramakrishnan, and then got through with a lot to spare with a fine partnership between Azharuddin and Gavaskar.

Next, it beat England; there were consistent performances from Srikkanth, Azharuddin and Vengsarkar, and from Sivaramakrishnan and Shastri as bowlers. In the last match of Group A against Australia, all the bowlers were at their best and restricted Australia to 163—a score which the Indians chased comfortably.

The West Indies and New Zealand, as expected, had qualified from Group B. India played the runners-up from that group, New Zealand; and Pakistan played against the West Indies.

India was expected to beat New Zealand in the semi-final, and there were no surprises. Some late order biffing from Lance Cairns took New Zealand to a somewhat-competitive

206—Shastri and Sivaramakrishnan were again a handful for New Zealand to manage. While batting, India got through the target with a partnership of 105 at less than a-run-a-ball from Vengsarkar and Kapil.

Pakistan had, almost inconceivably, seen off the West Indies in the other semi-final, through the most unanticipated of sources. Mudassar Nazar, son of Nazar Mohammad, one of the stalwarts of early Pakistan cricket, wrecked the famed West Indies batting line-up, snaring 5/28 with his military medium-pace. The West Indies was all out for 159, Pakistan got the meagre target easily, and an India versus Pakistan final was set up.

India vs Pakistan, World Championship Cricket Final, MCG, Melbourne, 10 March 1985

The stage was ready for one of the most riveting rivalries in cricket. Both India and Pakistan were somewhat underrated in this series, and both had proved their detractors wrong. Pakistan had almost consistently upstaged India in Test matches in the previous decade, but in recent times, India gained the upper hand over Pakistan in ODIs.

Javed Miandad, Pakistan's captain, won the toss and decided to bat first. India opened the bowling with Kapil and Chetan Sharma. Roger Binny was injured and could not take the field. Chetan was an able deputy though, and he kept it tight at one end. From the other side, Kapil was having one of his champion days. That lovely late outswinger was testing Pakistan's openers, who had been quite successful in the tournament so far. Eventually, a couple of false strokes from Mudassar and Mohsin gave Kapil his wickets, but he had earned them through his consistency and flair. Soon after, he got Qasim Umar bowled on the first ball. Pakistan was 3 down for 29, and Kapil had already turned the match towards India's favour. Captain Miandad and former captain Imran had a decent, albeit slow partnership, but the lower-middle order could not chip in with much. Eventually, Pakistan made 176/9 at the end of 50 overs—a target that was very reachable for the strong Indian batting line-up.

Imran Khan and Azeem Hafeez bowled tight spells to start the innings, but no wicket was forthcoming. Shastri played conservatively initially, but Srikkanth on the other end was waiting for an opportunity to launch. The first memorable stroke from him came in the 10th over, when he picked Hafeez up from good length to launch him over long off and into the stands. Once Imran and Hafeez completed their first spell and the change bowlers, Tahir Naqqash and leg-spinner Wasim Raja, came in, the fidgety, aggressive opener from Tamil Nadu went on the attack. He lifted Wasim Raja over long off, and just managed to clear Raja's cousin Ramiz, stationed there for exactly that shot. By the time Srikkanth played one stroke too many, holing out to Wasim off Imran in his second spell, India was on 103 in over 23, and the match was virtually won. Azharuddin came in at 3. He dispatched the innocuous medium-pace bowling of Salim Malik to the sight screen, then flicked Naqqash to the mid-on boundary, and got bowled by the same bowler. Shastri and Vengsarkar then got India home without further drama.

Shastri was chosen as the man-of-the-tournament for his all-round performance, and was presented with an Audi. Azharuddin, Chetan, Sivaramakrishnan, Viswanath and Malhotra had fine tournaments in varying degrees, and were all youngsters that India expected much from in the coming years. It seemed that Indian cricket was in the right hands.

Kapil gave a post-match statement, 'We have done it twice, so nobody can say it was a fluke again.' And fluke it was not. The West Indies was undoubtedly still the best team in the world, but it wasn't invincible. India was one of the best suited to take advantage of any slip, at least in limited-overs cricket.

SCORECARD

Pakistan: 176/9 in 50 overs (Miandad-48, Imran-35; Kapil-3/23, Sivaramakrishnan-3/35)

India: 177/2 in 47.1 overs (Srikkanth-67, Shastri-65*; Imran Khan-1/28, Naqqash-1/35)

Result: India beat Pakistan by 8 wickets

17

THE SIX THAT SUNK INDIA

India's win in the 1983 Cricket World Cup and World Championship of Cricket in Australia in 1985, beating Pakistan, had given the nation a justified claim to have stolen a march over their feuding sibling, Pakistan, in limited-overs cricket.

Sharjah, the Hub of Cricket in the 1990s

But things were about to change, and the tipping point for this change in fortunes of the two cricketing siblings was played out in the desert lands of the United Arab Emirates (UAE). Sharjah, in the UAE, has diminished as a cricketing venue today, but during a point in the 1980s and the 1990s, it was a major cricket centre. Abdul Rahman Bukhatir, a Sharjah-based businessman, who had started organizing international tournaments there, nominally played for a 'Cricketers' Benefit Fund'. The Sharjah Cricket Association Stadium specialized in three or four-nation one-day tournaments.

Sharjah was a happy hunting ground for India. India had won the Asia Cup in 1984 there; and the Rothmans Four-Nations Cup with Pakistan, Australia and England, in 1985. This tournament included an unforgettable win against Pakistan, where, after getting all out for 125 in the face of an unstoppable 6/14 by Imran Khan, the Indians got up, brushed themselves off and dismissed the entire Pakistan line-up for 87.

In 1986, an Austral-Asia Cup was organized there, with five teams in the fray: India, Pakistan, Sri Lanka, Australia and New Zealand. Since Sri Lanka was the winner of the 1986 Asia Cup, it got a pass to the semi-final. The other four teams played in the quarter-finals: India beat New Zealand by 3 wickets in the first of them; Pakistan beat Australia by 8 wickets in the other; and New Zealand qualified for the semi-final as the losing quarter-finalist with the lower margin of defeat. India was to meet Sri Lanka in the semi-final, and Pakistan with New Zealand.

In the first semi-final, India beat Sri Lanka but not without a scare. Chasing Sri Lanka's 205, India got off to a bright start, thanks to openers Gavaskar and the quick-scoring Srikkanth who had hit the purple patch. After they fell, India lost a few more quick wickets. From being in a comfortable position on 170/2, India was suddenly in a precarious position at 194/7. They squeaked across the line in the last over of the match, thanks to the dogged Shastri.

With Pakistan defeating New Zealand for 64, in the other semi-final, the great rivals met again, for perhaps one of the greatest limited-overs encounters of all-time.

Pakistan's bowlers, especially leg-spinner Abdul Qadir and 19-year-old left-arm tearaway Wasim Akram, were in tremendous form, but the batting line-up tended to underperform, especially Pakistan's best batter, Javed Miandad. He had had a pedestrian tour of Sri Lanka just prior to this tournament. The India team, on the other hand, was a well-oiled machine in the limited-overs format. The team was identified by certain features—steady battership, a handful of medium-pace bowling all-rounders, and suffocating spin bowling; add to that decent ground-fielding, and we had a team of quality.

India vs Pakistan, Austral-Asia Cup Final, Sharjah Cricket Stadium, Sharjah, 18 April 1986

Imran Khan won the toss, and put Kapil's men in to bat first. After a sedate start, Srikkanth took the attack to the Pakistan bowlers. He started with carting Manzoor Elahi to the long-off fence. When Akram strayed outside the off-stump, Srikkanth flashed him over cover. The other opener, Gavaskar, too got into the act, square drove and then hooked Elahi for boundaries. Once the slow bowlers, Qadir and off-spinner Tauseef Ahmed were brought in, the scoring rate slowed a little, but not substantially. Srikkanth was still in his element. Qadir was lifted over his head, and then over long off for sixes. Eventually, Srikkanth played one stroke too many, and was caught at long-on by Akram off Qadir, for 75.

Gavaskar kept the scoreboard ticking with No. 3 Dilip Vengsarkar. The run-rate had plateaued somewhat, but after the initial thrust that was to be expected of the middle overs. Vengsarkar was eventually yorked by Akram, for a well-compiled 50, with India at 216. Gavaskar fell soon after, just 8 runs short of a deserved hundred. Akram and Imran bowled excellent finishing spells after that, to restrict India to 245/7. It seemed like a considerable but not impossible chase for Pakistan.

Pakistan's regular opening partnership of Mudassar Nazar and Mohsin Khan took the field. It did not get as good a start as India did. Mudassar fell LBW to Chetan Sharma even before the team was in double digits. Kapil got his premier left-arm spinner Maninder Singh in to bowl early, and he did the job for India, castling Rameez Raja. Mohsin Khan, after a bright start, played a poor shot to get himself bowled off Madan Lal. Miandad was struggling, and he and Salim Malik got a scratchy, edgy near-50-run partnership. Then disaster struck for Pakistan. Miandad and Malik got into a horrible mix-up, and Malik was run out.

Imran then sent in the dangerous floater Abdul Qadir to give the innings some momentum. The move paid off, with the partnership adding 71 runs in reasonably quick time. After that, Miandad bravely kept resisting the Indian bowlers, and was helped along by the lower-middle-order and the tail. However, the Indians were always in control of the innings. Miandad was batting out of his skin, but wickets continued to fall from the other end. First, Imran was dismissed and was then followed by Elahi. But Miandad, who had gone on to his hundred by then, had taken the match right to the very end.

Kapil and Chetan Sharma each had an over left, with a target of 17 runs. Kapil, the experienced professional, understood that if he bowled a good 49th over, the pressure on youngster Chetan would be less. He did just that, and gave just 6 runs in that over.

In the last over, Pakistan had 11 runs to win. Miandad slogged Chetan's first ball to long-on, and came back for a tight second run. However, Akram could not beat the throw and was run out. One run scored. Akram had run himself out. There were 10 runs to get off five deliveries. The tenth batter for Pakistan, wicketkeeper Zulqarnain came in to partner Miandad. India was still well in control.

Miandad pulled Chetan's next ball to cow corner for a four. Six was needed off 4 balls. Pakistan was back in the game. Chetan bowled an over-pitched one on middle-stump next, and Miandad almost swept it towards the fine leg boundary—

another four would almost win Pakistan the match. But Roger Binny made an excellent diving stop at short fine leg, resulting in only 1 run. Five runs were needed off 3 now—and Zulqarnain was on strike. Had Binny won the match for India?

Zulqarnain was not much of a batter, and a fast, straight one from Chetan evaded his desperate slog, and ended up crashing into the stumps. The ninth wicket had fallen. Pakistan was left with the last wicket, and 5 runs off 2 balls. Pakistan's No. 11, Tauseef Ahmed, came in to bat.

Miandad was screaming at Tauseef, 'Run at everything.' The fifth ball, another straight one of good length, Tauseef blocked and went out for a run. But the ball had gone to India's best fielder, Azharuddin. Would he hit the stump at the bowler's end and get Tauseef run out? He didn't. Azhar missed by an inch. The Pakistanis were still alive in the game.

Last ball was left and 4 runs were needed to win. India had been ahead of the game throughout the match, but could not land the killer blow. Theoretically, Pakistan was still in the game—improbable as the last ball might be a four.

Chetan, a quick, hit-the-deck bowler, came in for the last delivery. He planned for a yorker. If he could nail the yorker, a four was well-nigh impossible, and he would have won India the match.

What happened next became history. Chetan missed the length, and the ball came out as a knee-high full toss. Miandad was perfectly poised for that specific delivery. He launched it high over the square leg boundary, and the ball sailed into the crowds. It was a six, off the last delivery.

Miandad did not even look at the ball after he hit it—he knew that the match was won! He raised both his fists to the air, and started running towards the pavilion, a huge smile plastered on his face. The Indians were shell-shocked. They had lost a match they were winning from the first delivery to the second-last, only to lose it on the last delivery of the match.

That last-ball six by Javed Miandad was a bugbear for subsequent Indian teams for a long while. After that win, from the late 1980s to the 1990s, Pakistan's teams consistently had an upper hand over Indian teams right up to the end of the last millennium. Perhaps only the next millennium would see the Indians get back on an even keel with the Pakistanis and exorcise the ghost of a short, squat, mustachioed man with two arms raised and a beaming grin on his face.

SCORECARD

India: 245/7 in 50 overs (Gavaskar-92, Srikkanth-75; Akram 3/42, Imran Khan-2/40)

Pakistan: 248/9 in 50 overs (Miandad-116, Mohsin-36; Sharma-3/51, Madan Lal-2/53)

Result: Pakistan beat India by 1 wicket

18

POWER PLAY

India was one of the leading nations in world cricket in the mid-to-late 1980s, especially in the limited-overs format. The reigning champion also had the World Championship of Cricket under its belt. There was one lingering doubt. Could India host a top cricketing tournament successfully? The test would come in 1987, when it would play host to the fourth World Cup.

N.K.P. Salve was a modest politician, and a respected backroom negotiator of his day and age. Born to freedom-fighter parents, he was a staunch Gandhian and a Congress party member. As a man of self-respect and courage, he was an expert at the art of a win-win discussion. He was also a cricket fan, a university-level cricketer and had been president of the BCCI during 1982–85, the times of the greatest cricketing upheaval in India.

The shoots of democratization of cricket, away from the corridors of power at the MCC, stemmed from the day India won the World Cup in 1983. India's Ambassador to the US at the time, S.S. Ray, was, like Salve, a university-level cricketer. He happened to be in London at the time and expressed a wish to attend the finals. Salve, as the BCCI chairman, had asked for two extra tickets for Ray and his spouse to attend the finals; it was well within his rights as the BCCI chairman. He was, however, rebuffed rather curtly by the MCC. Not even priced tickets were made available. It was a loss-of-face for Salve.

The gentlemanly Salve responded in the only way he knew—through diplomacy. Over the next couple of days, Salve arranged a meeting with Noor Khan, head of the Pakistan Cricket Board. Plans were afoot to have the next edition of the World Cup hosted in the subcontinent.

Cricket was still very much ruled by England and Australia, and their cricket boards vetoed every move that Salve and Khan made. Eventually, after a pitched legal battle, there was a nominal agreement that an India–Pakistan Joint Managing Committee (IPJMC) could explore the option of a subcontinental World Cup, if finances could be arranged.[29]

At Salve's behest, Rajiv Gandhi, the then PM, allowed the release of foreign exchange, paving the way for an Indian corporate to sponsor the tournament (remember, economic liberalization only came five years later). Dhirubhai Ambani, the patriarch of Reliance Group, pitched in with a literal blank cheque. The fourth edition of the World Cup was a subcontinental tournament. It was the Reliance World Cup, 1987.

There were eight teams in the World Cup in a very linear format. Two groups of four teams each were to play against one another twice. India's Group A consisted of Australia, New Zealand and Zimbabwe, the associate nations team. Group B had Pakistan, England, the West Indies and Sri Lanka. These were two equally-balanced groups, with the eventual expectation that India and Pakistan would meet each other in the finals.

---

[29]Bhatti, Gulhameed, 'Against All Odds, the Reliance Cup Will Be the Biggest Ever', *India Today*, 15 October 1987, https://bit.ly/3nNhwfl. Accessed on 4 April 2023.

The group stage results were largely along expected lines. There were a couple of exciting matches—Australia beat India by one run in the first Group A encounter; Pakistan and West Indies played out a scintillating last-ball finish, memorable for Courtney Walsh refusing to run-out the last man Saleem Jaffer—who had backed up too much in the second-last delivery of the match, leaving Abdul Qadir to then get the required runs off the last ball to beat the West Indies.

Besides, New Zealand and the West Indies played out a modern-day thriller, the highlight of which was a brilliant 142 by Zimbabwe's star player David Houghton, and Martin Crowe's great catch to dismiss Houghton and win the match for New Zealand. Viv Richards, the pre-eminent batter in the world, proved his class with a breathtaking 181 against Sri Lanka.

Eventually, India and Australia qualified from Group A, and Pakistan and England from Group B. The West Indies not making it to the semi-final was a bit of a surprise, but England had beaten the team in both its group-stage matches. So far, so predictable. India would play England, and Pakistan would play Australia in the semi-final.

That predictability went out of the window in the semi-final, as Australia beat the previously-imperious Pakistan quite comfortably at Lahore, and England beat India—with the English captain Graham Gooch sweeping everything that India's two frontline left-arm spinners, Maninder Singh and Ravi Shastri, could throw at him. There was heartbreak across the border. We could not see the famous India versus Pakistan rivalry in the finals. But there was an even older, immortal cricketing duel between Australia and England. This was to be the last match of a precise, well-run tournament, with moments cast in memory and sparks of magic. And keeping aside our biases, we could agree that the best two teams would play in the finals.

England was a team of experienced professionals and was considered to be a favourite for the finals. Gooch was in the form of his career, and there were also the solid captain Mike Gatting and the swashbuckling Allan Lamb to bolster the batting. Though Ian Botham was not playing the tournament, England had a capable deputy in Phillip DeFreitas, and there was also the off-spinner John Emburey in the ranks. It also had impressive quick bowling options in Neil Foster and Gladstone Small, along with DeFreitas; spinner Eddie Hemmings complemented Emburey.

Australia was a curious case. The early to mid-1980s were not the best times for the Down Under. Some stalwarts of the '70s had retired, and after a rebuilding stage under the doughty veteran, Allan Border, a fine team had started to emerge by the time of the World Cup. Key batters Dean Jones, David Boon and Geoff Marsh were coming to their peaks, along with Border, who had a claim to being one of the best batters in the world. The youngster of the side was Steve Waugh, who went on to have a storied career. The Aussie quick bowling ranks had seen a recent upsurge, with the emergence of two excellent fast bowlers, Craig McDermott and left-arm beanpole Bruce Reid.

Australia vs England, World Cup Final, Eden Gardens, Calcutta, 8 November 1987

The World Cup final at Eden Gardens, Calcutta, on 8 November, started with Border winning the toss and deciding to bat. The successful opening partnership of Boon and Geoff Marsh started the proceedings for Australia. It was a fine start, steady and measured. A 75-run partnership, dominated by Boon, ended when Marsh was bowled by Foster. Dean Jones came in, and Boon and he continued in the same vein for another steady 76-run partnership. Jones departed next with the score on 151, and burly fast-bowler McDermott was sent up the order to provide some momentum. After a couple of lusty blows, he fell, and Boon departed soon after. With a few overs remaining, but with a solid platform for the innings already created, captain Border had an important partnership with Mike Veletta. Veletta played one of the most underrated knocks of the World Cup finals—a brisk 45 off 31 deliveries, filled with smart placements and intelligent running-between-the-wickets to set up the match for Australia. The team finished at 253/5, a competitive score but not an unsurpassable one.

In reply, England did not get off to a good start. Tim Robinson fell to McDermott in his first over. Gooch and Bill Athey steadied the innings, and by the time Gooch fell to all-rounder Simon O'Donnell, the team had stitched together a 65-run partnership. It was slow, the required run-rate was high, but there was a platform now. Gatting came in next, and started off like a dream. The run rate was hurtling along, with Gatting imperious and Athey steady.

Captain Border brought himself on to bowl his innocuous left-arm spin next. Gatting was picking up runs quite comfortably through conventional methods against Border's bowling, when he had a brainfade. He tried a reverse sweep and looped a catch, which the Australian wicketkeeper Dyer gladly accepted. Gatting had fallen for 41, England was 3 down for 135 and the momentum had shifted back in favour of Australia.

It was a momentum that the Australians did not lose. English wickets fell at regular intervals. There were a few lusty blows from Lamb and DeFreitas, but they were in fits and starts.

England was never really out of the match, but Australia was always in the driver's seat. Right up until the last over, there was a possibility that a couple of really good overs could turn the tide for England. But that impetus never came, and Australia walked away with a 7-run victory. Somehow, the margin of victory seemed a lot closer than the match actually was.

Border's young turks had won the World Cup, and the dawn of a new cricketing order was starting to emerge. This Australian team was the precursor to the dominant Australian teams of the next two decades. On the administrative front, by staging this tournament successfully, India had shown the world that an event of such magnitude could be held and managed adroitly by subcontinental officials. Jagmohan Dalmiya and I.S. Bindra, important officials of the IPJMC organizing committee, eventually shaped the cricketing world in the coming days. This tournament and this match was the harbinger of changing times.

SCORECARD

Australia: 253/5 in 50 overs (Boon-75, Veletta-45*; Hemmings-2/48, Foster-1/38)

England: 246/8 in 50 overs (Athey-58, Lamb-45, Gatting-41; Waugh-2/37, Border-2/38)

Result: Australia beat England by 7 runs

19

THEN CAME A NEW GOD

'Suddenly I heard a squeaky voice: "Mai khelega."'

—Navjot Singh Sidhu[30]

That voice was of a 16-year-old, who had been struck on the nose by a ferociously quick bouncer from Waqar Younis. The cherubic face of the youngster, spluttered with blood, was that of Sachin Ramesh Tendulkar. He said he would play, and that was the moment he grew in stature in front of his teammates and the world. Through his career, he played his way into the hearts of a billion Indians. This is the story of the match in which the boy rose up and became a man.

In the latter half of the 1980s, Indian cricket was at a crossroads. Its greatest ever batter, Sunil Gavaskar, had bowed out of the game. The talisman all-rounder, Kapil, had begun to feel the burden of carrying the bowling attack for a decade. The country as a whole was grappling with economic crisis and communal violence. Major trade and fiscal deficits, decline in investor confidence and dependence on bailouts from the World Bank and the International Monetary Fund had crippled

---

[30]"Discon 2010-Navjot Singh Sidhu-3", YouTube, https://bit.ly/431wAX1. Accessed on 4 April 2023.

Sachin Tendulkar

the Indian economy. India was also reeling under the conflicts with supporters of the Khalistan movement and the impending threat of the Liberation Tigers of Tamil Eelam. Indian cricket, and the country itself, was in need of a hero—someone to rally behind, someone who could provide hope amid gloom.

It was during this time that the Bombay cricket grapevine was buzzing with news of the emergence of a prodigious talent coached by the famous Ramakant Achrekar. The young boy, Sachin Tendulkar, had lit up the school cricket scene in Bombay. News of his achievements first flashed across the world in February 1988. His school, Shardashram Vidyamandir was taking on St Xavier's in a Harris Shield semi-final. He and fellow Achrekar trainee Vinod Kambli put on a partnership of 664 runs. This was then the highest partnership for any wicket in any class of cricket. Tendulkar followed this with yet another triple hundred in the Harris Shield final. It was now only a matter of time before he made his Bombay debut.

The then 15-year-old scored a hundred on his Ranji Trophy debut and amassed 563 runs in the season. Tendulkar was already being talked about as the successor to Gavaskar, as the next great Bombay and Indian batter. In an interview conducted by Tom Alter just before the selection of the Indian team for the tour of the West Indies, Tendulkar was asked whether he felt it was the right time for him to be selected, considering the fearsome pace of the West Indies attack—with Marshall, Curtly Ambrose and Patrick Patterson. A confident Tendulkar said that he did not have any trouble facing fast bowlers, and preferred playing fast bowling as the ball came on to the bat.[31] As it turned out, Tendulkar was not selected.

India's tour to the West Indies ended in misery, as the visitors were decimated 5-0 and 3-0 in the ODIs and Test series, respectively. That was also a time of great controversy in Indian cricket, as a group of players including Kapil had gone on a tour of North America, despite the board warning them against it. There was the possibility of the team members concerned being banned from the tour to Pakistan in the winter.

Back home, Tendulkar was about to play one of the most important innings of his career. Appearing for the Rest of India against Ranji champions Delhi, he made a brilliant unbeaten 103 in the second innings.

---

[31]"When Tom Alter Interviewed Sachin Tendulkar for the First Time: "Part of Being a Cricket Star"", *Indian Express*, 30 September 2021, https://bit.ly/3lrE58I. Accessed on 20 March 2023.

When the time came to select for India's tour of Pakistan in 1989, one of the selection committee members, Akash Lal, recalled that Tendulkar's selection for the tour to Pakistan was not unanimous, but a 3-2 decision. The selectors were worried about putting a 16-year-old against the pace and skill of the Pakistani attack featuring Wasim Akram, Imran Khan and Waqar Younis (who was also making his debut against India). However, the selectors in favour of Tendulkar argued that his techniques were among the finest in the country when it came to handling fast bowling, and the younger he made his debut, the longer he would serve the country.[32] Thus, the youngest cricketer to play Test cricket for India was selected for an arduous series against India's arch rival. At the age of 16 years and 205 days, Tendulkar made his Test debut at Karachi.

India batted second and its innings got off to a disastrous start, with 4 wickets quickly lost. At the fall of Manoj Prabhakar's wicket, Tendulkar came in. The Pakistani bowlers were about to show Tendulkar no mercy. His brief stay at the wicket ended, as he missed a sharp, incoming delivery from Waqar. Tendulkar was bowled out for 15 runs. The teenager was visibly shaken by the gulf in class between first-class level and Test level.

Coming back to the Test match, India managed to eke out a draw, with Sanjay Manjrekar making a superb hundred in the second innings. As far as Tendulkar was concerned, his teammates recognized the immense talent that the young man possessed and encouraged him to give himself time, when he got the opportunity to bat again.

---

[32]Ray, Suman, 'Selector's Secret Diary on Sachin's Selection Unravelled', *India Today*, 13 November 2013, https://bit.ly/3LBg0Ho. Accessed on 20 March 2023.

At Faisalabad, in the second Test, Tendulkar batted with great patience, making 59 off 172 balls with a crucial 143-run partnership with Manjrekar. This Test also ended in a draw and so did the third encounter played on a featherbed at Lahore. So, it was 0-0 in the series, going into the final match at Sialkot.

India vs Pakistan, 4th Test, Jinnah Stadium, Sialkot, 9-14 December 1989

As expected, the Indians were presented with a green pitch. The Pakistan bowlers got first use of the juicy track, as Imran Khan won the toss and elected to field. India's two batting mainstays in the series, Manjrekar and Azharuddin, put up a classy 128-run partnership, and Sachin made a quick-fire 35 runs off 51 balls as India posted a competitive score of 324.

Prabhakar and Kapil had consistently made inroads into the Pakistan top order with their swinging deliveries all through the series but had little back up. However, this time, it would be the young right-arm fast medium bowler Vivek Razdan, playing only his second Test, who made the biggest impact. He bowled with great penetration, taking a haul of 5 for 79, as Pakistan was bowled out for 250. For the first time in the series, India had a first innings lead. Inexplicably, this became Razdan's last Test for India.

After conceding a lead of 74, the Pakistan bowlers knew that they had to pull off something truly special to make a match of it, and claim the series victory that they must have expected when the two teams had lined up in Karachi for the first Test match. The Indians, on the other hand, had played resolutely and considered a drawn series a satisfactory result.

The Pakistan bowling attack stormed in at the Indians in the second innings. Srikkanth, Manjrekar, Azharuddin, Shastri, all perished, with the Indian score at just 38.

It was now up to Navjot Singh Sidhu, along with Tendulkar playing his first international series, to ensure India's safety. Disaster struck early into Tendulkar's innings, as he was hit bang on the nose by a Waqar Younis delivery. Everyone, including his batting partner Sidhu, thought that his innings was over. Not only did Tendulkar recover and continue batting, he struck the next delivery from Younis for a boundary. Tendulkar went on to make a vital 57 off 134 balls.

This highly-regarded youngster not only proved that he was blessed with precocious talent, but that he had the courage and maturity that went beyond his years. In the words of senior journalist Gautam Bhattacharya, 'In any case, the 1989 tour was more about his courage to stand up to pace bowlers (at Sialkot, he was hit by a Younis bouncer, started bleeding, but stood up instantly to resume play) than about his genius.'[33]

After Tendulkar's dismissal, Sidhu batted on to make 97. The Indian lower-middle order also stood firm, as the Test match finished with India on 234/7. Sidhu was deservingly named Man of the Match. However, it was the baby-faced Indian who had captured the imagination of an entire nation.

Indian cricket, yearning for a batting superstar post the retirement of Gavaskar, had a new hero—a hero who would fill millions of hearts with joy with his stunning performances in the years to come. From this moment on, the nation held its breath when Sachin Ramesh Tendulkar went out to bat. His rise coincided with India opening its doors to the world through economic liberalization. As a new India emerged, tales

---

[33]Rao, Meenakshi, '1989 Was About Sachin's Courage, Not Genius', *The Pioneer*, 17 November 2013, https://bit.ly/3mdmNwE. Accessed on 10 April 2023.

of the exploits of India's new batting superstar started to spread throughout the world. With Tendulkar's rise, the popularity of Indian cricket reached its zenith. Cricket became a religion in India, and Tendulkar its God.

> **SCORECARD**
>
> **India**: 324 all out (Manjrekar-72, Azharuddin-52; Akram-5/101, Imran Khan-2/61) and 234/7 (Sidhu-97, Tendulkar-57; Imran Khan-3/68, Akram-2/41)
>
> **Pakistan**: 250 all out (Rameez Raja-56, Saleem Malik-34; Razdan-5/79, Prabhakar-3/92)
>
> **Result**: Match drawn

20

THE DOMESTIC CLIFFHANGER

We have tried to touch upon significant domestic matches played in India, and thus we cannot skip arguably the best match played in the history of Ranji Trophy. It was perhaps one of the best long-form matches ever played, even rivalling the miracle at Eden Gardens a decade into the future.

The Bombay team of the early 1990s could compete with the best Bombay teams of the '60s and the '70s. Sunil Gavaskar had retired, but Sachin Tendulkar had announced his arrival. Passing on the flame of excellent Bombay battership from one little master to another was Dilip Balwant Vengsarkar.

Vengsarkar was a tall, gangling man, with all the strokes in the book. He was a severe driver of the cricket ball, and was excellent at square-of-the-wicket shots. Blessed with a fine defensive game and with a knack of riling the opposition, he had a successful international stint, with 17 Test hundreds in 116 Tests, and a special liking for the Mecca of cricket. He scored three hundreds at Lord's Tests in successive England tours.

In the 1991 Ranji Trophy season, the final was played between Bombay, the powerhouse, and Haryana. Haryana's only previous Ranji finals appearance had been in the 1985–86 season, where it had been comprehensively beaten by Delhi. But Haryana did have the greatest all-round player in the history of Indian cricket, Kapil. He had captained his team to a World Cup victory, but the Ranji Trophy had eluded him. This time, he had a team inspired and built in his shadow. He was ably supported by Chetan Sharma, a fine quick bowler as well as batter Ajay Jadeja and wicketkeeper Vijay Yadav. The luckless Amarjit Kaypee was one of the best Indian batters in the domestic circuit for a long while, but an international call eluded him.

Haryana vs Bombay, Finals, Ranji Trophy 1991, Wankhede Stadium, Bombay, 3-7 May 1991

Bombay had reached the final with comprehensive ease, and had in its ranks nine players who had played for India at some point, or would in the future. And of the two who didn't, Shishir Hattangadi was a domestic cricket stalwart, and left-arm spinner Sanjay Patil who later finished his first-class career with more than a hundred wickets. The rest was a virtual India team. Lalchand Rajput opened the batting for Bombay with Hattangadi. The middle-order was rather strong by domestic cricket standards—captain Manjrekar, Vengsarkar, Tendulkar and Kambli. Wicketkeeper Chandrakant Pandit had played for India, as had two of the three quick bowlers, Salil Ankola and Raju Kulkarni. The towering (6 ft 5 in.) Abey Kuruvilla, the other quick bowler, made his India debut in 1997. Bombay were also the favourite because the match was being played at the Wankhede Stadium, their home ground.

Kapil won the toss and decided to bat first. Dhanraj Singh was dismissed early by Kuruvilla, but then Ajay Jadeja and Deepak Sharma had a long 176-run partnership. Deepak had a moderate first-class career, but this innings was going to be the shining light of his career. Ajay Jadeja was dismissed six short of his hundred by the tireless Kuruvilla, and Kaypee came to the middle. A near hundred-run partnership followed, but towards the end of the day's play, Kaypee was dismissed by Kuruvilla. Haryana finished the day at 290/3, with Ajay Banerjee giving Deepak company.

On the second morning, Deepak stood steady while wickets tumbled at the other end. Ankola jolted the lower-middle order of Haryana by dismissing Kapil and Vijay in quick succession. After that came a fine partnership between the two Sharmas, the circumspect Deepak and the devil-may-care Chetan. After 80 more invaluable runs, Deepak's vigil was broken by Ankola, agonizingly one run short of his double-hundred. Haryana was all out for 522, a stroke after tea on Day 2.

Bombay's innings was a story of fits and starts. Seven of the top eight batters got to more than 25, but none could carry on the way Deepak did. Patil got the team's highest score of 85, and Rajput made 74. Off-spinner Yogendra Bhandari got 5 wickets, and Kapil, 3. Bombay were all out for 410, and it was already near the middle of the fourth day. In the Ranji Trophy, if an outright result is not achieved, the higher score in the first innings determines the winner. Haryana and Kapil were nearing their first Ranji triumph, and the lead was 112 runs.

Bombay had not become this juggernaut by throwing in the towel. Its bowlers attacked relentlessly, and before the close of Day 4, Haryana was 100/5. Kapil came in to join Ajay Banerjee, and carted the Bombay bowlers all around Wankhede. Just as he was taking Haryana to an unassailable lead, he was out, bowled by Kulkarni. Haryana finished at 242.

There were 355 runs to win and not even a day's play left. Bombay had to go for it, nevertheless. The start was not auspicious. Kapil and the nippy Chetan got rid of Hattangadi,

Rajput and Manjrekar within 34 runs, and now, two of the greatest exponents of the Bombay school of battership, at very different junctures of their careers, came together. Vengsarkar, at 35, was coming to the end of a storied career. Tendulkar, at 18, was at the beginning of his legendary one.

What happened next was absolute carnage. Tendulkar scored 96 runs off 75 balls off a 134-run partnership. He crashed Kapil back over his head for a six. He flat-batted Chetan into the crowd. He hammered the spinners. And just when he was taking the match away from Kapil's boys, he blasted a rank full toss from Bhandari into the hands of cover.

Kambli, Tendulkar's classmate from school, walked in to give Vengsarkar company. Vengsarkar was peppering the boundary rope now, and runs were in full flow. When not hitting boundaries, they kept the scoreboard ticking with quick singles. This was Day 5 of the match, and Vengsarkar's 35-year-old body creaked; he pulled a muscle, and had to ask for a runner. Rajput joined Vengsarkar as a runner.[34]

After an 81-run partnership, Kambli gave a return catch to Ajay Jadeja's innocuous medium pace. 106 runs to win, and we were within the 20 mandatory overs, with 5 wickets in hand. It was an even match, because Vengsarkar was still there, rolling back the years. The next 4 wickets fell cheaply. Bombay were suddenly 305/9, 50 runs adrift, with only the eleventh man Abey Kuruvilla giving Vengsarkar company.

Vengsarkar had not yet completed his hundred—he duly did so with a six off Bhandari. But this was not a time for personal glory. There was a seemingly impossible task to be

---

[34]Permission to take a runner has now been outlawed from every form of cricket. The rule was: If a player had injured themselves during the course of play, they could ask for a runner, who would essentially do the running between the wickets for the hurt batter.

achieved. He battered Bhandari for 26 runs in an over, and after that, all that was left was a battle of nerves.

Kapil struck Kuruvilla on his pads, and shouted out an appeal. The umpire was not moved and Kapil was furious. Was it going to be a case of so near yet so far for him? The scoreboard ticked forward since Vengsarkar was not averse to taking the singles. Bombay were hurtling closer to the target.

And then came the fourth delivery of the 18th mandatory over. Three runs were needed to win off 14 deliveries. Kuruvilla, the batter, connected, and the ball went towards Amarjit Kaypee. Vengsarkar's runner, Rajput, had started his run, but Kuruvilla hesitated. By the time he ran in full earnest, it was too late. The throw was in the hands of the fielder, and then onto the stumps. Kuruvilla was run out. Haryana became the Ranji Trophy champion for the 1990–91 season.

The people who were in the ground that day say that Vengsarkar was on his knees, sobbing uncontrollably, long after the celebrations in the Haryana camp were over. That one trophy that had eluded Kapil during most of his illustrious career was in his hands finally. Even in interviews 25 years later, Kapil mentioned this as the best victory of his career.

SCORECARD

Haryana: 522 all out (Deepak Sharma-199, Chetan Sharma-98; Kuruvilla-4/128, Ankola-3/77) and 242 all out (Banerjee-60*, Kapil-41; Ankola-39/3, Patil-3/65)

Bombay: 410 all out (Patil-85, Rajput-74; Bhandari-5/118, Kapil-3/54) and 352 all out (Vengsarkar-139*, Tendulkar-96; Sharma-2/59, Bhandari-2/124)

Result: Haryana beat Bombay by 2 runs

21

TIGERS AT HOME

In the limited-overs format, India had carved out an identity by the early 1990s. It was a team of steady battership, a handful of medium-pace bowling all-rounders and suffocating spin bowling. And it was one among a clutch of good limited-overs nations, with a few seriously good players: Kapil, Azharuddin and Tendulkar. In Test cricket though, after the 1970s with the spin quartet, India did not have a true identity. And if truth be told, while the spin quartet was exceptional, India's memorable Test performances were more about sparks of brilliance rather than a sustained pattern, with a clear winning formula.

In early 1990, Mohammad Azharuddin was given the captaincy of the Indian team, replacing K. Srikkanth after the 1989 Pakistan series. Azharuddin was a quiet, shy, reticent man, a gorgeous batter of exceptional, fragile beauty and understated power and arguably the greatest fielder that India has produced. He might not have naturally been seen as a leader, the way Tiger Pataudi, Sunil Gavaskar or Kapil Dev were. Nevertheless, he ended up having a long, rather successful and also a controversial career as a captain.

In his early days of captaincy, Azharuddin had the benefit of having an expert coach to help him strategize. That man was Ajit Wadekar, former Indian captain of the glorious double triumph in the West Indies and England in 1971. With a shrewd cricketing brain, he also became a successful banking professional later in his life. Azharuddin and Wadekar had a superb partnership as captain and coach. They devised, in our opinion, the first consistent Test match winning formula for the Indian national team, albeit only in home conditions.

Azhar's first four series as captain all resulted in defeats—losses in New Zealand and England, a thorough battering in Australia and prior to this series, a close 1-0 series loss in South Africa (the country that had re-entered the Test match arena not long before, after its apartheid-related exclusion). Statistics show that India's Test team was at its lowest ebb, having won only one of its last 25 Tests, and that was at home against Sri Lanka.

Then came England's tour to India in 1992–93. England stepped in India as favourites, with a batting line up of grizzled veterans in captain Graham Gooch, Mike Gatting and Robin Smith, and talented up-and-coming Michael Atherton and Alec Stewart. And the team also had Graeme Hick, the Zimbabwean-born, who was rewriting the record-books in county cricket. He had to wait a fair few years before he became England-eligible. But he was in the English Test team now, and while he had not had the best of start in international cricket, England had high hopes from him. There was a bit of controversy in team selection for the tour, because David Gower, widely perceived as England's best player of spin, had not been chosen.

England believed that it had better spin bowlers—left-armer Phil Tufnell was in excellent form, and veteran off-spinner John Emburey was back after his ban for a tour to South Africa. There was also genuine quick bowling from Devon Malcolm, Paul Jarvis and Chris Lewis, another young player from whom the English had great expectations.

Indian spinners perhaps did not have the name recognition that the English did, but in Venkatapathy Raju, Rajesh Chauhan and Anil Kumble, Azharuddin and Wadekar believed that they had a trio that could deliver. Along with swing-bowling all-rounders in the great Kapil and the combative Manoj Prabhakar, there was the partnership of Azhar and Tendulkar. This was also the debut series for Kambli, Tendulkar's classmate and friend. Lewis bowled to Kambli in one of the tour games, and supposedly remarked, 'I reckon I can get this guy out any time I want to.'[35]

The first Test was played in Calcutta in January 1993. There were a few quirks: England had taken leg-spinner Ian Salisbury along as a net bowler, but he impressed so much during the practice sessions that he was chosen above Tufnell for this Test. Eden Gardens was Azharuddin's favourite hunting ground; he had scored a hundred in his debut test there, the last time England had visited India. As captain, he did not disappoint in the first innings, and scored a glorious 182 in 197 deliveries. India made a total of 371. England, in response, was all out for 163, with the three Indian spinners getting 3 wickets apiece. Following on, England could again not muster up much of a challenge against Kumble, Raju and Chauhan, and set India a target of 79 to win. India got to the target comfortably, with the loss of two wickets, and won the first of the three-match series. England's chief selector, Ted Dexter, complained about the smog in the air in the aftermath of the match!

The second Test began from 11 February 1993 in Chennai. However, just before the match, England had a bout of

---

[35]Smyth, Rob, 'Fumbles, Fallouts and Faulty Planes: England's Nightmarish 1993 Tour of India', *The Guardian*, 8 November 2016, https://bit.ly/3KwqAhS. Accessed on 4 April 2023.

misfortune. Captain Gooch, Mike Gatting and Robin Smith, all fell ill. It was rumoured that Gooch and Gatting had shared a plate of prawn curry, and that had led to the illness. Gooch could not take the field, but Smith and Gatting did. Stewart captained England in Gooch's absence, and handed over the keeping gloves to Yorkshire youngster Richard Blakey. India batted first and piled on the runs. Tendulkar got a massive hundred. Sidhu, a real character of an opener, scored a hundred and India declared at 560/6.

England yet again had no answer to the Indian spinners, and was all out for 286. The team would have to follow on for a second time in the series. Before the second innings, the wickets were largely shared by the three spinners. But in this innings, the best of the Indian spin triumvirate truly came into its own. Lewis managed a rearguard hundred, his first in tests, but it was all Kumble with his 6 wickets in the second innings. England lost by an innings and 22 runs.

Anil Kumble is possibly the greatest spinner and the greatest match-winner in the history of Indian cricket. He was initially underrated as a bowler; he did not have the leg spinner's stock delivery of the big loopy leg break that turned from leg stump to beyond off stump. In fact, before this series, Keith Fletcher, the England coach, announced that precisely because of that reason, he did not believe the English batters would have problems with Kumble. A tall, quick-armed spin bowler, Kumble indeed did not have a big turner, and depended on beating the batter with length and subtle variations in pace and angle. An expert in reading a batter's weakness, he made a great career out of hustle, persistence and will-power. This series was the first blossoming of greatness, when the gangling, bespectacled young man from Bengaluru made the cricketing world sit up and take notice.

India vs England, 3rd Test, Wankhede Stadium, Bombay, 19-23 February 1993

With the series already lost, the England spirits absolutely crumbled in the third Test in Bombay. Gooch was back, but this was a face-saving mission destined to end in failure. England's first innings was impressive for an innings of 178 by Hick, his first in Tests. An innings of great focus and concentration, it was also a display of fine stroke-play. The world perhaps did not see the best of Hick in Test cricket—it was a case of unfulfilled potential to an extent, but the potential was there and this brilliant innings was proof of that. Kumble and Kapil hacked through the rest of the English batters, and the rivals were all out for 347.

India, in return, scored 591. Everyone got starts—Sidhu, Prabhakar, Tendulkar, Azharuddin, Pravin Amre, Kapil—but there was only one who could really make the start count. And that was Vinod Kambli. In his first international match at his home ground, he scored 224. It was an innings of great strength and potential. Strong pulls, correct off-drives, strong cuts off the back foot, the left-hander's natural elegant flicks, allied with the correct defensive technique. It seemed that the future of Indian battership was secure for the next decade and a half, with Kambli to complement Tendulkar.

England was completely mentally sapped by now. Again, Kumble, Raju and Chauhan took apart the English batters. Kumble cut through the unsure English defensive strokes. Richard Blakey panicked and was bowled first ball by Kumble. And there was again an innings defeat. It was deja vu for England.

This was perhaps the worst series for England as a touring party, but Azharuddin and Wadekar had chanced upon a winning formula. This involved playing on dust bowls—which were good for batting on the first two days, but would break up like breadcrumbs on the remaining days. India had a lethal weapon in Kumble to exploit these dust bowls. The Indian batters would pile up big runs in the first innings, and then Kumble and his able supporting cast of spinners would run through the opposition.

This series, along with the dust bowl formula, gave us Kumble (the dour, intense leg spinner) and Kambli (the flashy, talented batter). While Kumble ended up having a legendary career, Kambli's was a career of a thousand 'what-ifs'. Perhaps, he could not handle the fame. Perhaps, he got injured at the worst times. Perhaps, he should have been given a few more opportunities to come back. We do not know, but for that Test at Wankhede, his home ground, he was indeed king.

SCORECARD

England: 347 all out (Hick-178, Lewis-49; Kapil-3/35, Kumble-3/95) and 229 all out (Smith-62, Gatting-61; Kumble-4/70, Prabhakar-3/28)

India: 591 all out (Kambli-224, Sidhu-79, Tendulkar-78; Tufnell-4/142, Hick-2/97)

Result: India beat England by an innings and 15 runs

22

DARKNESS UNDER FLOODLIGHTS

The hallowed turf of Eden Gardens in Calcutta has given Indian cricket some of its most iconic moments. It has also seen some of Indian cricket's darkest days. From violence and a bonfire in the stands on New Year's Day in 1967—amid which Conrad Hunte was seen trying to recover the West Indies—and a stampede over tickets during a match against Australia in December 1969, which killed six people, the stadium has had its fair share of tragic moments. However, to the generation that we, the authors of this book, belong to no incident strikes as much sorrow as the 1996 World Cup semi-final against Sri Lanka. The match showed how, at times, the passion for the game in India can work to its own detriment.

With pitches tailor-made to India's strengths and spinners who could take advantage, the Indian team became almost invincible at home. The Test success was replicated in the limited-overs arena as well, with victories in multi-nation tournaments, such as the Hero Cup, the Singer World Series in Sri Lanka (featuring Australia, Pakistan, India and Sri Lanka), the Wills World Series (featuring New Zealand and the West Indies as the other teams) and the Asia Cup in the UAE. Hence, when the 1996 World Cup—to be jointly hosted by India, Sri Lanka and Pakistan—started, the Indian cricket fans expected nothing short of a second World Cup trophy.

The group stage of the World Cup was barely smooth sailing for India. There was Sri Lanka's convincing victory over India at the Feroz Shah Kotla ground (now known as the Arun Jaitley Stadium) in Delhi, powered by a ferocious assault by the Sri Lankan openers, Sanath Jayasuriya and Romesh Kaluwitharana, after India posted a commanding total of 271, with a brilliant 137 from Tendulkar. The Indians also had another reversal at the Wankhede Stadium, when they were beaten by 16 runs by Mark Taylor's Australia. Wins against Kenya, the West Indies and Zimbabwe ensured India made the quarter-finals comfortably.

The quarter-final against Pakistan at the M. Chinnaswamy Stadium was a momentous occasion. The high intensity match was filled with drama—from Ajay Jadeja's remarkable ball-striking against Waqar Younis, to the bitter tussle between Venkatesh Prasad and Aamir Sohail. In the end, the Indian team kept its nerves to claim a famous 39-run victory. Indians must have felt that the World Cup trophy was now within their grasp.

India faced a familiar foe in the semi-final—Sri Lanka, which had put up yet another scintillating batting display as it disposed of England in the quarter-final. Sri Lanka had beaten India before in the tournament, but surely the former's experience and superior talent would tell on the big occasion. However, the Sri Lankans were unfazed, taking each match as one more step to completing a fairytale journey. Their experienced cricketers, Asanka Gurusinha, Aravinda de Silva, Arjuna Ranatunga in the line-up had lived up to their billing, while a new superstar had emerged in world cricket—Sanath Jayasuriya.

India vs Sri Lanka, World Cup Semi-Final, Eden Gardens, Calcutta, 13 March 1996

In front of a packed crowd at Eden Gardens, numbering close to a lakh, Mohammad Azharuddin won the toss and elected to field first. This decision, which has attracted controversy for many years, was probably done to negate the Sri Lankan strength of chasing.

The crowd was in delirium, as Javagal Srinath dismissed both Sri Lankan openers in the first over. But the Indians still had a major hurdle to cross: Aravinda 'Mad Max' de Silva. He took on the Indian bowlers, picking Venkatesh Prasad for special treatment. Of the team's first 48 runs, he scored 43. Aravinda hardly played a ball in the air, yet seemed to find the gaps with ease. A quicker one from Kumble ended an extraordinary innings of 66 off 47 balls, and that turned the momentum in India's favour. A resolute half century from Roshan Mahanama and some hefty blows at the end from Chaminda Vaas guided Sri Lanka to a decent score of 251 for 8.

In those days, to the Indian fan, Indian batting only meant Sachin Tendulkar. With each stroke by him, Indian hopes grew, while a Tendulkar dismissal would lead to millions switching off their television sets. Much to the Indian fans' delight, he seemed to be batting with great confidence at Eden Gardens. When he was at the crease, the Eden Gardens pitch looked like a flat batting deck. Playing the Sri Lankan bowlers with ease after India lost Sidhu early, Tendulkar notched up his half century in the 17th over.

Then, calamity struck in the 23rd over, as a delivery from Jayasuriya hit Sachin's pads, and in almost a reflex action, Sachin stepped out of his crease for a brief moment—that was all it took for Kaluwitharana to affect a superb stumping.

What followed next can be described as nothing short of a tale of horror. The pitch suddenly seemed to change character and turned into a minefield. Azharuddin and Manjrekar fell in quick succession, as the Sri Lankan spinners started to scythe through the Indian batting. India sent Javagal Srinath in at No. 6 to throw the Sri Lankan spinners off their length, but alas, he was run out before making any significant impact. Ajay Jadeja, Nayan Mongia and Ashish Kapoor also had no answer to the Sri Lankan spinners, as a stunned Vinod Kambli watched in shock at the other end. India was at 120/8. The nation was seeing its hopes sink.

An incensed crowd expressed its anger by throwing bottles on the ground. Upul Chandana, the Sri Lankan leg-spinner, was one of the first to be struck. The umpires had no choice but to temporarily halt the game. After the initial burst of crowd dissent, the police somehow managed to bring the situation under control and the game was about to restart. However, another spurt of bottle-throwing from the life membership block forced match referee Clive Lloyd to come out. The frenzied crowd was voicing its disgust over the Indian collapse from all corners. The match referee had to take a hard call, and he did. The match was awarded to Sri Lanka by default. Kambli left the crease in despair. The image of his trudging off the field in tears is one of the most painful in Indian cricket.

Cricket is more than a game for Indians. Results of cricket matches dictate moods as people go about their work. Cricket drives dinner-table discussions. Cricketers are worshipped. Fans, who show cricketers so much adulation, also vent out their frustration in the most extreme manner. Sometimes, the love and passion for the game just boils over. Indian cricket hung its head in shame that day. It was a truly dark, dark day for Indian cricket under the floodlights of the Eden Gardens.

SCORECARD

Sri Lanka: 251/8 in 50 overs (De Silva-66, Mahanama-58, Srinath-3/34, Tendulkar-2/34)

India: 120/8 in 34.1 overs (Tendulkar-65, Manjrekar-25, Jayasuriya-3/12, De Silva-1/3)

Result: Sri Lanka beat India by default

23

THE LORD'S PLAY

To say Lord's has had a significant role in shaping the history of Indian cricket would be an understatement. The home of cricket has played host to era-defining matches in Indian cricket, be it India's introduction to Test cricket in 1932 or its first World Cup victory in 1983.

The second Test of India's series against England at the venue in 1996 was yet another of those distinctions. The most formidable batting line-up in Indian cricket history, and arguably world cricket history, had taken shape. No longer did hopes of Indian fans fade when Tendulkar was dismissed. No longer were television sets switched off the instant the Little Master departed from the crease. A stylish left-hander from Bengal and a resolute right-hander from Karnataka, around the same age as the legendary Mumbaikar, announced their arrival to the world of cricket at Lord's and gave Indian fans two new reasons to dream.

India's tour to England was the next major assignment after the former's tragic exit from the 1996 World Cup. The squad for the ODIs and Test series featured two young batters who had been knocking on the doors of the selection panel through strong domestic performances for quite a while.

One was Rahul Dravid, a classy, technically equipped batter from Karnataka. The other was Sourav Ganguly, an elegant left-hander from West Bengal, who had made his limited-overs debut in the Benson & Hedges World Series in 1992, and had not played for the country since. Ganguly had been criticized during and after the tour for his attitude; it was rumoured that he had refused to even carry the drinks.

Ganguly's selection for England attracted a fair amount of criticism from former cricketers, with some questioning his approach and others calling his selection a result of the quota system. Well, they were about to be proven wrong.

Ganguly and Dravid both made their first international appearances in England in the last match of the ODI series, which turned out to be a nightmare for the Indians, as they lost 0-2. All throughout, the Indians had seemed clueless in the early English summer against the England seam bowling line-up.

Off the field, there was drama in the Indian camp, as Sidhu left the tour citing differences with captain Mohammad Azharuddin. Former BCCI Secretary, Jaywant Lele, in his book, *I Was There: Memoirs of a Cricket Administrator*, said that Sidhu thought Azharuddin was constantly abusing him. Azharuddin, with his personal life in turmoil, had also become increasingly distant from his players.[36]

The first Test at Edgbaston saw India crumble to an 8-wicket defeat, in spite of a stunning second innings with 122 by Tendulkar. The rest of the batting line-up continued its struggle in conditions that aided seam and swing. India's strategy of playing an extra bowler had backfired, and it was clear that the Indians needed to beef up the batting for the next game.

---

[36]PTI, 'Lele Reveals Why Sidhu Walked out of 1996 England Tour', *The Times of India*, 25 October 2011, https://bit.ly/3ZGpaFQ. Accessed on 4 April 2023.

India vs England, 2nd Test, Lord's Cricket Ground, London, 20-24 June 1996

There was more strife for the Indians, as Manjrekar had to withdraw from the second Test at Lord's due to an ankle injury. Thus, the door opened for Ganguly and Dravid to make their Test debuts at Lord's.

India won the crucial toss and elected to field. Javagal Srinath and Venkatesh Prasad, who put in lion-hearted performances throughout the series, took advantage of helpful conditions, with 3 and 5 wickets, respectively. India at one point had reduced England to 107 for 5. Then wicketkeeper Jack Russell and Graham Thorpe staged a superb recovery, with a partnership of 136. England's innings ended on 344, and Russell top scored with 131.

India was jolted early in its innings, with Vikram Rathour perishing for 15. Ganguly came out to bat at No. 3 at the fall of Rathour's wicket. On Day 2, he impressed many former cricketers in the audience, with his precise footwork against the moving delivery. India ended Day 2 with 2 wickets down, and with Ganguly and Tendulkar at the crease.

On the third day, Tendulkar was bowled by Lewis for 31. Azharuddin and Ajay Jadeja also fell without adding much to the scoreboard. At the other end, Ganguly was in sparkling form. His silken shots through the offside reminded many English supporters of the elegant David Gower. 'On the offside, first there is God, then there is Dada' was a famous quote by Rahul Dravid, and Ganguly's brilliance on the offside was in full view that day. Dravid joined Ganguly at the crease, with India at 202 for 5.

Together, the debutants guided India towards a position of strength. The right-hander from Karnataka impressed with

Sourav Ganguly

his determination and solidity. Another exquisite cover drive from Ganguly brought up a memorable century.

His stunning knock of 131 was ended by Alan Mullally. India was at 296 for 6. After Ganguly's dismissal, Dravid found two able allies in his Karnataka teammates Kumble and Srinath, as India moved past 400. Dravid's resolute knock ended an agonizing 5 runs short of a well-deserved hundred, dismissed by Lewis. India finished on 429, with a lead of 85.

The Indian bowlers put up a brave effort in the second innings, with Srinath and Prasad picking 2 wickets each, and Kumble bowling a marathon spell of 51 overs, conceding 90 runs and claiming 3 wickets. In the end though, there was simply not enough time left in the match. The Test came to a close with the English innings on 278/9.

Ganguly notched up another century in the final Test at Trent Bridge, becoming only the third batter after Lawrence Rowe and Alvin Kallicharran to score centuries in their first two Test innings. Tendulkar also played a superb knock of 177 as India posted a mammoth first innings of 521. However, the pitch was too flat for any team to force a result, as the English batters replied with an even bigger score.

The series was lost 0-1 to India. But amid this defeat, there was a ray of hope for the future. India had found two young batters who could stand up to pressure and excel in overseas conditions. Ganguly's stunning stroke play and Dravid's resilience and technique became a feature of India's batting in the years to come. Soon, they were joined by the classy Hyderabad right-hander V.V.S. Laxman. Together with Tendulkar, they formed the Fab Four of Indian batting, which would scored 45,000 runs between them in Test cricket. Their performances became the foundation for many famous Indian victories. Looking back, one can conclude that the seeds of the glorious era of the Fab Four were planted on that afternoon at Lord's, when the Prince (Ganguly) and the Wall (Dravid) etched their names into Indian cricket folklore.

SCORECARD

England: 344 all out (Russell-124, Thorpe-89; Prasad-5/76, Srinath-3/76) and 278/9 declared (Stewart-66, Irani-41; Kumble-3/90, Prasad-2/54)

India: 429 all out (Ganguly-131, Dravid-95; Mullally-3/71, Lewis-3/101)

Result: Match drawn

24

AN UNEXPECTED COLLAPSE

To an earlier generation of Indian cricket followers, nothing will surpass the despair felt when Javed Miandad hit 6 off the final ball by Chetan Sharma that day in April 1986. To a different generation of Indian cricket followers, the nadir was reached 11 years later, on 31 March 1997, at Kensington Oval, Bridgetown, Barbados.

India was coming off a chastizing 2-0 defeat at the hands of the South Africans, having been routed by the rivals' quick bowling attack led by the fearsome Allan Donald in its 1996–97 tour to South Africa. India's over-dependence on Tendulkar to be the saviour in overseas conditions was reduced with the arrival of Dravid and Ganguly in 1996, but they were both still finding their feet as international players. Laxman debuted in the latter part of 1996, and was even more raw. However, two stalwarts of the previous decade, Azharuddin and Sidhu, were still there in the team.

The West Indies was a far cry from the world-beaters of the '70s and the '80s. The legendary fast-bowling partnership of Curtly Ambrose and Courtney Walsh was past its prime but still formidable. Ian Bishop had returned to cricket after a long layoff necessitated by an injury. Among the batters, there was the peerless Brian Lara, and the talented but inconsistent Carl Hooper. Shivnarine Chanderpaul, the quirky master of the patient game, had made his appearance a few seasons back. Altogether though, this West Indies side had many who were a few notches below their brilliant predecessors.

The Indian bowling had been severely impacted by the loss of the spearhead Srinath. Venkatesh Prasad, a fine bowler but without the pace of Srinath, was burdened with shouldering the pace-bowling attack. Abey Kuruvilla and Dodda Ganesh were brought in to support Prasad. The leg-spin of Kumble and the left-arm orthodox of Sunil Joshi would complement them.

This was to be a five-Test and four ODI series. It was widely considered that this was a good chance for India to win another series in the Caribbean after the class of 1971. The fiery tracks of Kensington Oval, Bourda and Sabina Park were, however, a thing of the past. The newly-laid tracks often played slow and low, making both quick run-making and wicket-taking difficult. Attritional cricket was often the order of the day.

The first Test at the Sabina Park was a staid draw. Some scintillating stroke-play from Lara and Hooper, and a spirited marathon bowling performance from Kumble were the take-homes from this match.

The second Test at Queen's Park Oval, Trinidad, followed much of the same pattern. If anything, it was even more of a snooze fest. Sidhu, famous for his towering sixes against Shane Warne back home, scored a laborious 201 off nearly 500 deliveries. The West Indies blocked their way through both their innings. A result was out of the question.

West Indies vs India, 3rd Test, Kensington Oval, Bridgetown, Barbados, 27-31 March 1997

This was the background in which the third Test was played at Kensington Oval. It was a testing track, with considerable grass and the expectation of uneven bounce as the game progressed. The West Indies had a major misfortune on the eve of the match, when captain Walsh complained of a hamstring injury and could not play. Bishop was brought in to replace him. Since the Kensington Oval track was quite green, India chose to field three quickies and replaced Joshi with his state mate, Ganesh.

Lara captained the West Indies for the first time in his career, standing in for Walsh. Indian captain Tendulkar won the toss and elected to send the Caribbeans in first. On the green, bouncy track, Prasad provided one of his best displays in Test cricket, and troubled all batters—all, except Chanderpaul, who batted throughout the innings, having come in at the fall of Sherwin Campbell's wicket. He remained not out for 137, and the West Indies were all out for 298.

India struggled against the four-pronged West Indies attack as well, and except for a patient 170-run third-wicket partnership between Dravid and Tendulkar, there was no other substantial partnership in the innings. Sidhu, Ganguly and Azharuddin got starts but could not convert them into substantial scores. There was some contribution by Kumble in the lower-order, and India ended up with a meagre 21-run lead at the mid-point of the match.

The West Indies' second innings was all about the Indian quick bowlers. Kuruvilla was a tall, fast-medium bowler, who had had a stellar first-class career as the spearhead of the Mumbai bowling attack in the '90s. This was his great moment—playing for India. He got a 5-wicket haul. Ganesh, another stalwart of the Indian domestic game, also performed creditably, and Prasad carried his form from the first innings. The West Indies was all out for 140, almost right at the end of the third day, and India went on to bat on the fourth day with victory only 120 runs away.

What followed, on the fourth day of play, on 31 March 1997, was perhaps the most difficult moment for many Indian cricket fans. Early in the innings, Sidhu was caught in the slips, fending at a lifting delivery from Franklyn Rose. There was agony for the player and the Indian fans when replays showed that Rose had overstepped and it was a no-ball—a call missed by umpire Lloyd Barker. Rose, who was from Jamaica, had a flowing chest-on bowling action, excellent pace and exuberant celebration but often lacked control. This morning, he was right on the money. Bowling from wide of the crease, he got one to straighten to Dravid, and the Indian edged a catch to the wicketkeeper. India was two down for 16. Next, a slightly short-of-good-length ball from Rose kept low and knocked back Laxman's off stump. Three down for India.

Ian Bishop came back now to bowl a lovely out-swinger to Tendulkar. The Little Master edged, and Lara plucked up a fine catch at first slip. India was wobbling now at 4 down for 32. Then came a tentative partnership between former captain Azharuddin and Ganguly. They edged and missed and continued to push the score forward. Ambrose came back into the attack, and tested Ganguly thoroughly for an over of sustained hostility, eventually castling him. The West Indies could see the end now: an unlikely victory. India was still 75 runs short, and had lost half its team.

Ambrose then got through Azhar's defence with a ball that kept low. The rest of the innings was a procession. Bishop and Ambrose wiped out the tail, and India was all out for 81. The team batted for only 35.5 overs. India had failed to chase the 120-run winning target. The West Indies had won by 38 runs.

The rest of the series was largely washed out by torrential rain. The West Indies won 1-0. Tendulkar was gravely disturbed by this failure, and mentioned in an interview[37] much later that he had considered retiring from cricket after this failure. Thankfully, he didn't. He, however, relinquished the captaincy after a few more failures, and that marked the start of the next chapter of Indian cricket.

> **SCORECARD**
>
> **West Indies:** 298 all out (Chanderpaul-137*, Ambrose-37; Prasad-5/82, Ganesh-2/70) and 140 all out (Lara-45, Dillon-21; Kuruvilla-5/68, Prasad-3/39)
>
> **India:** 319 all out (Tendulkar-92, Dravid-78; Rose-4/77, Bisho-3/70) and 81 all out (Laxman-19; Bishop-4/22, Rose-3/19)
>
> **Result:** West Indies beat India by 38 runs

---

[37]'After Barbados Defeat, Sachin Tendulkar Considered Quitting Cricket', *The Indian Express*, 3 November 2014, https://tinyurl.com/6xhjnc66. Accessed on 26 September 2023.

25

DESERT STORM!

Imagine a scenario. You return from school, eagerly switch on your television set to watch the match. With bated breath, you watch a nearly impossible target being set by a nearly unbeatable opposition. It is late in the evening; your mother literally has to drag you away from the television set for dinner. You stuff your face with some morsels and go back to watch the match. You see one short, stocky, powerfully-built young man take on the might of the Australian team. He goes on to take on the weather gods—the searing heat of the deserts, and even a sandstorm. This was our Desert Storm!

Desert Storm! To a generation of Indian cricket fans, those two words evoke myriad memories of childhood or adolescence. This was the Sharjah-special tri-nation one-day tournament, with Australia and New Zealand participating in the tournament along with India. The initial round-robin league where the three teams played each other twice was followed by the two top teams playing the finals. The official name of the tournament was the Coca-Cola Cup, named after the sponsors.

Only three days prior to the start of this 1998 Coca-Cola Cup tournament, India and Australia were involved in another three-nation cricket tournament along with Zimbabwe, played in India and sponsored by Pepsi, the rival soft drink company.

Australia had won that tournament, beating India in the finals.

Sharjah was not a happy hunting ground for India. Miandad's last-ball six against Chetan at the 1986 Sharjah Cup had been a blow to the Indian cricketing psyche. After that win, from the late 1980s to the 1990s, Pakistani teams had consistently had an upper hand over Indian teams right up to the end of the millennium. Pakistan was not playing this tournament. Australia, however, was arguably the best team in the world across all formats around that time.

In the first match of the tournament, India beat New Zealand on the back of a ton from Ganguly. In the subsequent match, New Zealand was brushed aside by Australia by 6 wickets. Australia gave the same treatment to India next, winning comprehensively by 58 runs. At this point, Damien Fleming, the swing bowler from Australia, could control the ball as if on a thread and he bowled excellently against both New Zealand and India.

The real shock came in the first reverse fixtures. A slew of runouts saw India crumble for 181 against New Zealand, and the latter got across the line. A charged-up New Zealand then played out of their skins against Australia, but the Aussies eventually managed to defeat their Trans-Tasman rivals.

Everything hinged on the last match of the league stages, where India had to win or lose a close-contested match against Australia to reach the finals.

On that day, Australia scored a handsome 284/7, with the help of an elegant 81 from opener Mark Waugh and a typically industrious 101 from Michael Bevan. By the time India came out to bat, there were mini-sandstorms lashing at the Indian batters. However, Tendulkar remained unbeaten that day. He continually stepped out and pulled Michael Kasprowicz, a bowler of respectable pace by all means. While other Indian batters were struggling from the other end, Tendulkar was in the zone. The bowlers were no match.

And then came the only presence that could stand a chance against the Little Master in that mood. Mother Nature intervened. A huge sandstorm engulfed the stadium and stopped the match, temporarily. After nearly half an hour, when the match could be restarted, the umpires decided to truncate the match to 46 overs for India. The victory target was 276 runs now, and the qualification target was 237, in 46 overs. Tendulkar was in no mood to relent. Wickets continued to fall from the other end but he continued—6 off Steve Waugh, 4 off Fleming, then another 6 off Waugh. Then there was a stroke of luck: Damien Martyn missed a tough chance to catch Tendulkar at deep mid-wicket.

Now, 48 runs were needed off 28 balls to win—and one man was not thinking of qualification, he was thinking of the win. A towering 6, and then a 4 off Fleming followed. And then with 32 needed of 19 balls, Fleming bowled one short to Tendulkar and he went for a pull. It was too high, and he missed. But did he get a faint edge? Wicketkeeper Gilchrist appealed and Fleming pleaded, both desperate. Umpire Ian Robinson was convinced though—it was not out. And then suddenly, we saw the anguish in the Australian faces change to joy—Tendulkar was walking away. He felt an edge, and he was doing the honest thing. Laxman and Hrishikesh Kaniktar blocked through the last three overs. India had qualified, and lived to fight another day.

Thus, ended Desert Storm version 1.0. The Australians had won the match, but had they? They were certainly rattled, their veneer of invincibility dented by the genius of one man.

India vs Australia, Final, Tri-Nation Tournament, Sharjah Cricket Stadium, Sharjah, 24 April 1998

Australians were known to not buckle easily—they kept faith in the team that got them this far. And then came the final. With renewed confidence, Australian captain Steve Waugh won the toss and decided to bat first. But they did not have the best of starts. Within the first six overs, India's opening bowlers Agarkar and Prasad had snared 3 Australian wickets. Then came a controlled partnership between Gilchrist and Bevan. The former played an uncharacteristically quiet innings, and Bevan, the most consistent limited-overs batter of the times, gave the Australians a platform to launch themselves. By the time they had fallen for identical 45 runs, Australia had a platform. Captain Waugh and Darren Lehmann could now attack the Indian bowlers.

And attack they did. The next 15 overs yielded 103 runs, and both Waugh and Lehmann finished on identical 70 runs. At the end of 50 overs, Australia was 272/9. India had to get 273 to win, a very competitive score in the conditions.

But India had Tendulkar. If Desert Storm 1.0 was heavy-metal cricket, Desert Storm 2.0 was classic rock. There were sporadic shows of violent power, but that was engulfed by serene, complete control. The iron fist that was thrown at the Australians was sheathed in velvet gloves.

Tendulkar started slowly. However, a massive on-drive, which missed taking the head of non-striker Ganguly by a whisker, showed his intent. Ganguly had scored the bulk of the runs when he was dismissed in the ninth over. Pinch-hitter Nayan Mongia was sent up the order, but all the pinch-hitting was done by Tendulkar now. Once his biggest rival, Warne, came in to bowl his first over from around the wicket. Then, Tendulkar stepped out and lifted Warne over the long-on boundary.

By the time Mongia got out, halfway through the innings, India was on 128. Captain Azharuddin walked in, another big-match player. With absolute control and minimal fuss, Tendulkar and Azharuddin built up a dominant 120-run partnership. Regular hits to the boundary made sure that the change bowlers for Australia, Tom Moody and Waugh, could never settle into a rhythm.

Warne received the maximum punishment. The champion batter had decided that the challenge had to be taken with someone of his own exalted stature, the greatest leg-spinner of all time. Fleming and Kasprowicz were repeatedly smashed back over their heads. This was an all-time great, in his zone. In the 45th over, with the match won for all practical purposes, Tendulkar received perhaps the worst decision of his lifetime from umpire Steve Bucknor, and was given LBW to Kasprowicz, to a ball pitched outside leg stump, and missing the off stump by a fair distance. Not to be left behind, the other umpire Javed Akhtar managed to outdo Bucknor by giving Azharuddin 'caught behind down the leg-side' when there was clear daylight between bat and ball. There were just 12 runs to win off four overs then, and Ajay Jadeja and Hrishikesh Kanitkar made sure of the victory.

India had won the Coca-Cola Cup. It was perhaps one of the multitudes of tri-nation tournaments of little significance played during the late '90s, but this specific one was made forever memorable by those two breathtaking knocks.

These were the last embers of the 'Sachin is India and India is Sachin' phenomenon that overwhelmed Indian cricket in the 1990s. As the new millennium drew near, Dravid emerged as the most dependable No. 3 batter. Ganguly and Laxman consolidated their positions to provide the Indian team with the Big-4—a middle-order to compare with any other. Virender Sehwag emerged as the most distinct of opening batters. With Kumble, Srinath, and later Harbhajan Singh and Zaheer Khan, India emerged as the only team to compete toe-to-toe with the Australians of that vintage—perhaps, the greatest team the world had ever seen.

> **SCORECARDS**
>
> **League Stage**
> **Australia:** 284/7 in 50 overs (Bevan-101, Mark Waugh-81; Prasad-2/41, Tendulkar-1/27)
>
> **India:** 250/5 in 46 overs (Tendulkar-143, Mongia-35; Moody-2/40, Fleming-2/46)
>
> **Result:** Australia beat India by 26 runs (revised)
>
> **Final:**
> **Australia:** 272/9 in 50 overs (Lehmann-70, Steve Waugh-70; Prasad-2/32, Kanitkar-2/50)
>
> **India:** 275/4 in 48.3 overs (Tendulkar-134, Azharuddin-58; Fleming-2/47, Kasprowicz-2/48)
>
> **Result:** India beat Australia by 6 wickets

26

MAGIC IN KOTLA

7 February 1999. Feroz Shah Kotla. Pakistan was on 201 for 9 in the fourth innings, facing certain defeat. Srinath bowled a short of a good length delivery. Younis rocked back and hit a skier that seemed to be going over the head of square leg. Sadagoppan Ramesh, playing his second Test, ran back to try and take the catch. The ball fell away from him. The whole Kotla crowd and the Indian team heaved a sigh of relief. In usual circumstances, there would be disappointment at a missed opportunity, but that afternoon in Delhi was different. This is the story of the afternoon when history was made.

To understand the makings of the epic feat, which lies at the heart of this chapter, one must go back to September 1992 to the Irani Trophy match between the defending Ranji Trophy champions Delhi and The Rest at the same ground. Bowling with great discipline, on a pitch that had started to get more and more up and down, as the game wore on, Kumble had destroyed the Delhi batting in both innings, picking up a match haul of 13 for 138. This match had ensured that Kumble came back into the Test side after being out for more than two years following his debut Test. Kotla was his favourite hunting ground, where he picked up 58 wickets in just seven Tests at an average of 16.79.

Anil Kumble

The first Test series between India and Pakistan since Tendulkar's debut series in 1989 was as much about diplomacy as it was about the contest on the field. The series almost did not happen, as certain groups instigated major protests, determined to stop the tour at any cost.

On 6 January 1999, supporters of Bal Thackeray's Shiv Sena barged into the Feroz Shah Kotla stadium, the proposed venue for the first Test, and dug up the pitch. It took a series of assurances from the government, the BCCI and the Delhi cricket administration and the direct intervention of the then Indian PM to ensure that the tour went ahead.[38] This resulted in a change in schedule, with Chennai being allotted the first Test and Delhi hosting the second.

---

[38]Goldenberg, Suzanne, 'Hindu Extremists Begin Pitch Battle to Stop Pakistani Tour', *The Guardian*, 8 January 1999, https://bit.ly/3lnCtNr. Accessed on 21 March 2023.

The Chennai Test was a thriller. Battling a bad back, Tendulkar played one of his finest Test innings, making 136 as India threatened to chase down the fourth innings target of 271, after being 5 down for 82. However, Tendulkar was dismissed with the Indian score on 254, and a familiar collapse of the Indian tail ensued. It was a heartbreaking 12-run loss for the hosts. Saqlain Mushtaq was the star for Pakistan with a 5-wicket haul in each innings. The knowledgeable Chennai crowd then gave a standing ovation to the Pakistan team, as they made a lap of honour around the M.A. Chidambaram Stadium.

India vs Pakistan, 2nd Test, Feroz Shah Kotla, Delhi, 4-7 February 1999

On to our featured match at Kotla. At 0-1 down in the series, the pressure was completely on the home team. Azharuddin won a crucial toss electing to bat first on the Kotla pitch, notoriously tough to bat on in the fourth innings. There was also the question of how well the pitch had been salvaged, post the damage inflicted by the Shiv Sena.

Despite a good start by the openers, the Indians could only put together a score of 252 in the first inning. Saqlain picked up his third consecutive 5-wicket haul, as the last 7 wickets fell for 61 runs. Captain Azharuddin was India's top scorer with 67.

When it was Pakistan's turn to bat, Kumble, reunited with his beloved Kotla turf, did the bulk of the damage, running through the Pakistan middle-order. Ijaz Ahmed, Inzamam-ul-Haq and Yousuf Youhana all fell to the tall leg spinner from Karnataka. Kumble picked up 4 for 75. The Pakistan innings folded for 172, giving India a vital lead of 80 runs.

Magic in Kotla

In the Indian second innings, the left-handed opener Ramesh played superbly and was dismissed, agonizingly on 96, caught and bowled off by Mushtaq Ahmed. After losing a few quick wickets, Ganguly and Srinath notched up a potentially match winning 100-run eighth-wicket partnership. Ganguly was elegant as ever, making an unbeaten 62. India scored 339 runs in their second innings, setting Pakistan a huge target of 420 runs.

The Pakistan openers Saeed Anwar and Shahid Afridi started the innings with gusto. Launching into attacking strokes at the slightest opportunity, the Pakistan openers romped to a hundred-run partnership. Kumble's first six overs went for 27 runs. The Indian fielding and body language too appeared lacklustre, and incredibly it seemed that the Pakistanis had wrested the initiative. Then, Azharuddin made the crucial shift of bringing Kumble on from the pavilion end. The move worked like magic.

With the score on 101, Afridi attempted to hit a Kumble delivery on the off stump. However, the ball landed in Mongia's hands. There was a loud appeal for caught from the Indians, and umpire A.V. Jayaprakash raised his finger almost instantly. Ijaz was dismissed LBW off the very next ball, with a full and straight delivery. There was no stopping Kumble from then on.

Inzamam, Youhana and Moin Khan fell in quick succession. Kumble's accuracy and pace off the track made him almost impossible to play against under these conditions. He just needed the odd ball to turn, to implant doubts in the minds of batters.

Anwar who had seen the carnage from the other end was eventually dismissed with the Pakistan score on 128. Only 4 wickets remained between India and a squared series. Also, just 4 wickets remained between Kumble emulating the almost mythical feat of Jim Laker at Old Trafford way back in 1956, against Australia. Whispers of a perfect 10 started floating around the Kotla.

After staging a brief recovery with Akram, Saleem Malik went to pull a short of a length delivery from Kumble with the score on 186. To his shock, it missed his bat and struck the top of middle stump. This was yet another example of a batter beaten by the sheer pace that Kumble generated off the wicket. The Pakistan spin duo of Mushtaq and Saqlain were the next two to succumb to the brilliance of the Karnataka leg spinner. There was 1 wicket to go.

Srinath bowled the 60th over of the innings. He was instructed to bowl way outside off stump, and he duly obliged. It could all have gone pear-shaped if Ramesh had taken that catch, which we spoke about at the beginning of this chapter. However, this day was destined to go down in history and it was Kumble who had the final word. On the third ball of the 61st over of the Pakistan innings, Akram inside-edged a delivery to forward short leg, and Laxman took a sharp catch. Akram was dismissed for a brave 37. Pakistan were all out for 207. India won by 212 runs. Series ended at 1-1. However, in the minds of the audience, none of those numbers mattered. The only figures that mattered were 10 for 74.

There could have been no Indian bowler more deserving of this feat. Kumble has a strong case of being considered India's greatest match-winner of all time. Through his remarkable persistence and class, he made India a dominant force at home, and later in his career, overseas as well. One of the greatest spinners the world has ever seen, Anil Kumble walks into our all-time Indian Test XI.

SCORECARD

India: 252 all out (Azharuddin-67, Ramesh-60; Saqlain-5/94, Mushtaq Ahmed-2/64) and 339 all out (Ramesh-96, Ganguly-62; Saqlain-5/122, Akram-3/43)

Pakistan: 172 all out (Afridi-32, Malik-21; Kumble-4/75, Harbhajan-3/30) and 207 all out (Anwar-69, Afridi-41; Kumble-10/74)

Result: India beat Pakistan by 212 runs

27

A VERY VERY SPECIAL MIRACLE

Of all the remarkable numbers associated with India's monumental victory over Australia in 2001, at the Eden Gardens, we think '335 for no loss' stands out. With their team facing certain defeat, two batters mastered the pressure of the occasion, a fourth-day pitch, and a truly great bowling attack—with two brilliant fast bowlers and the greatest leg spinner to ever play the game. And it was this fourth day that turned the course of one of the most extraordinary Test series ever played on the Indian soil. It was this day that kickstarted a golden era for Indian cricket, which had been ravaged by the match-fixing scandal only a year before. This day and the eventual victory gave new identity to Indian cricket. This is the story of V.V.S. Laxman and Rahul Dravid, of Harbhajan Singh the Turbanator and a resurgent Indian team under their firebrand captain, Sourav Ganguly.

Laxman's whole stint as a Test opener had largely been a disappointment, barring one shining effort at the SCG at the Test on New Year's in 2000. His 167 filled with magical stroke play against the Australian pace battery and the great spinner Warne was one of the most breathtaking exhibitions of batting ever by an Indian on Australian soil. However, he knew that for him to achieve the level of greatness he had promised in this innings on a consistent basis, he would have to move down to his more familiar middle-order role. Laxman decided to return to domestic cricket where he set the stage alight. He scored a record 1,415 runs in the Ranji Trophy season with a sensational 353 against Karnataka in the semi-final and a 111 against Mumbai in the final. He finally got a spot in the middle-order for the first Test against Zimbabwe in Delhi in November 2000.

However, it must be mentioned that despite his Ranji Trophy heroics, it would have been difficult for Laxman to earn a spot in the middle-order if Dravid, Tendulkar, Ganguly and Azharuddin had all been eligible for selection. But that was not to be. The reason: the biggest scandal to ever hit Indian cricket. Let us take a closer look.

The Match-Fixing Scandal

After the disastrous tour of Australia, India was due to play a two-Test series at home against Hansie Cronje's South Africa. Tendulkar, clearly distraught at the team's performance in Australia, decided to step down from the captaincy. However, he remained captain for the Tests against South Africa. The series compounded the misery for Indian supporters, as an inspired South Africa convincingly beat the hosts 2-0. Ganguly took over as captain for the ODI series, which was won by India 3-2. However, the sweet taste of victory turned sour, when on 7 April 2000, Cronje was accused by the Delhi Police of taking money to fix the ODIs against India.

What followed was a dark phase for world cricket, with a series of denials, exposés, investigations, testimonies and finally confessions. On 15 June 2000, Cronje confessed to taking $100,000 in bribes from gamblers since 1996. He also told the King Commission that Azharuddin had introduced him to a bookie, who then offered Cronje money to throw a match.[39]

Parallelly *Tehelka*, an independent website released the documentary 'Fallen Heroes: The Betrayal of a Nation'. This documentary was the result of the work done by Manoj Prabhakar, who had travelled throughout India with secret recording equipment and taped meetings with friends and former teammates. What emerged shook Indian cricket to its foundations. The deep-rooted links between bookies and many Indian players were revealed. In November 2000, the BCCI slapped a life ban on Mohammad Azharuddin, along with Ajay Jadeja and Ajay Sharma, all of who were found guilty. The year 2000 was truly annus horribilis for Indian cricket off the field, and some landmark performances were needed to dispel the gloom.

Border-Gavaskar Trophy, 2001

Laxman retained his spot in the Indian squad, when the team for the three-Test home series against the mighty Australians was selected. The Indian squad for the series against Australia had a notable exclusion. Kumble, India's strongest weapon in home conditions, was out due to a shoulder injury he had sustained in October 2000. Enter Harbhajan Singh. Harbhajan, thought to be a great talent, had had an underwhelming Test career till then, with a best haul of 3/30 in eight Test matches. He had not played for India since the latter half of 1999. It is now well known that Ganguly had heavily pitched for Harbhajan's inclusion against Australia.

---

[39]Ravindran, Siddharth, 'A Decade's Worth of Scandal', *ESPNcricinfo*, 3 July 2010, https://es.pn/407FqAv. Accessed on 22 March 2023.

The Indians went for the Border–Gavaskar Trophy as massive underdogs in a home series, after a long time. The Australians were coming into the series on the back of 15 consecutive Test match victories. They were not only considered the best side of their era but one of the greatest of all time. All that remained was conquering, in Steve Waugh's words, 'the final frontier'. Australia's last series win in India came in late 1969 under Bill Lawry. However, this time the Australians came into the series as the undisputed No. 1, with a batting line up that had dominated bowling attacks around the world, and a superb bowling line-up featuring Glenn McGrath, Jason Gillespie and Shane Warne.

The worst fears of Indian supporters came true when Australia destroyed India in the first Test at Mumbai in three days. None of the Indian batters barring Tendulkar, who played a superb innings of 76 and 65, seemed comfortable against the Australian pace attack. With the bat, Adam Gilchrist was especially severe on the Indian bowlers making 122 off 112 balls, while Matthew Hayden scored 119 off 172 deliveries. The Australians were here not only to win but dominate. India, on the other hand, were left searching for answers as they made their way to the famous Eden Gardens for the second Test.

India vs Australia, 2nd Test, Eden Gardens, Kolkata, 11-15 March 2001

On 11 March 2001, Ganguly and Steve Waugh lined up for the toss at the Eden Gardens for the 2nd Test of the Border–Gavaskar Trophy, but they did not arrive at the same time. Waugh was famously made to wait by Ganguly, which did not please the Aussie captain at all. Ganguly later clarified that it was not intentional. Australia won the toss that day at the Eden and predictably elected to bat on what looked like a very good batting wicket.

The Australians started their first innings in imperious form, belting the bowlers all around the Eden Gardens. Hayden picked up right where he had left off at the Wankhede Stadium, dominating both pace and spin. In two sessions, the Australians lost just 1 wicket. Then, with Hayden just 3 runs away from a second consecutive century, he played Harbhajan uppishly on the leg side only to find the substitute Hemang Badani on the boundary. Zaheer Khan struck another important blow, picking up Justin Langer for 58. Mark Waugh fell next, caught behind off Harbhajan.

In the second delivery of the 72nd over, with the score on 252/4, Harbhajan bowled a flattish off break to Ricky Ponting. The ball did not turn much, and trapped Ponting right in front of his stumps. Gilchrist was dismissed LBW off the very next delivery, another flat and straight one from Harbhajan. Harbhajan was on a hat-trick. In the next few seconds, the Eden crowd erupted with joy. Harbhajan had become the first Indian bowler to take a Test match hat-trick. Describing his thoughts on the hat-trick ball, Harbhajan told *Sportstar*, 'You don't bowl to take a hat-trick. It happens. It was a team hat-trick.'[40]

Australia were at 252 for 7, and India were firmly in the ascendancy. However, they still had to get the redoubtable Australian captain, Steve Waugh out. With the tail providing stubborn resistance, the Australian captain brought up yet another courageous century. Australia were finally dismissed for 445, a formidable score against an out-of-form Indian batting line-up.

---

[40]Lokapally, Vijay, 'Harbhajan Singh Relives Eden Gardens Hat-Trick Feat', *Sportstar*, 11 March 2020, https://bit.ly/3JswHSw. Accessed on 22 March 2023.

The Australian bowlers resumed their dominance over the Indian batting as soon as the Indian innings started. McGrath, Gillespie, Kasprowicz and Warne kept striking at regular intervals as India was reduced to an embarrassing 129/9. Only Laxman stood tall among the ruins, playing some superb strokes as he made a sparkling 59. India ended up with a total of 171, 274 runs behind the Australian total. Steve Waugh enforced the follow-on.

The Indian openers for the second innings Shiv Sunder Das and Ramesh put on a resolute half century partnership. With India's score at 52, Warne struck, forcing Ramesh to edge the ball to slip off a deflection from Gilchrist. Laxman was next on the crease, as he had been promoted to No. 3. It was John Wright, who had given Laxman the news of his promotion, asking him not to take off his pads when he came into the dressing room after being the last man out in the Indian first innings. Laxman was delighted, as he had batted at No. 3 right from junior cricket.

Das played a steady hand of 39 till he stepped on to the stumps, while trying to play a short of a length delivery from Gillespie on the onside. Tendulkar was next to go, playing a very loose shot to a Gillespie delivery on off stump, edging to Gilchrist. With India at 115/3, hopes were fading away.

Ganguly and Laxman set about rebuilding the Indian innings, with the left hander playing some sparkling strokes, especially on the offside. The two put together a partnership of 117 runs and inched India towards parity. With the score on 232, Australia struck, McGrath dismissed Ganguly who was caught behind.

At the other end, Laxman was not out on 95, batting with great fluency. On 232/4, Warne dragged a ball short and Laxman pulled the ball to the mid-wicket boundary for 4. He brought up his hundred, with a nudge off Warne to fine leg. Together with Dravid, he guided India to 254/4 at the close of Day 3, still 20 runs short of making Australia bat again.

India started Day 4 with Dravid scoring only 2 runs off his first 23 deliveries. Dravid had struggled against Australia in recent times with 166 runs in his last 9 innings against the world champions. The Aussies believed he would crumble if they put enough pressure on him. However, the Wall was made of sterner stuff. He soon shifted gears, making 33 runs in his next 50 deliveries. Soon, India overhauled the Australian lead.

Laxman was playing with remarkable ease. His strokes against Warne left the Australian team and ex-cricketers watching the match in awe. While taking to *The Hindu*, Ian Chappell said: 'If Laxman comes three paces out of his crease and hits an unbelievable on-drive against the spin and you then flight the next delivery a little higher and shorter to invite another drive and instead he quickly goes onto the back foot and pulls it, that's not bad bowling. That's good footwork.'[41]

India went for lunch at 376/4, Laxman on 171 and Dravid on 50. India led by 102 runs. After lunch, Laxman continued his imperious form, bringing up his double hundred. Dravid soon followed with a landmark of his own. At 476/4, he danced down the wicket and drove Warne on the onside for a boundary. At hundred, he celebrated with more gusto and aggression than he had ever before. This was a reply to the critics who doubted his ability to perform against the best in the world. At tea, India were 491/4.

---

[41]'Laxman's 281 among Ian Chappell's All-Time Great Knocks against Spin', *The Hindu*, 29 March 2020, https://bit.ly/3JZaBbI. Accessed on 22 March 2023.

V.V.S. Laxman and Rahul Dravid

After tea, Laxman broke the record for the highest Test score by an Indian, easing a ball on the onside off Hayden for a single. Aussies were now resigned to using part timers. Dravid, at the other end, had begun suffering from cramps. It must be noted that Laxman too played the match with back spasms and slept on the floor at night due to his disc being tilted on one side. Anyhow, such was the resolve of the two batters that they just kept batting. India ended Day 4 on 589/4, with Laxman at 275 and Dravid at 155.

On Day 5, the greatest Test innings by an Indian was ended on 281 by McGrath. Despite Laxman's early dismissal,

Ganguly did not declare, wanting to keep the Australians on the field till India had set an insurmountable target. Dravid was run out for a brilliant 180. India finally declared on 657/7, setting the Australians a target of 384.

By general consensus, Ganguly had left the declaration too late. There were just not enough overs for India to bowl out a rampant Australian batting line-up. Hayden and Michael Slater started off with aplomb, raising hopes of an unlikely Australian victory. The first breakthrough came with the score on 74, with Slater gloving a rising off break from Harbhajan to Ganguly at leg slip. Justin Langer and Mark Waugh soon followed, leaving Australia on 116/3. Australia had still maintained a quick run rate, scoring at almost 4—surely with 3 wickets down, they would pull down the shutters.

Hayden and the Australian captain Steve Waugh had different ideas. With the score on 166, Harbhajan made the crucial breakthrough. Waugh failed to negotiate the bounce generated by Harbhajan and the substitute, Badani, picked up the catch at leg slip. The hapless Ponting, who was mesmerized by the Turbanator throughout the series, perished in the same over.

India found an unlikely bowling hero in Tendulkar. In a spell of crafty leg spin bowling, Tendulkar took the wickets of Gilchrist, Warne and the all-important wicket of Hayden. It was left to Harbhajan to add the finishing touches to a historic victory. In the third delivery of the 69th over, McGrath padded up to an off break from the man of the moment, Harbhajan. Umpire S.K. Bansal had no hesitation raising his finger. The crowd of almost one-lakh people at the Eden Gardens went wild with joy and so did the rest of the nation, who were glued to the match on their television sets. India had won by 171 runs, after following on—the third ever team to achieve this feat, after Andrew Stoddart led England's win at Sydney in 1894, and the famous Botham inspired England win at Headingley in 1981 against Australia. We too were among the millions following every single delivery of the match, and still have goosebumps thinking of that moment.

Harbhajan ended with a second wicket haul of 6/73; 13 wickets in the match. India now had a world class off-spinner, to partner their champion leg-spinner Kumble, on his return after healing from the injury. Harbhajan continued his remarkable run with a 15-wicket haul in the next Test in Chennai and hit the winning runs, while India hung on for a thrilling 2-wicket win.

India won the series 2-1, thus stopping Australia's streak of 16 consecutive Test victories at the Eden Gardens. This series win filled the team with a renewed confidence in themselves, which, in turn, gladdened the hearts of Indian fans who were still recovering from the shock of the match fixing revelations of 2000. The Indian fans could now look at the Indian team as a beacon of hope again. The entire country got behind Ganguly and the Indian team, which went on to provide all of us with immense delight over the next four years. Some of the greatest wins for India, under the captaincy of Ganguly, are covered in the next few chapters. Even while reading those chapters, we feel every reader would look back on the 'Miracle of Eden' and particularly on 14 March 2001 as the day when a very special batter and the Wall brought about a renaissance of Indian cricket.

SCORECARD

Australia: 445 all out (Steve Waugh-110, Hayden-97; Harbhajan-7/123, Zaheer-2/89) and 212 all out (Hayden-67, Slater-43; Harbhajan-6/73, Tendulkar-3/31)

India: 171 all out (Laxman-59, Dravid-25; McGrath-4/18, Kasprowicz-2/39) and 657/7 declared (Laxman-281, Dravid-180; McGrath-3/103, Gillespie-2/115)

Result: India beat Australia by 171 runs

28

THE YOUNG LORDS RISE

With a target of 326 runs, Sachin Tendulkar got bowled by Ashley Giles for 14 at Lord's on 13 July 2002. India was at 146/5 with 180 runs remaining, Sehwag, Ganguly and Dravid all gone. The nation wondered whether it was time to switch off the television sets, as yet another final loss beckoned. 'Not so fast,' said two young guns.

The Very Very Special miracle at the Eden Gardens in 2001 had rejuvenated Indian cricket. Indian cricket's pride had been restored, and one could look ahead to the future with great hope. However, when it came to the limited-overs game, this renewed optimism did not translate into results, but that was until the summer of 2002.

There was a silver lining: the emergence of a crop of talented young players. Prominent among them was Yuvraj Singh, the Man of the Series in the 2000 U19 World Cup in Sri Lanka. Against Australia in the 2000 ICC (International Cricket Council) Knockout quarter-final, the left-hander batted his way to a magnificent 84, displaying sensational power and timing. He failed to live up to his billing in the next few tournaments and series, as he only scored a single half century in the next 23 limited-overs innings. This eventually led to him being dropped.

India's Struggle with Limited-Overs Format

There were serious apprehensions about the Indian limited-overs team. The top order of Sehwag, Tendulkar and Ganguly looked strong, but from No. 4 onwards there seemed to be no batter who could take on the opposition bowling. The doubts about the Indian team only increased in their next ODI series, as they fell behind 1-2 to an unfancied but competitive Zimbabwe team. Yuvraj made a resounding comeback to the team in the last two matches, playing blazing knocks as the series against Zimbabwe was salvaged 3-2.

Questions about the Indian batting depth remained. There was a sharp fall in talent, after No. 6. A shake-up was necessary, and John Wright and Ganguly put their master plan into action, when India played the West Indies in an ODI series in May–June 2002.

There were two fundamental elements to the reengineering of India's limited-overs XI. Firstly, Tendulkar was asked to drop down to No. 4 in order to provide experience and solidity in the middle-order. The second and most important change was Dravid keeping wickets. The Indian team now had the much-needed batting depth it was lacking, with Mohammad Kaif, the winning captain in the 2000 U19 World Cup batting at No. 7. This team also had outstanding fielders in Yuvraj and Kaif. This was an Indian team for the new age, at least on paper. Would it translate into performances on the field?

The answer was a resounding yes. India won the limited-overs series against the West Indies 2-1, with contributions from across the squad. The real test came in England, against a well-balanced England side that had performed exceedingly well against India in India itself. Sri Lanka were the third side as a much-anticipated NatWest Triangular series started.

England vs India, Final, NatWest Series, Lord's Cricket Ground, London, 2002

Any doubts the Indian supporters had about the quality of the team that went to England for the NatWest Series were dispelled in India's first match at Lord's in June 2002. India's new-found batting depth and striking ability in the middle-order, propelled India to a 6-wicket win, as they chased down a target of 272 with 7 deliveries remaining. The highlight of the match was an unbroken 131-run fifth-wicket partnership between Dravid and Yuvraj. India made the final of the NatWest Series with ease, losing only a single match in the group stage (to England at the Oval). Their opponents were the hosts.

Chasing in finals had always been a bugbear for India, and when the England captain Nasser Hussain won the toss in the final at Lord's, he predictably elected to bat first. After losing Nick Knight, with the England score on 42, Hussain came out at No. 3. At the other end, Marcus Trescothick was in fine form, hitting the Indian bowlers all over the park. Trescothick went on to play a superb innings of 109 before he was bowled by Kumble.

Hussain had started out in scratchy fashion but started to find the middle of the bat more often as his innings progressed. His innings of 115 was not the most memorable exhibition of batting that the Lord's faithful had seen, but his celebration on reaching his hundred will surely be remembered for a long time. Pointing to his jersey number of 3, he raised three fingers and gestured to all his critics, in response to the latter questioning his batting position. England's innings ended on 325 for 5.

After the break, the opening partnership of Ganguly and Sehwag came, and revitalized the Indian fans at the Mecca of Cricket and the millions watching at home. Ganguly, who got off to a roaring start, reached his half century in the 12th over with a stunning shot off Andrew Flintoff. Sehwag joined the party, with 4 boundaries off the next over by Ronnie Irani. It was a blitzkrieg of a start, with India crossing 100 in the 14th over. Ganguly's dismissal with the Indian score on 106, triggered a collapse. Sehwag, Mongia and Dravid departed in quick succession. Then came Tendulkar's wicket. Now, we go back to the action we were talking about in the beginning of this chapter.

Yuvraj and Kaif were not going to go down without a fight. Yuvraj was the first to step on the gas, with a spectacular on drive off Ronnie Irani with the score on 148. More stunning shots followed. Yuvraj brought up the India 200, with a huge six off Ashley Giles. Kaif, at the other end, was also batting well and the spectacular running between wickets was a sight for sore eyes for Indian supporters. Indian fans had started to dream again. 'Could the youngsters carry on this astonishing act of defiance?' the experts wondered. Harsha Bhogle mentioned the 'fear of winning' on commentary. With 10 overs to go, India needed just 69 runs to win.

Yuvraj's sensational innings came to an end with the Indian score on 267. He caught Alex Tudor-bowled Paul Collingwood for a remarkable 69. The England team must have breathed a sigh of relief on seeing the back of Yuvraj. They were reminded by Kaif that India was still very much in the game. In the very next over, Kaif hit Ronnie Irani for a 6. Kaif in the company of the Turbanator looked in total control, hitting the ball to all parts of the ground. With three overs to go, India needed just 14 runs to win. Four wickets were remaining. India were firm favourite now.

The lionhearted Flintoff struck twice in the 48th over, dismissing both Harbhajan and Kumble. This did not deter Kaif who was playing a flawless knock. Probably his only stroke of luck came on the last ball of the 49th over by Darren Gough. Trying to heave it on the offside, he top-edged the ball to a vacant fine third man. Four runs. India now needed just 2 runs off the last over.

It was the third delivery of the 50th over. Flintoff bowled a full toss to Zaheer Khan. Zaheer hit it to Irani, who threw the ball past the stumps as Kaif dived to make his ground. No one backed up for England. Kaif called Zaheer back for the second. India won. The two batters, Kaif and Zaheer jumped for joy. At the balcony, the Indian team was elated. Captain Ganguly, in an exhibition of impudence the Lord's crowd had never seen, took off his shirt and waved it in the air. He launched into a volley of expletives, punching the air. In his mind, Flintoff had insulted Indian cricket at Wankhede and it was his turn to pay it back.

The run of final defeats was over. Ganguly and Wright's master plan had worked wonders, the seventh batter had carried the Indian team to victory, with a magnificent 87. Two young men played fearless cricket, and signalled the beginning of a new era for India in the limited-overs game. This was a team built by an aggressive captain who believed in his players. The Indian team became a very successful outfit in the limited-overs game, as in a few months they were crowned joint champions in the ICC Champions Trophy in Sri Lanka. A great performance in the 2003 World Cup followed, but more on that later. The team always looked back on that landmark moment at Lord's as the moment when the rise of the Indian ODI juggernaut began in the twenty-frst century. On that July afternoon at Lord's, powered by the young lords Yuvraj and Kaif, a new Indian team emerged, which could outperform the opposition.

SCORECARD

England: 325/5 in 50 overs (Hussain-115, Trescothick-109; Zaheer-3/62, Kumble-1/54)

India: 326/8 in 49.3 overs (Kaif-87*, Yuvraj-69; Giles-2/47, Flintoff-2/55)

Result: India beat England by 2 wickets

29

MURDER IN THE DARK

Readers may be wondering why a chapter on such a joyous moment for Indian cricket has such a gruesome title. We had a heated debate, but finally we both concluded that nothing else could accurately describe the assault against the third new ball by Tendulkar and Ganguly, which underlined India's dominance in this Test match—a Test match that set in motion a phase in Indian cricket where they became a formidable force away from the comforts of home conditions. This is the story of (at least in the authors' minds) India's most complete performance overseas.

Post the successful 2001 Border–Gavaskar Trophy at home, India faced a string of disappointing results in Tests overseas: a drawn series against Zimbabwe, a 1-2 series loss to Sri Lanka and an 0-1 series loss in South Africa. The series in South Africa is mostly remembered for the controversy caused by Mike Denness handing punishments to six Indian players during the second Test at Port Elizabeth.

A tour to the Caribbean marked the beginning of India's overseas campaign in 2002. India got off to an encouraging start, with a creditable draw in Guyana and a historic win at the Queen's Park Oval, Trinidad (India's first win in the West Indies since 1976). However, things soon turned sour with defeats in the third Test at Barbados and the fifth at Jamaica, that too in conditions that provided a fair bit of assistance to seamers. The tag of 'tigers at home, lambs abroad' was beginning to haunt Indian cricket again.

England vs India, 3rd Test, Headingley Stadium, Leeds, 22-26 August 2002

India's next trip to Lord's, after the epic NatWest series final, ended in misery—a familiar defeat to start off an overseas Test series. The English bowlers led astutely by Nasser Hussain's captaincy stifled the Indian batting. The standout performance for India was an amazing hundred by Ajit Agarkar batting at No. 8.

In the second Test at Trent Bridge, India were left fighting against a 260-run deficit, going into their second innings despite a stunning hundred in the first innings from their new opener, Sehwag. What followed was a stunning rearguard action by India's famed middle-order. Dravid made a superb hundred, a sign of even greater things to come. As for Tendulkar, it must be noted that there were whispers before this innings that he was no longer the Sachin of old. But the Little Master let his bat reply for him with a stroke-filled 92. Ganguly played a resolute knock as well, just falling one short of a well-deserved hundred. A draw was salvaged.

For the third Test at Headingley, India brought in Sanjay Bangar to replace Jaffer at the top of the order. His selection revolved a lot around the bowling attack India selected for the Test. India elected to play both spinners Harbhajan and Kumble on a pitch tailor-made for seam bowling. Ganguly's logic was simple: He wanted to pick bowlers capable of picking 20 wickets irrespective of the conditions. Bangar provided India a third seam bowling option to complement Agarkar and Zaheer.

On an overcast morning and a damp pitch, Ganguly won the toss and to everyone's surprise, he elected to bat first. A stunned Botham, who was doing the toss interview, asked Ganguly again to make sure he had heard correctly. Ganguly outlined the team strategy clearly during the interview. India was playing two spinners, and wanted to bowl last.

The Indian batters responded to their captain's call with aplomb. After losing Sehwag early, Bangar and Dravid put on a magnificent partnership under hostile conditions. The ball was swinging, seaming, rising off a length as both batters were wrapped on the fingers, struck on the helmet, shoulder and chest. The two batters took the blows and batted with remarkable courage. Bangar's 68 off 236 balls is often forgotten due to the brilliance of the middle-order that followed him, but his innings played a vital part in India's success. India was 185/2 at the fall of Bangar's wicket.

Tendulkar joined Dravid and together they took advantage of an English attack, frustrated at their failure to make inroads on conditions that were perfect for them. With the score on 219/2, Dravid flicked a ball on the onside off the bowling of Matthew Hoggard for 4. Century for Dravid! It was a career-defining knock from the Wall. All his attributes of patience, determination, resolve, courage and superb technique were displayed in this innings. Dravid's heroic innings of 148 ended in the 114th over of the Indian innings. By then, he and Tendulkar had guided India to a formidable position. The Indian total was 335 when Ganguly joined Tendulkar.

Ganguly continued the tempo set by Tendulkar and Dravid in the morning session. The Prince of Calcutta feasted on the left arm spin of Ashley Giles and also played the fast bowlers with confidence. Tendulkar was also in brilliant form, hitting the hapless England bowlers all over the park. With an on drive of Giles, Tendulkar brought up his thirtieth Test century, surpassing the legendary tally of 29 hundreds by Donald Bradman; only Gavaskar remained ahead of him. The batters piled on the misery for the English attack, with Ganguly becoming more and more aggressive as the innings progressed. Meanwhile, the light had started to fade. Nasser Hussain took the third new ball, hoping that the Indians would take the offer for bad light and end his bowlers' ordeal for the day. The Indian captain, however, did not take the bait.

Tendulkar and Ganguly launched an attack, which is scarcely believable even today. 11 overs with the third new ball cost England 96 runs, with 5 sixes and 9 fours. This was nothing short of a massacre. At one point, it seemed that every delivery was destined for the fence. Andrew Caddick's befuddled expression, as Tendulkar whacked another good length delivery on the onside, said it all. The English bowlers were clueless. Indian batting had never seen a phase of play overseas, where they had made the opposition look so helpless. Amid the assault, Ganguly also brought up his century. With the conditions almost pitch dark, Ganguly missed a straight ball from Tudor with his score on 128. India walked off the field soon after.

Tendulkar failed to bring up his double century the next morning, falling for a memorable 193. India declared their innings on a mammoth 628/8.

It was over to the spinners now, and they did not disappoint, picking 3 wickets each in the England first innings. On the fourth morning, England were all out for 273 with Stewart—the highest scorer—making an unbeaten 78. Ganguly had no hesitation in imposing the follow on.

The second innings followed a familiar script with wickets falling at regular intervals. The old firm of Alec Stewart and

Nasser Hussain (who made a superb hundred), were the only English batters to offer any semblance of resistance. Deservingly, Kumble, who had endured years of defeats overseas, struck the final blow trapping Caddick LBW. England was all out at 309. India had won their first Test in England in 16 years, and had won with spin taking 11 wickets, on a wicket where even the legendary Shane Warne had a bowling average of around 90. Also, they didn't just win, they thumped England, winning almost every single session in the match. India had won by an innings and 46 runs, let it sink in again: AN INNINGS AND 46 RUNS!

India were no just there to make up the numbers on overseas tours. They went on to draw the series 1-1 after a draw on a featherbed of a pitch at the Oval. In the next few years, they drew a series against Australia, on the home turf of the world champions, and beat Pakistan in Pakistan itself in a historic series. The same core went on to win a series in the West Indies and England, in their next Test tours there, under the leadership of Dravid. Few of those remarkable triumphs, particularly those under Ganguly, are featured in the chapters to come. For now, let us look back and smile at an astonishing performance by the Indian team, particularly their champion batters who had all stood up together. It was Dravid's colossal 148 that laid the groundwork, and it was the massacre under the fading light by Tendulkar and Ganguly that put the icing on a batting show for the ages.

SCORECARD

India: 628/8 declared (Tendulkar-193, Dravid-148, Ganguly-128; Caddick-3/150, Tudor-2/146)

England: 273 all out (Stewart-78, Vaughan-61; Harbhajan-3/40, Kumble-3/93) and following on 309 all out (Hussain-110, Stewart-47; Kumble-4/66, Bangar-2/55)

Result: India beat England by an innings and 46 runs

30
CUTTING A PATH TO IMMORTALITY

We, the sports fans, are a greedy bunch. We not only crave victories and extraordinary feats from our heroes but also seek a defining performance by our favourite sportsperson for the world to remember. In fact, we are not even happy with a defining performance, we seek one singular moment of glory from our heroes, which will be etched in our minds for time immemorial. Several of the legendary sportspeople have given us those moments: from Usain Bolt's jog to the victory line at Beijing to Bob Beamon's leap of faith at Mexico City to Michael Jordan's game winning shot against the Jazz in the 1998 NBA finals.

In the minds of Indian cricket fans, Sachin Tendulkar needed that one moment to almost show the world that the greatest batter in the world is Indian. The Master Blaster had carried the weight of expectations since the age of 16 and had carved out a remarkable career. Yet there were some who said that he didn't have 'that' moment. That moment arrived at Centurion in the 2003 World Cup against the arch rivals Pakistan and the fastest bowler in the world, Shoaib Akhtar.

A Brief Background

In between India's win at the 2002 Champions Trophy (India were joint winners with Sri Lanka) and the 2003 World Cup, there were reverses that threatened to disturb India's status as one of the premier ODI teams. India narrowly lost a limited-overs series to the West Indies at home and then succumbed to a humiliating 2-5 series defeat against New Zealand Down Under on some very green pitches. The only bright spot in New Zealand for India came in the form of two stunning hundreds in the limited-overs series by Sehwag. Tendulkar himself had a miserable series, scoring only 2 runs in the 3 ODIs he played. The No. 4 role was no longer yielding the benefits that the NatWest Series promised. Many experts, and perhaps Tendulkar himself too, felt it was time for the Little Master to return to his beloved opening position in the ODI game.

The World Cup of 2003

With such performances, it was only natural that the Indian supporters were once again apprehensive of the team's prospects, when the latter landed in South Africa for the 2003 ICC World Cup. India opened their campaign with a match against the Netherlands in Paarl, and Tendulkar made his return to the opening spot. India's campaign began with an unconvincing 68 run win.

In India's next encounter, the Indian batting came a cropper against the rampant Australian pace attack of Mcgrath, Lee and Gillespie, as India were dismissed for a paltry 125. The Aussies reached their target in just 22.2 overs. This defeat left Indian fans irate. A wave of demonstrations followed, and once again the passion of Indian cricket fans boiled over. Effigies of the captain, Sourav Ganguly, were burnt and Mohammad Kaif's house was vandalized in Allahabad (now Prayagraj).

Wins against Zimbabwe and Namibia somewhat restored India's campaign, with Tendulkar leading the way with a half century against Zimbabwe and a century against Namibia. It was the next game at Kingsmead, Durban, against England that gave the Indian World Cup campaign the momentum it needed.

India won the match comprehensively against a strong English squad, by 68 runs. Tendulkar blazed a trail with a half century, and there were useful contributions from Dravid and Yuvraj. With the ball, Ashish Nehra took centre stage with a breathtaking spell of swinging left-arm quick bowling for a haul of 6/23.

India vs Pakistan, ICC World Cup, SuperSport Park, Centurion, 1 March 2003

However, the next clash with Pakistan was about far more than a Super Six berth. It was more about pride and passion. The pressure of the occasion often reflected on the players themselves, and for the last decade and a half it was Pakistan who had handled the pressure better. It must be said that for most of that period, Pakistan had the superior side. There was an exception of course when it came to World Cups. India had faced Pakistan thrice in World Cup history: at Sydney in 1992; Bengaluru in 1996 in that memorable quarter final; and in 1999, at Old Trafford. On each of those occasions, India had emerged triumphant.

Pakistan won the toss and elected to bat first, on a hard pitch at the SuperSport Park. The Indian bowlers were faced with a formidable foe in the Pakistan opener, Saeed Anwar—a remarkable limited-overs player who routinely stepped up against India. Anwar batted resolutely, defending the good balls and putting the bad balls away at every opportunity. He played a well-crafted knock of 101. The ever-reliable wicketkeeper Rashid Latif contributed some handy lower order runs, making 29 off 25 balls as Pakistan posed a very respectable score of 273.

Tendulkar and Sehwag came out to open the innings yet again and once more a tactical change was made. Tendulkar, who usually batted at No. 2, decided to face the first delivery of the run chase. A crashing back foot drive through the covers followed on the third ball—Tendulkar had signalled his intentions early. As the second over approached, it was time for the clash that everyone was talking about going into the game: Sachin Tendulkar vs Shoaib Akhtar.

Akhtar had announced his arrival on the big stage with two spectacular bowled dismissals off back-to-back deliveries at the Eden Gardens in 1999. The batters were Dravid and Tendulkar. Tendulkar's wicket off a rapid reverse, swinging full delivery, had stunned the crowd into complete silence. Since then, Tendulkar had faced up to Shoaib on a few occasions, but the electricity in this clash at Centurion was something else. Akhtar had the opportunity to stamp his authority on the Little Master on the grandest stage of all.

It took only one delivery to destroy Akhtar's lofty ambitions. In the fourth ball of the second over, Akhtar pitched a 150.9 kmph ball short to Tendulkar outside the off stump. Rocking back, Tendulkar played a ferocious square cut, which sailed into the crowd for six. The Indian section of the crowd erupted with joy; the Pakistan supporters gasped in awe. The Tendulkar fanatics finally had The Signature Moment from the Little Master. This shot was replayed for years to come. The next ball, at 151.9 kmph, was stroked off Tendulkar's bat on the leg side with superb timing, finding the square leg boundary for 4. The last ball of the over, at 154.1 kmph, was punched by Tendulkar straight past mid-on for an exquisite boundary. He made 6-4-4 off 3 balls that had an average speed of 152.3 kmph. In the course of these three balls, Tendulkar turned the fortune of this match and the India–Pakistan rivalry on its head. India was 27 for no loss in just two overs.

Akhtar reportedly told his teammates that he was done and could not bowl. The exact nature of what Akhtar said is disputed, but it was clear that the Tendulkar assault had affected him mentally. Sehwag also got into the act, with his trademark 'upar cut' for 6 off Waqar Younis. India brought up their 50 in just the fifth over.

In the sixth over, Waqar Younis struck twice, dismissing both Ganguly and Sehwag. India's hero at the NatWest final at Lord's, Mohammad Kaif, came in next. Kaif ran like a hare and rotated the strike expertly giving the Little Master maximum deliveries to face. Tendulkar, who was stroking the ball magnificently, had one reprieve when he was dropped by Abdul Razzaq. Post that, Tendulkar continued his blazing form, displaying extraordinary timing and class. Kaif and Tendulkar had a 102-run partnership, before Afridi took Kaif's wicket.

After the fall of Kaif, Tendulkar, although still batting with supreme confidence, started to suffer from cramps. With the Indian score on 175, he took a quick single, which aggravated his condition further. Tendulkar took a runner, with his score on 98, something which he had never been comfortable with. In the 28th over, Shoaib bowled a quick ball into Tendulkar's rib cage. A cramping Tendulkar failed to counter Shoaib's pace for once, and Younis Khan picked up an easy catch. India were at 177/4 when Tendulkar was dismissed for a masterful 98.

Tendulkar's thrilling knock had ensured that even after his dismissal, India only needed to score at a run rate of around 4.5 runs an over.

Dravid and Yuvraj ensured that Tendulkar's brilliance did not go to waste as they cruised to the target in 44.5 overs without losing any more wickets. Yuvraj showed the world why he was considered one of the most talented players in the world game, with a superbly stroked 50. Dravid brought up the winning runs with a pull off Waqar Younis. The old warhorse had also played his part, with a determined 44.

India had beaten Pakistan for the fourth consecutive time in the World Cup. However, this was not an Indian side that played above themselves and upset the apple cart. This was an Indian side that expected to win, and believed that they were the better side. The emergence of Kaif and Yuvraj meant India had a young core of batting that would serve them for years to come. They now had a seam attack in Zaheer, Srinath and Nehra that could compete with Pakistan. From the match at Centurion to when this book was being written, the record stands at 26-21 in favour of India—a definite turnaround in fortunes. Nowhere was India's dominance more complete than in the World Cup, with India winning the encounters between the two sides in 2011, 2015 and 2019 as well.

The last word in this chapter must belong to the Little Master. After thrilling fans since 1989, Tendulkar finally had a defining moment on the grandest stage of them all. No one could ever again dispute Tendulkar's ability to perform in high pressure situations. Though India could not clinch the title, his extraordinary tally of 673 runs at the 2003 World Cup is still a record, and he went on to win the Man of the Series at this tournament. His return to the top of the batting order had been triumphant, and he kept adding chapters to his legendary career.

SCORECARD

Pakistan: 273/7 in 50 overs (Anwar-101, Younis Khan-32; Zaheer-2/46, Nehra-2/74)

India: 276/4 in 45.4 overs (Tendulkar-98, Yuvraj-50; Waqar-2/71, Afridi-1/45)

Result: India beat Pakistan by 6 wickets

31

THE WALL AND V.V.S.

'Dravid sometimes underestimates his own talent'

—V.V.S. Laxman[42]

This was a very apt statement by the cricketer from Hyderabad about the great Karnataka batter. Rahul Dravid's career was characterized by, in Laxman's words, 'grit, determination, fighting spirit and professionalism'. Dravid had an array of strokes at his disposal, which he used to play for the greater good of the team. However, as the Indian team began to grow in confidence, so did Dravid's penchant to express himself. In the Test arena, nowhere was this transition more visible than at the Adelaide Oval in 2003, and in that glorious performance, his partner in crime was the familiar figure of V.V.S. Laxman.

Writing for the *Deccan Herald*, Laxman recollected a time when he was representing Hyderabad U19 against Dravid's Karnataka U19 (Laxman was only 16 at that time), 'There was a spark, an electricity that translated itself through his body language and his mannerisms. It was easy to make out that

---

[42]PTI, 'Sheer Hard Work Brought Dravid Close to Sachin: VVS Laxman', *The Quint*, 23 February 2017, https://tinyurl.com/5xbhhhdp. Accessed on 21 September 2023.

this was no ordinary player."[43] Dravid had got a hundred in that encounter. Dravid and Laxman played together for the South Zone. Their batting styles complemented each other—Laxman was the more naturally aggressive player and had the gift of remarkable timing, while Dravid's game was built on determination and a watertight technique. There was no doubt that on that occasion, Laxman was the lead actor with Dravid playing the ideal supporting role. In the context of this match, if not necessarily the partnership, the roles were reversed at the Adelaide Oval where India scripted a famous win.

India arrived in Australia in late 2003, determined to reverse the years of humiliating defeat in Down Under. Captain Ganguly was seen as a true leader of men in blue; he built a strong core of young players who served India for many years in the foreseeable future. Among that group of brilliant youngsters, the Test side featured the talents of Zaheer Khan, Harbhajan Singh and the explosive Virender Sehwag. The Australians, on the other hand, were missing a few stalwarts in the bowling line-up. However, India knew it was up for a supreme challenge when Ganguly and Steve Waugh lined up for the toss at the Gabba, Australia's fortress.

The standout player for India in the first Test was none other than their captain. The Australians had made it public that they would be targeting the Indian captain before the series. They had sensed that Ganguly had a major weakness against the short delivery, and they wanted to make sure that Ganguly faced plenty of chin music. Ganguly took on the short delivery with aplomb and capitalized with exquisite shots through the covers, whenever the Australian bowlers

---

[43]"VVS Laxman on Dravid's Intensity, Passion", *Deccan Herald*, 9 March 2012, https://bit.ly/3FILojl. Accessed on 24 March 2023.

pitched it up. He made sure to attack the leg spin of Stuart MacGill. Ganguly's classy knock of 144 in the first innings was a statement knock. India had not arrived in Australia to be rolled over. The rain-affected Test ended in a draw.

Australia vs India, 2nd Test, Adelaide Oval, Adelaide, 12-16 December 2003

Injuries ruled out Zaheer and Harbhajan for the second Test at Adelaide. So, this meant a debut for the young left arm swing bowler from Baroda, Irfan Pathan, and the return to the XI for the leg-spinner legend Kumble.

Australia won the toss and elected to bat first on a pitch that was ideal for batting, with a reputation of breaking up as the match progressed. Pathan made an instant impact as Hayden, almost walking into the delivery, edged an away-moving ball into the hands of the wicketkeeper Parthiv Patel. Ponting then played a fantastic knock of 242 studded with 31 glorious boundaries. The Australians piled up a mammoth score of 556 in just 127 overs. There was a notable exception to the sorry tale of the Indian bowling. The returning Kumble had put in a marathon effort and earned 5 wickets as a reward.

After a quick start powered by the belligerence of Sehwag, who blasted his way to 47, the Indian innings had a collapse and was in troubled waters at 85 for 4—a massive 471 runs behind the Australian total. Even avoiding the following on seemed like a distant possibility. India once again looked towards Dravid and Laxman. The miracle workers did not disappoint.

Dravid was the early aggressor in the partnership with some punitive blows off Jason Gillespie and Andy Bichel. Soon, Laxman joined the party displaying his glorious repertoire of strokes. Laxman's timing was a joy to behold. Dravid also kept unleashing a few superb strokes every now and then, in between keeping the good balls out, with his copybook technique. A key moment in the game came when Ponting dropped an opportunity presented by Laxman off a delivery from Brad Williams, with India still more than 340 runs behind the Australian total. Just before lunch, Laxman played one of his trademark wristy shots through the onside off MacGill. India went into lunch on 252 for 4, just over a hundred runs short off the follow-on target, but still a long way from any sort of parity in the game.

After lunch, Dravid brought up his hundred in an unusually attacking fashion, as he pulled a ball for 6 off Gillespie. This shot epitomized the kind of mental state Dravid was in. This was a completely different Dravid to the batter that came to Australian shores four years back. That Dravid used to ever-so-often withdraw into his shell, but not this one. This Dravid believed he could assert his superiority over any bowling attack. Laxman brought up his century soon after, and quite aptly was called 'the scourge of Australian cricket' by Alan Wilkins on commentary. Laxman always performed his best when faced with the best team in the world, and this tour was no different. Laxman and Dravid continued to frustrate the Australian bowlers and carved another 300-run partnership. After Laxman's dismissal, Dravid continued his rich vein of form. Dravid brought up his fourth double century very early into Day 4. India's innings got wrapped up in the first session of Day 4 for 523—Dravid was the last man out for an epic 233.

At that point, it seemed India had a strong chance to draw a Test match, which earlier seemed to be going away from them at 85 for 4. The thought of a victory may not have crossed the minds of too many Indian supporters. And then entered Ajit Agarkar. With the Australian score on 10,

Justin Langer was dismissed LBW by a brisk inswinger from Agarkar, which, replays showed, might have been going over the stumps. Ponting was next to go, hitting a short off a length delivery from Agarkar, straight to Akash Chopra at gully. Ashish Nehra, Kumble and the golden arm of Sachin Tendulkar struck some crucial blows as India kept pegging Australia back with wickets at regular intervals. From then on, it was Agarkar, show as the Mumbai speedster ran through the Australian lower order, bowling at a brisk pace on a pitch that was just skidding through, with the odd ball keeping low. Agarkar ended with a career-best haul of 6 for 41, as the Australian innings folded for 196. India had to get 230 to claim a landmark victory.

The Indian second innings got off to a decent start, with Sehwag playing in typically aggressive fashion. After losing Chopra with the Indian score on 48, Dravid came out to bat and greeted the next delivery from a fiery Gillespie with a straight bat, with the ball striking the maker's name. With the Indian score on 73, Dravid edged a Brad Williams delivery to a diving Adam Gilchrist who failed to cling on to a difficult chance. Aussies, however, found a reason to cheer very soon, as Sehwag was dismissed by MacGill. Tendulkar, who had made just 1 run in his 2 innings so far in the Test series came out to join Dravid. Together, the greatest No. 3 and No. 4 in Indian cricket history guided India to a position of strength with a partnership of 70 runs. After Tendulkar's dismissal, India was on 149/3, with 81 runs to go. Ganguly fell soon after, and it was Laxman's turn to once again join his fellow miracle worker. It was fitting that it was Dravid and Laxman who came together and put the final nail in the Australian coffin with a partnership of 51. This was an Indian team that did not have 'the fear of winning' and Laxman's quick-fire 32 at close to run a ball was an embodiment of the belief that existed in the Indian side. At the other end, Dravid was batting with the calmness of a monk. There was no celebration when he raised his half century, just a cursory 'half-raise' of the bat. There was a job at hand that needed to be finished.

Laxman got out with the Indian score on 221, trying to hoick Simon Katich on the onside. Dravid continued playing in a serene fashion. With a deft stroke on the leg side off Katich, Dravid levelled the score and punched the air. Then, on the fourth ball of the 73rd over bowled by MacGill, Dravid hit a square cut through the covers to claim India's first win in Australia since the famous Kapil-inspired win in 1981. Dravid finished on 72 not out. Finally, Dravid celebrated, raising his arms aloft, as he stood in the centre of the Adelaide ground.

Rahul Dravid was the cynosure of all eyes. Like the famous win at Eden, it was the partnership between Dravid and Laxman that was present at the core of the victory. However, this time, Dravid no longer played second fiddle. He ended the series with 619 runs at an average of 123.80. The series ended at 1-1, with Australia winning the third Test at the MCG. The third Test will always be remembered for Sehwag's blistering 195 on the first day. In the final Test, Steve Waugh played the last of many rearguard knocks that characterized his career, as Australia drew a Test match, which India dominated for a large part. The series was drawn, but it was India who held aloft the Border–Gavaskar Trophy, as they had come into the series having won the previous series between the two. In many ways, this result was a culmination of Ganguly and Wright's concerted effort to make India into a force, away from the subcontinent. India had now drawn its last series in England as well as its last series in Australia, results which seemed a distant possibility in the '90s.

At the heart of both amazing performances was the legendary batter from Karnataka, Rahul Sharad Dravid, whose performances in Australia echoed memories of a young Gavaskar in the West Indies in 1971. Lord Relator's famous calypso can rightfully be modified for India's rock—'Just like a Wall, the Aussies couldn't out Dravid at all, not at all.'

SCORECARD

Australia: 556 all out (Ponting-242, Katich-75; Kumble-5/154, Nehra-2/115) and 196 all out (Gilchrist-43, Steve Waugh-42; Agarkar-6/41, Tendulkar-2/36)

India: 523 all out (Dravid-233, Laxman-148; Bichel-4/118, Katich-2/59) and 233/6 (Dravid-72*, Sehwag-47; Katich-2/22, Macgill-2/101)

Result: India beat Australia by 4 wickets

32

THE SULTAN OF MULTAN

While selecting the 50 matches for this book, we had an epiphany: The great India–Pakistan rivalry perhaps acts as a soft leitmotif for all these chapters. Siblings born of the same earth, separated arbitrarily, the pain of Partition is the lived reality even after more than 70 years of independence.

No matter how hard we try, the spectre of politics looms large in discussions about the rivalry. We have written about the tense series between the two teams in 1952, followed by the equally sombre 1954 tour of Pakistan by the Indian team. There were long intermediate breaks in between full fledged tours of India to Pakistan and vice versa—the first between 1961 and 1978, the second between 1989 and 1999, and the third ongoing one as of 2023—for political reasons. The subcontinent is a geopolitical hotspot, and cricket, at the end of it, is just a game. We would write about a fleeting moment in time, when all seemed good with the world, where cricket really mattered and about one of the most uplifting, rousing, competitive yet friendly series between the rivals.

We had the drawn series in Pakistan in 1989, which marked the arrival of two generational talents, Sachin Tendulkar and Waqar Younis. In the aftermath of the subsequent break in cricketing relations between the two nations, we had witnessed green shoots of normalcy in relationships between the two nations: India toured Pakistan for three ODIs and then we had Pakistan's 1999 visit of India, with vivid memories of Akhtar's 1-2 against Dravid and Tendulkar at the Eden Gardens; Sachin Tendulkar playing perhaps one of his greatest innings in Chennai; and after Pakistan's win, the Chennai crowd giving the Pakistanis a standing ovation.

India's then PM, the avuncular Atal Bihari Vajpayee, was keen on resuming friendly relations between the two nations. His famous Indo-Pak Bus diplomacy continued through the Kargil War and was only stopped after the 2001 attack on the Indian Parliament. However, Vajpayee was a supporter of cricket diplomacy. Eventually, India's 2004 tour came about as a culmination of years of planning and negotiation. Vajpayee, sending the Indian players off, handed a bat to the Indian captain, Sourav Ganguly, with the inscription '*Khel hi nahin, dil bhi jitiye* (Not just the game, win the hearts too).'[44]

India's Tour of Pakistan

It was planned to be a five-ODI and three-Test series. The teams were reasonably equally balanced: Pakistan had the legendary Inzamam-ul-Haq and Mohammad Yousuf; the unfulfilled talent of Imran Farhat, Taufeeq Umar and Yasir Hameed; the fire of Shoaib Akhtar and Mohammad Sami, backed by the all-round steadiness of Abdul Razzaq; the wiles of Danish Kaneria; and the dying embers of Saqlain Mushtaq. India had the famed Big Four in the middle-order, the unflagging determination of

---

[44]'Atal Bihari Vajpayee, a Cricket Bat and India's Historic 2004 Tour of Pakistan', *Deccan Chronicle*, 17 August 2018, https://bit.ly/4Oco7hX. Accessed on 24 March 2023.

Anil Kumble and the emerging quick-bowling talent of Irfan Pathan and Lakshmipathy Balaji. Zaheer Khan, the best Indian quick bowler of the post-Javagal Srinath era, was still trying to find his niche, and so were two other talented quicks, Ajit Agarkar and Ashish Nehra.

Virender Sehwag had arrived in the Indian cricketing scene in the late 1990s and made his Test debut in 2001. He played a distinctive brand of cricket. 'See ball, hit ball' was his philosophy towards batting. He had the most magnificent run-making abilities, the most still of heads, hardly any foot movement, a complete disregard of the coaching manuals and the crucial ability of forgetting the previous delivery as soon as it was over. His batting was all sunshine and light. For a decade and a half, he gave unparallelled joy to the cricketing world. The first Test match of the series was the moment he truly announced himself to the cricketing world as a legend in the making.

Pakistan vs India, 1st Test, Multan International Cricket Stadium, Multan, 28 March–1 April 2004

The first Test was held at Multan International Cricket Stadium between 28 March and 1 April 2004. Ganguly, the Indian captain, was injured and Dravid captained India in this match. He won the toss and decided to bat. What followed set the tone of the series. Sehwag laid waste to the Pakistani bowling attack with some audacious stroke play—by the time the first wicket had fallen, of his Delhi compatriot Aakash Chopra, India had 160 on board and it wasn't even the 40th over of the day. Dravid, the No. 3, was soon dismissed, and Tendulkar joined Sehwag at the crease.

Sehwag had admitted to modelling his batting around

Virender Sehwag

Tendulkar. He was a fan, and in his stocky built and his punchy off-drives, one could see shades of the Little Master. But he left even the great Tendulkar behind in his audacity at the wicket, and in their partnership that followed; Tendulkar was certainly the steadier, quieter half. It was a massive partnership, filled with the most innovative stroke play, and the scoreboard hurtled along. The 200 came along, then the 300 and by the end of the day, India was in the driver's seat with 356/2. Sehwag was not out with 228, and Tendulkar was not out on 60.

The next day followed similar patterns; if anything, Sehwag was even more adventurous and a terror to the bowling attack. The 400 came up early on Day 2 and, soon, Sehwag got to 300, with a massive six. He was out soon after, for a sparkling, scarcely believable 309. He was off on 375 deliveries, with 39 fours and 6 sixes.

The rest of the innings seemed like the lull after a storm. The only other notable event was Dravid declaring the innings with Sachin not out at 194, just 6 runs off his double hundred. India had declared at 675/5.

The Meek Performance of Pakistan

Pakistan was rattled by India's youthful quick-bowling partnership of Pathan and Balaji. Both snared a wicket each before Pakistan got to a hundred. Yasir Hameed and Inzamam steadied the innings with a fine 160-run partnership, but after they both departed in quick succession, the rest of the wickets fell in regular intervals, and Pakistan were all out for 407. India had a lead for 268, and since this was the starting of Day 4, Dravid decided to impose the follow-on and asked Pakistan to bat again.

If the Pakistan first innings' bowling honours were reserved for India's young quicks, the second innings was all about the old warhorse, Anil Kumble. A fourth-day track on subcontinental conditions, and Kumble was one of the most difficult to face in the history of world cricket. Despite a stylish 112 by Mohammad Yousuf, the rest of the batters could not sustain a challenge against the wiles of Kumble, and folded for 216. Kumble took 6 wickets as reward for his consistency. India won the match in the first hour of Day 5 by an innings and 52 runs.

Following the first Test win, the following test, in Lahore, was won by Pakistan by a comfortable margin of 9 wickets. As was usual for such a competitive, topsy-turvy series, India came back to win the third Test by an innings and 131 runs, on the back of an epic 270 by Dravid. India thus won the series by 2-1. This series was marked by a great sense of bonhomie between the fans of both the teams, and also between the players. Unheralded players prior to the season—Balaji, Pathan and Sehwag—were popular favourites of the Pakistani fans. As requested by the PM, India not only won the matches (albeit after a very competitive series) but also the hearts.

SCORECARD

India: 675/5 declared (Sehwag-309, Tendulkar-194*; Sami-2/110, Farhat-1/31)

Pakistan: 407 all out (Hameed-91, Inzamam-77; Pathan-4/100, Tendulkar-2/36) and following on 216 all out (Yousuf-112, Farhat-24; Kumble-6/72, Pathan-2/26)

Result: India beat Pakistan by an innings and 52 runs

33

OVERPROMISED, UNDER-DELIVERED

The Indian team selected for the 2007 World Cup was one of the most talented squads ever to represent the country. And yet, you would not think this was a perfect family, would you? There were strong personalities in this team. Ganguly, Dravid, Tendulkar, Sehwag, Laxman, Kumble, Pathan, Harbhajan, Yuvraj, Kaif, Zaheer and Nehra were distinct individuals, and one would not associate them with meekness. There was a lot of flinty determination in that team. In the post-facto interviews about those times, one gets not only a sense of lots of different contrasting views but also a unit that was pulling in the same direction. Perhaps, the self-effacing personality of John Wright helped in that. The other successful foreign coach of the Indian national team, Gary Kirsten, shared that personality trait of Wright's. As we are not insiders, we are not in a position to comment.

However, between the immensely successful stints of Wright and Kirsten, there was also the stint of another foreign coach—a former player of considerably higher repute. Greg Chappell was, during his time, one of the best batters in the world. He had also, in time, become a batting coach of repute, and Ganguly had consulted him during a particularly bad patch and benefitted from Chappell's consultation. When Wright's successful five-year stint came to an end at the end of the

2004–05 season, Chappell was chosen to become India's next national team coach.

Expectations were sky-high. Chappell's methods were renowned to produce results in one-to-one situations. Even though he had less experience than a few of the other applicants to the job, Ganguly was a fan and had seconded his selection. Chappell was coming into a team with an abundance of talent, perhaps the best middle-order in world cricket, with an opener like Sehwag, two quality spinners in Kumble and Harbhajan Singh, and genuine quick-bowling talents in Zaheer Khan, Irfan Pathan, Ashish Nehra, Munaf Patel and Ajit Agarkar. Could Guru Greg take this Indian team to even greater glory and topple perhaps the greatest team of all time, the Australians?

Rift between Chappell and Team India

As time went on, this association did not quite seem to work out as well as expected. By the end of 2005, there were talks of in-fighting within the team. Then there was an email leak. Ganguly was first demoted from the captaincy, then sacked from the team. In his 2014 autobiography, *Playing It My Way*, Tendulkar mentioned Chappell's attitude as that of a 'ringmaster'.[45]

This controversy continued throughout Chappell's tenure, and through multiple statements, denials and controversies, the World Cup runners-up struggled through campaign after campaign. By the end of 2006, Ganguly was back in the team. This was also the beginning of Ganguly's new avatar—as the master of comebacks. Though India lost the series 2-1 against South Africa, Ganguly was the highest run-scorer for the Indian

---

[45]Tendulkar, Sachin, *Playing It My Way*, Hodder & Stoughton, London, 2014.

team. When the team for the World Cup was chosen, Ganguly's name was there.

India vs Bangladesh, ICC World Cup, Group B, Queen's Park Oval, Port of Spain, 17 March 2007

The 2007 World Cup was held in the West Indies. India, captained by Dravid, were considered one of the favourites—their recent form notwithstanding, which was less than stellar—especially away from home. By the luck of the draw, India managed to get into one of the easier groups, Group B, with Sri Lanka, Bangladesh and Bermuda. There were four groups, and two teams from each group would qualify to the Super-8 stage. Bangladesh had recently received Test status, and had not yet become the elite limited-overs team of the late 2010s and early 2020s. Sri Lanka were a fine team though, and the India vs Sri Lanka match was expected to determine the champions of the group.

India's first match was against Bangladesh at the Queen's Park Oval, Port of Spain, Trinidad. Dravid won the toss against Bangladesh captain Habibul Bashar, and decided to bat first. On the first delivery of the third over of the match, with the score on 6, Sehwag played on to Bangladesh's quickest bowler Mashrafe Mortaza. Ganguly, along with the No. 3 Robin Uthappa, struggled against the tight line and length of Mortaza and the other opening bowler, Syed Rasel.

Uthappa's vigil ended on the seventh over, when he edged a drive to point off a Mortaza outswinger. Tendulkar joined Ganguly in the middle, and Bashar brought in his army of left-arm spinners, starting with Abdur Razzak and the young turk, Shakib Al Hasan. They extracted a vice-like grip over the experienced Indian batters, and the runs came in a trickle.

Ganguly especially was completely in his cocoon, struggling to get the ball away from the in-fielders.

The main wicket for any Indian team was that of Tendulkar. At the stroke of the 15th over, Razzak got his man. Tendulkar missed the line of a straighter delivery from Razzak, and an inside edge from his bat popped up after ricocheting from the pad. The wicketkeeper Mushfiqur Rahim gladly held on.

Captain Dravid came in at No. 5, and the pace of run-scoring dipped further. Like Ganguly, Dravid too was failing to clear the in-field and get the scoreboard ticking. At the halfway point, with India at less than 3 runs an over, Bashar at last got his main bowler, the third of the left-arm spinners, Mohammad Rafique to bowl. And on his first ball, Rafique skidded one through to find Dravid's pad in front of the wicket. At the stroke of the 25th over, India had lost their three main batters, and were at 72/4.

Yuvraj came in, and was the only batter who looked remotely comfortable against the Bangladeshi left-arm spinners. The scoreboard got some momentum, though from the other end, Ganguly was continuing his horrid day. Eventually, Yuvraj fell in the 43rd over, with the score at 147 and that led to a collapse. Within 2 more runs, Ganguly, wicketkeeper Dhoni, Harbhajan and Agarkar lost their wickets. India were at 9/159, and the end was near. Zaheer and Munaf extended the inevitable, and took the team to 191.

Bangladesh got there quite comfortably in the end. The three teenage stars of Bangladesh cricket, 18-year-old opener Tamim Iqbal, and 19-year-olds wicketkeeper-batter Mushfiqur Rahim and all-rounder Shakib Al Hasan got Bangladesh past India's score with 9 balls to spare, playing risk-free cricket.

The Bangladeshis were jubilant. The Indians were shell-shocked. This was a jolt that made the team realize in one stroke that changes needed to be made in the set-up. There was still a fair bit to go in the tournament, but India was hanging on to their World Cup dreams by a thread.

The shock of the first match was impossible for the Indian team to get over. India played Bermuda next, and beat the Associate nation handsomely—the match only made memorable by perhaps one of the best catches of the World Cup, by the 20-stone Bermuda player Dwayne Leverock. Sri Lanka, in fine form in the World Cup, was in a different league though. The punch-drunk India team lost by a yawning 69 runs against them, and their World Cup was over at the group stages. Chappell's stint as coach ended with him being Enemy No. 1 for the Indian cricket fans. He resigned soon after the tournament. An appointment that started off with much promise ended with a whimper. September that year saw the ICC World T20 in South Africa. An experimental team was sent for the tournament, with Dhoni as India's captain.

SCORECARD

India: 191 all out in 49.3 overs (Ganguly-66, Yuvraj-47; Mortaza-4/38, Rafique-3/35)

Bangladesh: 192/5 in 48.3 overs (Mushfiqur-56*, Shakib-53; Sehwag-2/17, Munaf Patel-2/39)

Result: Bangladesh beat India by 5 wickets

34

DHONI'S DEVILS

There were four very distinct similarities between India's astonishing 1983 ODI World Cup triumph and the equally remarkable 2007 ICC World T20 win:

1. The team had played very few games in the format, compared to their competitors. In the case of the ICC World T20, India had played a grand total of one T20I before the tournament.
2. There was a general disregard and almost disrespect among the country's cricket fraternity for the format.
3. The Indians were rank outsiders before the tournaments. No one even gave the team a chance to make the semi-final, let alone lift the trophy.
4. Both the wins were epoch-making. The 1983 win set in motion a process that shifted the power base of the sport from the traditional powerhouses—Australia and England—to India, both on and off the field. The 2007 ICC World T20 provided cricket its greatest commercial and marketing opportunity. It also provided cricket with accessibility to a wider audience.

As India warmed to its heroes and celebrated their triumph at the ICC World T20, India also embraced the format itself, leading to the creation of the most lucrative cricket tournament of all time, the IPL. What made the IPL special and how it impacted the world of cricket will be covered in the next chapter. For now, let us look back on the incredible moments that unfolded on 24 September 2007 and the events that led to that.

After India's shock exit from the 2007 ODI World Cup, the team had a mini resurgence with wins in a limited-overs series against South Africa in Ireland and a Test series win in England after 21 years. However, the Indian cricket fans needed success at a global tournament to get over the horrors of the World Cup in the Caribbean. A world event in a new format offered India a chance for redemption.

Mahendra Singh Dhoni, the dynamic Indian wicketkeeper known for his ferocious hitting power with the bat, was selected to lead a team of youngsters into the 2007 ICC World T20. The squad did not include Tendulkar, Dravid or Ganguly, all of whom had withdrawn from the tournament. The team, of course, had a few experienced hands in Sehwag, Harbhajan, Yuvraj and Agarkar.

T20 World Cup 2007

India was placed in Group D with arch rivals Pakistan and Scotland. All the matches in the group were to be played at the Kingsmead in Durban. After their match against Scotland was rained off, India faced off against Pakistan, needing a win to guarantee themselves a berth in the Super-8 stage. This match saw the first bowl-out in an ICC tournament (both teams had scored 141 in their 20 overs). India held their nerves to claim a tense victory.

In their first match of the Super-8s, India lost to New Zealand by 10 runs, failing to negotiate the wily left arm spinner

Daniel Vettori in the middle overs. Then, it was India's turn to return to the Kingsmead, Durban, for a must-win encounter against England. This match is remembered for what happened in the 19th over of the Indian innings. Yuvraj, the brilliant Punjab left-hander, launched into such an assault on Stuart Broad that the world of cricket never forgot.

6, 6, 6, 6, 6, 6—the Durban crowd watched in awe as one ball after another sailed across the fence. Yuvraj made history becoming only the second batter in international cricket to hit six sixes in an over. He reached his 50 in just 12 balls, the fastest half century ever in international cricket. India posted a mammoth total of 218/4, and proceeded to win the match by 18 runs. South Africa were up next, with a semi-final spot up for grabs.

Rohit Sharma in his first T20I innings played a brave knock of 50, as India posted a competitive total of 153. The Indian bowlers, led by the brilliance of Rudra Pratap Singh, then ran through the South African top order and eventually restricted the hosts to 116 for 9—37 runs behind the Indian total—and were incredibly out of another ICC tournament at home. The Indian team against all expectation, sans all its megastars, had qualified for the semi-final.

In the semi-final, the standout performer was again Yuvraj, who played a blistering knock of 70 off just 30 balls, featuring five towering sixes. Captain Dhoni played a vital hand, scoring 36 off 18 balls, as India posted a score of 188/5, and that put them very much in contention for a final berth. The bowlers then put on a courageous show against the imposing Australian batting. S. Sreesanth, bowling with swing and pace, took the key wickets of stand in captain Adam Gilchrist and Hayden. Unheralded Joginder Sharma bowled the last over, picking up the wickets of Michael Hussey and

Brett Lee. India won by 15 runs, and were into the finals of the first-ever ICC World T20.

India vs Pakistan, New Wanderers Stadium, Johannesburg, 24 September 2007

India's opponents were the arch-rival Pakistan. The venue, Wanderers Stadium (or The Bullring), Johannesburg. The excitement across the borders was at its peak. Close to a billion people tuned in to watch the match. The Pakistan side was more experienced on paper, with greater depth in the bowling line-up. India had grown in stature as the tournament progressed and had the psychological edge after their bowl out victory over Pakistan in the Group Stage.

Dhoni's golden run with the toss continued, and he predictably elected to bat first, considering the pressure of the occasion. Gambhir came out to bat with a new partner, Yusuf Pathan, elder brother of Irfan, who was making his international debut. Yusuf in his brief stay at the wicket struck some punishing blows, including a massive six in the first over off Asif. However, he played one shot too many as an attempted hoick off Asif found Shoaib Malik. Uthappa departed soon after, dismissed by Sohail Tanvir. Yuvraj, India's hero of the tournament so far, came out to join Gambhir. The Pakistan bowlers played with great discipline at the Punjab left-hander and were successful in becalming him. At the other end though, Gambhir was playing a sensational innings. Showing his class against spinners, Gambhir attacked both Afridi and Mohammad Hafeez, and thwarted any threat posed by them.

As the innings progressed, Gambhir started to take the initiative against the fast bowlers as well. With Yuvraj, Gambhir had a partnership of 63 runs in just 47 deliveries. Umar Gul, who ended up as the leading wicket taker in the tournament, struck twice in the middle overs, dismissing Yuvraj and Dhoni in quick succession. Gambhir hit a massive blow for six off Gul, before perishing to him in the 18th over. His knock of 75 showed that he was a player for the big occasion. After his dismissal, Rohit played a crucial hand, taking the Indian total to 157/5 in 20 overs.

So, 158 was the target for Pakistan to win the first-ever ICC World T20. The target was not an enormous one by any means, but in a big match, maintaining a run rate of close to 8 is always challenging. India struck early with R.P. Singh, who had a brilliant tournament taking 12 wickets, picking up Mohammad Hafeez in the very first over. He struck again as he sent Kamran Akmal's stumps flying with the score on 26. India got a crucial wicket in the sixth over, as a direct hit from Uthappa caused a run out of the in-form Imran Nazir, with the Pakistan score on 53. After that, Pakistan kept losing wickets at regular intervals. At the fall of Yasir Arafat's wicket, Pakistan were 104 for 7 in 16 overs, still needing 54 runs to win in four overs. India had the trophy within their grasp now.

Misbah-ul-Haq had other ideas. In the 17th over, Misbah struck Harbhajan for three massive sixes. Then, in the next over, Tanvir joined the party, striking two sixes on the onside off Sreesanth. Pakistan was right back into the game. It was then that Sreesanth bowled Tanvir with a perfect yorker. Two overs to go, 2 wickets remaining, Pakistan needed 20 more runs. R.P. Singh continued his stunning run in the tournament, bowling a superb penultimate over, including a sharp yorker that dismissed Gul. Pakistan needed 13 off the last over. Close to a billion people were now on tenterhooks. With the option of the experienced Harbhajan still available, Dhoni turned to the medium pacer Joginder, with a total experience of only seven international games behind him.

With 12 needed off 5, Joginder bowled a full toss that was carted over the long off boundary for a six by Misbah-ul-Haq. They needed just 6 off 4 balls, with Misbah, who was in the zone now, on strike. Over a billion cricket fanatics must have held their breath at the moment when Joginder ran in to bowl the third delivery. The ball was just outside off stump, but Misbah moved across the stumps trying to hit the ball on the onside over short fine leg. Misbah hit the ball in the air, but it looped to Sreesanth at short fine. The ball wobbled in Sreesanth's hand for a brief moment, but he held on. India had won by 5 runs and with that, they also won the inaugural ICC World T20.

The team charged onto the field. There was rapturous applause from the partisan Indian crowd. Back home, a whole nation was in ecstasy. Against all odds, a team without Tendulkar, Ganguly and Dravid had conquered the world. This was a team led by the 'ice cool' captain of just 26 years, Dhoni. This team never took a backward step, and improved throughout the tournament. They batted with the exuberance of youth married with immense maturity, whenever the occasion demanded. They bowled with pace and fire, and they fielded like tigers. This was a new Indian team, emblematic of the emerging young population of our country. Dhoni soon took over as the ODI captain and then the Test captain, and took India to the throne of the best team of the world in both limited-overs and Test cricket. The ascent of Indian cricket to the top of the mountain in the global game under Dhoni is covered in chapters to come. For now, let us bask in the memories of this iconic triumph at The Bullring.

SCORECARD

India: 157/5 in 20 overs (Gambhir-75, Rohit-30; Gul-3/28, Asif-1/25)

Pakistan: 152 all out in 19.3 overs (Misbah-43, Nazir-33; Pathan-3/16, R.P. Singh-3/26)

Result: India beat Pakistan by 5 runs

35

A MONKEY (GATE) OFF INDIA'S BACK

3 February 1992. An 18-year-old Tendulkar had started the day unbeaten on 31 at the fastest and the bounciest pitch in the world, the Western Australian Cricket Association (WACA) Ground. The team's score stood at 135/5. The opposition bowling line-up had included Craig McDermott, Merv Hughes, Paul Reiffel and Mike Whitney. Tendulkar had gone on to unleash a flurry of brilliant strokes, pulls, hooks, straight drives against a bowling line-up that had every other batter ducking for cover. That day, Tendulkar had brought up what he considered his best-ever hundred—114 brilliant runs. The entire batting line-up had crumbled around Tendulkar, as the young batter put on an astonishing exhibition of courage, technique and stroke play.

Cut to 16 January 2008. Tendulkar is back batting at the WACA, with the Indian score on 59/2. However, this time, he had a middle-order with him that can be counted among the greatest of all time. This time, the batters with him could counter the treacherous conditions with aplomb. This time, he had a team that believed they could beat the world's best team playing under conditions that suit the hosts down to the ground. Tendulkar and the entire team stood up, for those four days at the WACA, in a manner that was unimaginable a decade and a half back. They did so, not only under the pressure of a 0-2 series deficit but also amid a controversy that tested the mettle of every team member.

The leader of the team was among the toughest cricketers to ever put on an India shirt. Anil Kumble, in the twilight of his career, was given the captaincy before the Test series against Pakistan. India won the series 1-0. His next assignment was against a side that had won its past 14 Test matches.

The 'Monkeygate' Controversy

Fourteen became 15 very soon, as Australia disposed of an underprepared India in three-and-a-half days at the MCG. The next Test at Sydney was a fantastic contest, but was eventually remembered for all the wrong reasons. In the Australian innings, Andrew Symonds played a remarkable knock of 162 after the hosts were reduced to 134/6. However, the innings were marred by several umpiring errors. The Indian batters put up a brilliant reply, scoring 532, which was 69 more than the Australian score. Tendulkar and Laxman both made masterful hundreds. Tempers between the teams boiled over during the eighth wicket partnership between Tendulkar and Harbhajan. There was a verbal skirmish between Harbhajan and Andrew Symonds, in which the Aussie claimed that Harbhajan had called Symonds a 'monkey' or 'big monkey', with clear racist overtones. There was a formal complaint from the Australian team, and a hearing was scheduled for the end of the match.

Coming back to the on-field action, Australia stormed back into the match—courtesy the centuries made by Matthew Hayden and Michael Hussey, leaving India a target of 333 to get in around 72 overs. India's second innings was when the tussle became most heated. Once again, the umpires were at the centre of the controversy. Dravid was given out caught behind off a delivery that clearly just brushed his pad. Ganguly gave a low catch to Michael Clarke, which replays showed had possibly hit the ground. However, the umpires refused to go to the Third Umpire, asking Ganguly to take Clarke's word for it. The photograph of Ponting raising his finger before the umpire raised theirs circulated in all forms of media for many months to come. Then, in the 71st over under fading light, disaster struck as Clarke picked up 3 wickets in an over to dismiss India for 210. Australia won by 122 runs. The famous columnist Peter Roebuck called for the sacking of Ponting, which was also because of his poor behaviour. The Australian cricket team, who often used the choicest abuses in the garb of banter and 'mental disintegration', were called into question from the entire cricket fraternity.

Off the field, Harbhajan was given a three-Test ban for breaching Level 3 offence under the ICC's Code of Conduct by match referee Mike Proctor.[46] Tendulkar, who was batting with Harbhajan when the confrontation with Symonds happened, maintained that Harbhajan had made no racist comment, and in fact Harbhajan was saying '*Teri maa ki*', which was mistaken by Symonds as 'monkey'. The Indians threatened to call off the tour, unless Harbhajan's ban was overturned. The ICC brought in Ranjan Madugalle to bring in a truce between Ponting and Kumble. Steve Bucknor, who had given several poor decisions in the Sydney Test, was replaced for the next match by Billy Bowden. Harbhajan was allowed to appeal the decision, an appeal which was heard at the end of the series. 'Monkeygate', as the controversy was so named, severely strained relations

---

[46]Vaidyanathan, Siddhartha, 'Harbhajan Hit with Three-Test Ban', *ESPNcricinfo*, 6 January 2008, https://es.pn/3z99Er7. Accessed on 27 March 2023.

between the two teams, and there always seemed to be a degree of bitterness whenever the two teams faced each other.

Australia vs India, 3rd Test, WACA Ground, Perth, 16-19 January 2008

After being defeated at Sydney, albeit under controversial circumstances on a pitch suited to India's strengths, very few saw the Indian team mounting a comeback at Perth, which had been a fortress for Australia. Australia signalled their intentions of giving the Indian batters a thorough working over by picking four fast bowlers, including the South Australian 'Wild Thing' Shaun Tait, capable of bowling as quickly if not quicker than Brett Lee. A testing pitch and the Fremantle Doctor awaited India.

India won the toss and elected to bat on a pitch that promised plenty of assistance for the fast bowlers. Sehwag, making a comeback, and Wasim Jaffer started confidently, notching up a 50-run partnership in good time. The Australian pacers Mitchell Johnson and Brett Lee struck with 2 quick wickets. That united the old firm of Dravid and Tendulkar. Dravid was back at his customary No. 3 position. In 38.2 overs, they put on a superb partnership of 139 runs, with Tendulkar scoring 71. However, the remaining Indian batting line-up failed to counter the Australian pace battery, except for a fighting 28 by Irfan Pathan batting at No. 8. India's innings finished in the first session on Day 2 for a competitive total of 330.

The Indian seamers put on a stirring performance, getting appreciable movement from the WACA wicket. Australia lost their first 3 wickets for 14 and their first 5 wickets for 61, as R.P. Singh, Irfan Pathan and Ishant Sharma all bowled with fire and great discipline. Especially notable was the 19-year-old Ishnat's dismissal of Ponting, acknowledged by many as the world's best batter. Ponting failed to counter the bounce generated by Ishant off a good length and gave an easy catch to Dravid in the slips. Australia then attempted to come back into the game in a typical Aussie fashion. In just 17.2 overs, Gilchrist and Symonds put on a sparkling partnership of 102 runs. Just at that moment, the Indian captain struck, using the WACA bounce to his advantage. Symonds failed to negotiate a delivery that took off like a 'Jumbo' and gave a dolly of a catch to Dravid at slip. This was the legendary Kumble's 600th Test wicket. India wrapped up the Australian innings for 212 in just 50 overs. The Indian seamers could rightfully claim to have utilized the conditions far better than their Australian counterparts.

India was in trouble at 125/5 in the second innings, with the Australian pacers threatening to run through the Indian batting. Enter the scourge of Australian cricket, V.V.S. Laxman. A 35-run partnership with Irfan Pathan, who played a very courageous innings of 46, gave some stability to the innings. Then, Laxman forged two very important partnerships—75 with Dhoni (38) and then a 53-run partnership with R.P. Singh (30)—that effectively sealed Australia's fate, taking the lead to above 400. Laxman's defiant innings of 79 had his trademark stamp of class but also had the steely resolve, which is often overlooked while we gasp at the quality of his stroke play. India's innings ended on 294, late into Day 3. Australia needed 413 runs for victory. More importantly, 10 wickets remained between India and a truly landmark triumph.

Irfan Pathan took the first 2 wickets dismissing the openers Chris Rogers and Phil Jaques. Then after a partnership with Hussey, Ponting fell to a stunning spell of fast bowling from Sharma. The eighth over from Sharma in that inspired spell has gone down in Indian cricketing folklore. Kumble was about to take Sharma off, when Sehwag intervened and said, '*Ponting strike par hai. Usko ek aur over do* (Ponting is on strike, give him one more over).' Kumble asked Ishant, '*Ek aur over karega?* (Will you bowl one more over?)'[47] Ishant replied yes. With a superb delivery on off stump that just moved enough, Ishant dismissed the Australian captain for the second time in the match. From then on, the Indian bowlers kept the pressure on the Australians despite an impressive 81 from Clarke who was dismissed by a beautiful flighted leg break from Kumble. On his last tour to Australia, Kumble bowled better than he ever had on an overseas tour. After Clarke's wicket, Mitchell Johnson and Stuart Clark gave India a minor scare with a quick-fire 73 run partnership for the ninth wicket before the eventual Man of the Match, Irfan Pathan, dismissed Clark. Then, with the score on 340, R.P. Singh bowled a perfect in swinging yorker to Australia's No. 11 Shaun Tait. Bowled! India won by 72 runs.

Just like the Miracle of Eden in 2001, Australia had come into this match on a 16-game winning streak and just like Eden, it was India who stepped up and handed the world's best team a defeat when no one had given them a chance. The controversial last day at the SCG and the 'Monkeygate' controversy had galvanized the Indian team, and they played like a team possessed. From the determined performances by the senior batters, the fiery showing by their fast bowlers to the leadership of their captain, this was a complete team performance. This victory also served to remove the aura surrounding the champion Australian team, as they slowly

---

[47]Sharman, Aditya, 'SK Flashback: Remembering India's Win at Perth in 2008', *Sportskeeda*, 19 January 2017, https://bit.ly/3FTkzZG. Accessed on 27 March 2023.

slided from their undisputed No. 1 spot in the years to come. This victory at the WACA also showed that India was now ready to assume their place at the top of the world game. They went on to achieve No. 1 Test ranking under the captaincy of Dhoni, but it was this extraordinary performance under Kumble that gave this team the belief that they could overthrow the mighty Australians from the top. The captain smiled and celebrated with his more exuberant teammates, while Tendulkar could be seen flashing the widest smile one had seen from him in a long while as he hugged his teammates. He was no longer alone at the WACA.

> **SCORECARD**
>
> **India:** 330 all out (Dravid-93, Tendulkar-71; Johnson-4/86, Lee-3/71) and 294 all out (Laxman-79, Pathan-46; Clark-4/61, Lee-3/54)
>
> **Australia:** 212 all out (Symonds-66, Gilchrist-55; R.P. Singh-4/68, Ishant 2/34) and 340 all out (Clarke-81, Johnson-50; Pathan-3/54, Sehwag-2/24)
>
> **Result:** India beat Australia by 72 runs

36

A NEW WORLD ORDER

Cricket will never be the same again! When we did a quick online search of this phrase, much to our surprise, the IPL did not even feature in the first two search pages. Sachin Tendulkar's retirement, Kerry Packer World Series Cricket in 1977, the 1975 World Cup and even India's ICC World T20 win in South Africa came in before the IPL. But can anyone deny the transformative effect that the IPL (and following it, the other T20 leagues across the globe) has had on world cricket?

India's World Cup win in 1983 changed the power structure of the game—India became the headquarters of world cricket. The ICC World T20 win of 2007 hurtled India into this new world of 20-over cricket. You did not have to devote a full day to the match, just three hours would be sufficient. You want entertainment? Here are your *#brandname* maximums. You want more? Look there, the cheerleaders are dancing. Even more? There's Shah Rukh Khan, waving a banner. Cricket, the way we knew it, had changed.

And oh, the auction, it became an event—the simple, brutal judge of a player's suitability to a particular format. It was the month of the English Premier League's transfer madness packed into a crisp five-hour show. It was the first IPL show—in fact we, the writers of this book, considered dedicating a separate chapter for the auction itself.

The Changing Rhythm of Cricket

The IPL was the brainchild of Lalit Modi, a businessman and the scion of an old Indian business family. The ICC World T20 win was the trigger—Lalit Modi realized that the potential for a franchise-based T20 league across India could be a huge hit with the paying public. He joined hands with Andrew Wildblood, a senior executive at IMG, and eventually convinced the BCCI to sanction it. Then came the selling of the eight state-based franchises, all for a whopping $723 million. Bollywood megastar Shah Rukh Khan bought the Kolkata franchise (and went on to name it Kolkata Knight Riders or the KKR), and Mukesh Ambani's family snapped up Mumbai (the Mumbai Indians) for $111 million.[48] Vijay Mallya, India's so-called liquor baron, the owner of United Breweries, purchased the Bengaluru franchise and named it the Royal Challengers Bangalore or the RCB. Soon after, a 10-year television deal with Sony TV was negotiated, worth an estimated $908 million.

Cricket, an inherently passionate sport for Indians, was suddenly put under questions. India's cricketing God, Sachin Tendulkar would play for Mumbai. The question that arose was would he not be cheered when he would be playing in Delhi or Kolkata? Would Bangaloreans be cheering his dismissal? What would people in Chennai do when Rahul Dravid scores a boundary for Bangalore (now Bengaluru), or Sourav Ganguly steps out to lift a Chennai Super Kings spinner to the stands? And if Shane Warne, the captain of the Rajasthan Royals, gets Hyderabad's V.V.S. Laxman out, would there be cheers in the stands at Jaipur?

---

[48]'Mukesh Ambani Fast Facts', *CNN*, 30 August 2022, https://cnn.it/3LTmYr1. Accessed on 27 March 2023.

The cricketing world was changing around the fans, and the fans could feel it. We were in the world of infinite money. What we could also see, almost in our rear-view mirror was how the lives of the non-international players would change. We had grown up hearing horror stories of former first-class cricketers struggling to make ends meet in old age. The amount of money on offer in the IPL would ensure that a person getting an IPL contract would not have to worry about financial well-being. And we could not complain about that.

The first match of the IPL was between KKR and RCB, at the M. Chinnaswamy Stadium, the home stadium of the Royal Challengers. KKR was captained by the iconic Prince of Calcutta, Sourav Ganguly, nearing the end of his storied cricketing career. Kolkata was also bolstered by the presence of another icon, the Australian captain, Ricky Ponting. There was the aggressive New Zealander Brendon McCullum, the Australian utility-man David Hussey, Pakistan's Mohammad Hafeez, Indian international bowlers Ishant Sharma, Murali Karthik and Ajit Agarkar, along with Bengal stalwarts Laxmi Shukla, Wriddhiman Saha and Ashok Dinda.

Bangalore similarly had their own homegrown legend, Rahul Dravid leading them. Another of their local superstars, Anil Kumble was not playing this match, but later joined the team and had some brilliant performances. There was also South African Jacques Kallis, perhaps the greatest all-rounder the world has seen since Sir Gary Sobers, as well as his compatriot Mark Boucher, one of the greatest wicketkeepers of all time. India's opening bowlers, Praveen Kumar and Zaheer Khan were both in the Bangalore team, as well as Australian all-rounders Ashley Noffke and Cameron White. India's opener Wasim Jaffer opened the batting with Dravid, and there were also the local boys B. Akhil and Sunil Joshi. The baby of the

RCB team was Virat Kohli, the captain of the Indian team that was victorious at the U19 World Cup. This was a clash of the titans in the truest sense of the term.

IPL First Match: RCB vs KKR, Chinnaswamy Stadium, Bangalore, 18 April 2008

The stadium was packed to the rafters at 8.00 p.m., when the match began. Ganguly opened with McCullum. Praveen Kumar bowled the first over, which was a steady and tidy one. All the runs came from extras. The carnage began in the second over, bowled by Zaheer. Three fours on the leg-side, and one flash over third man for six—18 runs off the over and the IPL had started properly now. Ganguly continued to get the ball away, but McCullum was off like a runaway train. Two massive sixes off Noffke's fourth over yielded 23 runs. Ganguly's struggles ended in the sixth over when he edged Zaheer to Kallis at slips, but there was still no stopping danger man McCullum. Ponting joined McCullum, and at the end of the ninth over the score was a comfortable but not daunting 77/1.

Each of the next four overs yielded more than 10 runs, and while Ponting fell in the 13th, at the end of the 14th, KKR was at 130/2. McCullum was at 83 off 49 balls and ready for acceleration in the last six overs.

It was a carnage. Three of the six overs yielded more than 20 runs; 92 runs were scored in the last six overs, and McCullum scored 158 not out, with 10 fours and 13 sixes. The IPL had started off with an absolutely unforgettable innings, a masterpiece in 73 deliveries. Perhaps, with context in consideration, this innings is yet to be surpassed at the IPL in greatness stakes.

Kolkata put up a score of 222/3. Essentially, the match

was finished, bar the shouting. RCB was like a punch-drunk boxer now, reeling in the aftermath of the onslaught. Ishant and Dinda were too experienced to not take advantage of it. Agarkar took 3 wickets, and even Ganguly completed his full quota of four, taking 2 wickets. RCB was all out for 82, within 15.1 overs, and had lost by a whopping 140 runs.

The IPL begun with a bang! McCullum played an innings for the ages, and the cricketing world had no choice but to stand up and clap for the *#brandname* maximums. Welcome, dear world, to cricket rebooted.

SCORECARD

Kolkata Knight Riders: 222/3 in 20 overs (McCullum-158*, Ponting-20; Khan-1/38, Noffke-1/40)

Royal Challengers Bangalore: 82 all out in 15.1 overs (Praveen Kumar-18*; Agarkar-3/25, Dinda-2/9)

Result: KKR beat RCB by 140 runs

37

CHASING AWAY NIGHTMARES

It was 31 January 1999 in Chennai. A nation hung its head in despair, as Saqlain Mushtaq dismissed Javagal Srinath, sealing a famous 12-run victory for Pakistan. The Man of the Match that day was not from the winning side. It was Tendulkar for his magnificent innings of 136. Tendulkar did not come out for the presentation ceremony, as he knew that his dismissal had sealed India's fate.

Close to a decade later, Tendulkar came out to bat again at the M.A. Chidambaram Stadium—home of many of his greatest innings—with India on 141/2, chasing a mammoth target of 387 against England. This time, he had the last word. This is the story of the match, where Sachin Tendulkar earned redemption for the events of January 1999. However, the great Chennai chase in 2008 was not all about Tendulkar. It was also about Gambhir, Yuvraj and, above all, the freakish talent of Sehwag.

England Tour of India in 2008

India had beaten Australia 2-0 at home in a prior series in September–November 2008. That victory was built on a great team effort, as the batting line-up, the spinners and the seam bowling duo of Zaheer Khan and Ishant Sharma contributed in equal measure. That series also saw a changing of the guard in Indian cricket. India's captain at the beginning of the series, Kumble, decided to hang his boots after the third Test at his favourite Feroz Shah Kotla. Ganguly also retired at the end of the series in Nagpur. It was the turn of the aggressive wicketkeeper from Ranchi, Mahendra Singh Dhoni to take over a talented and well-oiled squad now coached by former South African opener Gary Kirsten. Together they plotted a road to the No. 1 spot in the Test rankings.

The road to the Test No. 1 position began with a two-Test series at home against Kevin Pietersen's England. The series was played in the backdrop of the terrible events of 26/11 in Mumbai that had shocked the entire nation. An iconic landmark of modern India, the Taj Mahal Palace Hotel in the heart of Mumbai, along with several other important centres in South Mumbai, Mazagaon and Vile Parle, faced terrorist attacks from 26–29 November 2008. The heinous attack had injured and killed hundreds of people. England, who had played the fifth ODI of a bilateral series in India, on 26 November itself at Cuttack, flew home after the events of that night.

However, when the dust had settled from the attacks, Mumbai rose up and moved on and so did cricket. England decided to travel back to India for the two-Test series, after a training camp in Abu Dhabi. The two Test matches were moved from Ahmedabad and Mumbai to Chennai and Mohali. The English cricketers, management and board earned plaudits from the entire Indian cricket fraternity for coming back to India to conclude the series.

England vs India, the Crucial 1st Test Match, M.A. Chidambaram Stadium, Chennai, 11-15 December 2008

England won the toss at the M.A. Chidambaram Stadium, and elected to bat first on a pitch that seemed good for batting but promised to help the spinners as the game progressed. The England innings got off to a bright start with Andrew Strauss and Alastair Cook putting on a 118-run opening partnership, till Harbhajan got a crucial breakthrough by dismissing Cook. From then on, the Indian spinners held sway, despite a superb hundred from Strauss. The England innings finished on 316, with both Harbhajan and Amit Mishra taking 3 wickets each.

If the Indians thought they would cruise to a large first innings lead, they were in for a rude surprise. The English spinners Graeme Swann and Monty Panesar gave India a taste of what was to come in four years' time, taking 5 wickets between them as India were bowled out for 241. The spirited Flintoff, who had always produced lionhearted efforts on the slow Indian wickets, also chipped in with 3 wickets.

A 75-run lead is considered very significant in subcontinental conditions (in fact most conditions) with the opposition scheduled to bat last on a wearing pitch. After losing 3 early wickets to leave England tottering on 3/43, Strauss and Collingwood ensured that England would not squander their advantage, and at a point of time threatened to take the game completely out of India's reach. They both made identical scores of 108, as England seemed to be headed for a lead over 400. However, a strong fightback by the Indian seamers ensured that the lead was limited to 386, with Pietersen declaring with England nine down.

At that moment, with around four sessions left in the match, a draw seemed like the best possible result for India, especially given India's collapse against the same opposition in Mumbai a couple of years ago.

Try telling that to the Nawab of Najafgarh. Sehwag blazed away in the initial overs, with his trademark cuts through the offside. India blitzed to 45 runs in the first five overs. A key moment in the match was when Cook spilled a difficult chance given by Sehwag off the bowling of Steve Harmison. Soon, Sehwag brought up his half century and continued his assault on the English bowlers. Sehwag's stunning innings of 83 came off just 68 deliveries, with 68 runs coming from boundaries and sixes. He was dismissed with India still 270 runs behind their target. However, this innings had completely turned the momentum of the match in India's favour.

India started Day 5 with 256 runs left to win and 9 wickets remaining. England drew first blood, with Flintoff claiming the wicket of Dravid. Tendulkar then joined Gambhir, who played a calm innings. Gambhir's knock of 66 was ended by Anderson with the Indian score on 183. After Laxman fell for 26, India was 224/4. England were back in the game.

Tendulkar was a picture of calm and determination. He had started the innings cautiously and focussed on rotating the strike. Yuvraj's innings gave Indian team the impetus it needed. Tendulkar also grew in confidence, as the innings progressed, and started to play more attacking shots. Scoring at close to four an over, Tendulkar and Yuvraj got India within 4 runs of the target with an hour of play still remaining. Tendulkar was on 99, Yuvraj on 85.

On the third delivery of the 99th over, Tendulkar hit a paddle sweep off Swann for a boundary. India had chased down 387, losing only 4 wickets! Tendulkar brought up his 41st Test century, and his very first in a winning effort in the fourth innings.

This innings and this victory were not just for the Indian cricket team but for the city of Mumbai, which was Tendulkar's home. Cricket in India is more than just a sport, and the outpouring of joy post this victory was a proof of that. Even in the darkest of times, an Indian cricket victory provides a glimmer of happiness in people's lives, and at the M.A. Chidambaram Stadium, the Indian cricket team provided another moment to cherish. This victory also showed the steely determination in the Indian team of that era, and set up India for a golden phase wherein they did not lose a Test series for three years. Sehwag was deservingly named Man of the Match for setting the tone for the extraordinary chase for India. However, it was fitting that it was Tendulkar—Mumbai's favourite son—who hit the winning runs, as this victory was Indian cricket's tribute to the people of Mumbai who, with their bravery and resolve, had showed that no terror could bring one of the most vibrant cities in the world to its knees.

SCORECARD

England: 316 all out (Strauss-123, Prior-53; Harbhajan-3/96, Mishra-3/99) and 311/9 declared (Strauss-108, Collingwood-108; Zaheer-3/40, Ishant-3/57)

India: 241 all out (Dhoni-53, Harbhajan-40; Flintoff-3/49, Panesar-3/65) and 387/4 (Tendulkar-103*, Yuvraj-85*; Swann-2/103, Anderson-1/51)

Result: India beat England by 6 wickets

38

CHIN MUSIC, DESI STYLE

To the new generation of cricket followers, Kingsmead, Durban, is the venue that brings back joyous memories of Yuvraj Singh's six sixes in an over, and triumphs against Pakistan (in a bowl out), England, South Africa and Australia during the 2007 ICC World T20. However, for cricket tragics and followers of Indian cricket in the '90s—categories to which the authors of this book proudly belong—the enduring image of Kingsmead is Allan Donald sending Sachin Tendulkar's stumps flying as South Africa rolled India over for 100 and 66 on a fiery pitch. One of the members of the South African team that destroyed India in 1996 was the left-handed opener Gary Kirsten. In 2010, Kirsten was the coach of an Indian team that was No. 1 in the world, and looked forward to reverse the years of struggle India had faced in South Africa, particularly in Test cricket.

Kirsten took over as the coach of India in March 2008, though he had travelled with the team during their tour of Australia in 2007–08. In comparison to Greg Chappell, who wanted to establish his authority over the team, Kirsten never wanted to be Guru Gary at all. During his tenure, he achieved the perfect blend of being a mentor and guide to the younger players and a friend to the senior ones. He was fortunate in that he inherited a mature team. However, his contribution in moulding the team to consistently deliver on the biggest occasions and in all conditions cannot be underestimated.

After achieving a series victory against England at home, Kirsten and Dhoni's Indian team travelled to New Zealand for a three-Test series, where India had won a Test series for the last and only time in 1968. It was a memorable series, as India went on to win 1-0, underlining India's stark improvement under overseas conditions.

In November 2009, India achieved the hallowed status of No. 1 in the Test rankings after sealing a 2-0 series victory over Sri Lanka at home. The process that had started under the stewardship of Ganguly and Wright saw its culmination.

The sternest Test of India's new-found status was the three-Test series in the Rainbow Nation against Graeme Smith's powerful South African side in late 2010 and early 2011. South Africa was a formidable proposition at home. The finest fast bowler of his generation, Dale Steyn, and the imposing Morne Morkel lay in wait.

Memories of past Indian batting collapses in South Africa came back when India were bowled out in 38.4 overs for just 136 runs in the first innings of the opening Test at Centurion. South Africa proceeded to put up a massive score of 620/4. The Indian batting showed their resilience in the second innings, with Tendulkar bringing up his 50th century and Dhoni making a fighting half century. However, their efforts could not prevent an innings defeat. Let us move on to the second Test at Durban, our featured match for this chapter.

South Africa vs India, 2nd Test, Kingsmead Stadium, Durban, 26-29 December 2010

Graeme Smith won the toss at Kingsmead and predictably sent India in to bat first. The conditions were overcast and the pitch had a greenish tinge promising plenty for the fast bowlers. Steyn tore his way through the Indian batting line-up. His haul of 6 for 50 was a masterclass in pace, swing and accuracy. Laxman and Dhoni were the top scorers for India with 38 and 35, respectively, as India had to be content with only 205.

The Indian bowling attack then put up a sterling effort of their own led by their senior members, Zaheer and Harbhajan. After early inroads by the seamers, the Turbanator recorded remarkable figures of 4 for 10, as India bowled out South Africa for a paltry 131. The Indian bowlers had bowled with great energy and discipline in helpful conditions.

A 74-run lead put India in a strong position. However, India still needed to post a competitive total in the second innings to put South Africa under pressure. India were rocked early, as the South African fast bowlers reduced India to 56 for 4 in 14 overs. It was left to the artist from Hyderabad to weave his magic again. Laxman, who had time and again rescued India from perilous positions, played another sensational innings at Kingsmead. The Indian resilience started with a 48-run partnership between Laxman and Dhoni. With India 8-down, Laxman and Zaheer put together a potentially match-winning partnership of 70 runs.

In our minds, Laxman's 96 must go down as one of the top-10 Indian innings ever on foreign soil. India was finally all out for 228, leaving South Africa a very challenging target of 303.

Sreesanth struck first for India, dismissing Smith with the South African score on 63. Alviro Petersen was the next to go, caught by Cheteshwar Pujara and bowled by Harbhajan for 26. South Africa was at 82/2. At the same score, Sreesanth struck again, getting Hashim Amla caught behind.

South Africa began Day 4 still needing 192 runs to win. India had the advantage, but South Africa's batting depth gave them a fighting chance. On the eighth over of the day, Sreesanth bowled a brute of a delivery to Kallis, and that rose off a length and went straight at him. Kallis almost jumped in the air to play it, but could only glove it to Sehwag, who gleefully accepted the catch. This was an Indian bowler who had made one of the greatest batters in the world appear helpless through sheer pace and bounce. India finally had an attack that could dish up their own dose of chin music. South Africa were 123/4. After that, the Indians put on a clinical performance with their veteran pacer Zaheer Khan leading the way with three lower order wickets. In the 73rd over, Lonwabo Tsotsobe was run out by Pujara. South Africa was 215 all out. India had won by 87 runs in conditions that were completely against what was traditionally thought to be their strength.

Kallis, who was the unfortunate victim of Sreesanth's fury, redeemed himself with a superb second innings century, as South Africa managed to draw the final Test match at Cape Town, at a time when Harbhajan threatened to run through the South African batting order. Make no mistake, it was India who ended the series in the ascendancy, their No. 1 spot secure. They had a legendary batting line-up, a champion spinner and a pace attack capable of instilling fear in the hearts of the opposition. This great victory at Durban provided all of India with an image that encapsulated the strength and the threat possessed by the Indian team—that of the champion all-rounder Kallis fending the ball against a young Indian fast bowler, Shanthakumaran Nair Sreesanth.

> **SCORECARD**
>
> **India:** 205 all out (Laxman-38, Dhoni-35; Steyn-6/50, Tsotsobe-2/40) and 228 all out (Laxman-96, Sehwag-32; Tsotsobe-3/43, Morkel-3/47)
>
> **South Africa:** 131 all out (Amla-33, Petersen-24; Harbhajan-4/10, Zaheer-3/36) and 215 all out (Prince-39, Smith-37; Sreesanth-3/45, Zaheer-3/57)
>
> **Result:** India beat South Africa by 87 runs

39

THE SHOT HEARD AROUND THE WORLD

'I want to go to war with this guy,' this was Gary Kirsten, the erstwhile coach of the Indian cricket team speaking about M.S. Dhoni, the man who led India to its second World Cup trophy in 2011.[49] The World Cup is nothing short of a war, especially when it is fought on home ground. The expectations of the fans and the hounding of the media can create panic in the calmest of minds. India in the 2011 World Cup was fortunate to have a captain whose temperament was that of a monk, and he worked hand in glove with an astute coach who brought the team together like never before. It was thus fitting that it was the captain who sent an entire nation into raptures through a shot that will forever echo in the minds of every Indian.

This is the story of that day when India became world champions on home soil, and the events that led to that moment of glory.

This chapter is also a tribute to the career of the man who made cricketers from small towns and non-established cricketing centres believe that they too could dare to dream and

---

[49]'I Would Go to War with Dhoni By My Side: Gary Kirsten', *DNA*, 29 September 2017, https://bit.ly/42Je5X9. Accessed on 27 March 2023.

make an impact on international cricket. In previous chapters, we have talked about Dhoni's rise to Indian captaincy and some sensational wins under him. So, in this chapter, we look at the initial years that began the extraordinary rise of India's greatest ever limited-overs captain.

The Dhoni Mania

Dhoni was no teenage sensation like Yuvraj. Even other players of his generation—Harbhajan Singh, Mohammad Kaif and Zaheer Khan—made their debuts at a much earlier age than the Ranchi wicketkeeper. In fact, while others of his generation were playing in a World Cup final in South Africa in 2003, Dhoni was working as a Travelling Ticket Examiner at the Kharagpur Railway Station in faraway West Bengal.

Dhoni's career received a shot in the arm when he was spotted by the BCCI's Talent Research Development Officer Prakash Poddar during a match at Jamshedpur. Poddar recommended Dhoni to the National Cricket Academy. 'Good striker of the ball'; 'has a lot of power but needs to work on his wicket keeping'; 'technically not very good'; 'is very good at running between wickets'—these were the initial observations on Dhoni by Poddar.[50] A selection for the India A team followed, and then a tri-series that included Pakistan A. Dhoni put on a remarkable performance scoring 362 runs in just six innings.

This catapulted him into the Indian team, where he was initially considered a limited-overs specialist. Despite a poor beginning to his ODI career, making 22 runs in his first four

---

[50]Bhaduri, Archiman, 'The Man Who Spotted MS Dhoni No More', *The Times of India*, 3 January 2023, https://bit.ly/3nn9GsR. Accessed on 27 March 2023.

innings, Dhoni soon had a major impact in the limited-overs game, making his first century in his fifth innings—a blistering knock of 148 against Pakistan at Visakhapatnam. From then on, Dhoni quickly established a reputation of being one of the most dangerous ball strikers in the world game. He also became known for his calmness, especially in run chases where he could rotate the strike when needed and launch into a ferocious assault in the later overs.

Then came his captaincy for the 2007 ICC World T20, and that has been chronicled in a previous chapter. A young man from a small town had achieved super-stardom in Indian cricket.

Let us now move forward in time to where we left off after the previous chapter. After the Test series in South Africa, India played a five-match ODI series where, despite being affected by injuries to key players, India put in a spirited performance, eventually losing the series in the final match at 2-3. The next assignment was the biggest tournament in the lives of the fortunate 15 who were picked for the 2011 World Cup.

This was a team that was being built by Dhoni ever since the tri-nation tournament in Australia in 2008. In order to meet the demands of the modern game and match up to the fielding standards of the top sides in the world, the team management had to take a call of dropping a few legends from the ODI side. Dhoni's team was built on athleticism and the exuberance of youth. With Kirsten in tow, a very well-balanced team emerged—a side that could shift gears when they batted and run like hares between the wickets; a side that had penetration with the ball in both spin and pace; and a side that could claim to be among the best fielding sides in the world. Above all, this was a side that was not afraid of the big occasion and raised their game at key moments.

Under Dhoni, India won major tournaments, such as the Commonwealth Bank Series in Australia in 2008 and the Asia Cup in 2010. The success of the team and the fact that India were playing at home meant that the Indian cricket fans went into the 2011 World Cup with immense expectations, and only the trophy would do.

The plethora of television channels, brand campaigns and the proliferation of social media created a frenzy hitherto unseen in the history of cricket. It was up to the Indian team now to either embrace the attention and expectations, or succumb to the pressure. India's campaign at the 2011 World Cup actually started away from the comforts of home. Their first match was against Bangladesh at the Sher-e-Bangla National Cricket Stadium in Mirpur, Dhaka. The Indian batters put up a dominant performance against the co-hosts with a massive 175 by Sehwag and a superb 100 by Kohli. India ended up victorious by 87 runs.

A thrilling draw against England at Bangalore followed, marked by spectacular hundreds from Tendulkar and Strauss. India won their next two encounters against associate nations Ireland and the Netherlands with relative ease, though many of their batters at times seemed to be lacking in fluency. However, Yuvraj was having a superb tournament with bat and ball and was Man of the Match against both Ireland and the Netherlands.

Next came, a disappointing defeat to a familiar foe, South Africa at Nagpur. After a brilliant start, powered by a blazing 73 from Sehwag and a superb century from the Little Master, India collapsed from 267/1 to 296 all out—a total which the Proteas chased down, albeit some hiccups in the middle.

India finished the group stage with a convincing win over the West Indies on a sluggish pitch at Chennai, with the bowlers coming good and Yuvraj striking a sensational hundred.

The quarter final against Australia was a tense clash, with India claiming a hard fought 5-wicket win. With the bat, Yuvraj again emerged the hero, making a match-winning 57 off 65 balls. The crashing drive through covers off Brett Lee sealed India's victory, and the subsequent image of Yuvraj celebrating with gusto, with Brett Lee bowing his head, was replayed for years to come as a signature moment of the Punjab left-hander's career.

The semi-final against arch rival Pakistan was won with relative ease despite some nervous moments during the Indian batting effort. Tendulkar played a scratchy but vital innings of 85, but it was Suresh Raina's 36 batting at No. 7 that propelled India to a competitive total of 260. The Pakistani chase never got any momentum, as the Indian bowlers bowled with great skill and accuracy. Each of the Indian bowlers picked up 2 wickets, as the Pakistan innings folded for 231. The entire nation rejoiced; India had reached its third World Cup final.

World Cup, India vs Sri Lanka, Wankhede Stadium, Mumbai, 2 April 2011

India's opponents in the final at a packed Wankhede Stadium were the formidable Sri Lankan side. They had disposed of their opponents in both the quarter-final and semi-final (England and New Zealand, respectively) with ease. They had a batting line-up brimming with experience and class. In bowling, they had the speed and skill of the unorthodox fast bowler Lasith Malinga and the magic of Muttiah Muralitharan.

Both sides appeared evenly matched, though India were given the slight edge by experts. Sri Lanka won what many felt was a crucial toss, and elected to bat first. Only twice had a team batting second won a World Cup final. Zaheer Khan stepped up to bowl the first over. In contrast to his wayward opening over in the 2003 final, the mature Zaheer bowled a superb first over, with only 2 runs conceded, off a bye and a leg-bye. In the initial overs, Zaheer had a stranglehold over the Sri Lankan batters. He got the wicket his stunning spell deserved when he dismissed Upul Tharanga in the seventh over. Tillakaratne Dilshan fell next, dismissed for an uncharacteristically slow 33 by Harbhajan.

The arrival of Jayawardene injected momentum into the Sri Lankan innings with Sangakkara also growing steadily in confidence. Jayawardene and Sangakkara put on 62 runs in 11.2 overs, till Sangakkara fell caught behind to Yuvraj. From then on, it was a Jayawardene masterclass at the Wankhede Stadium. The elegant right-hander showed remarkable touch and timing as he handled all the Indian bowlers with ease. A boundary off the fifth ball of the 48th over bowled by Zaheer brought up a classy hundred from the great Sri Lankan batter. The left-handed all-rounder Thisara Perera also had a major impact on the Sri Lankan innings striking 18 runs off the last four deliveries of the innings off Zaheer. Sri Lanka finished the innings with 274/6 in 50 overs. India needed to record the highest total ever achieved batting second to win a World Cup final.

Discussions abounded in living rooms, restaurants, shops with only one question on people's minds: Could India pull off this chase against the quality Sri Lankan bowling line-up? India's batting line-up was brimming with talent and depth, but the pressure of chasing in a World Cup final on home ground was an unknown entity to even the experienced Indian batting line-up. The entire nation looked forward to their batting line-up—particularly Tendulkar who was on the brink of 100 international hundreds—to rise to the occasion. India got off to the worst possible start, losing Sehwag for a duck in the very first over. Tendulkar soon sent the crowd into raptures with two beautifully stroked boundaries before disaster struck. On the first ball of the seventh over, Tendulkar edged a full-pitched away-going delivery from Malinga straight to Sangakkara. Tendulkar was out for 18. India was 31/2. There was a stunned silence in the crowd at Wankhede. Hopes of a second World Cup triumph seemed to be slipping away.

This Indian team, though, was not dependent on one man alone. The young Kohli and Gambhir, always reliable in big matches, rebuilt the Indian innings with a determined 83-run partnership, mixing attack with defence. Gambhir displayed superb technique against spinners and was not afraid to dance down the wicket and take the aerial route. He brought up his 50 off 56 balls. Then, with the score on 114, Kohli mistimed a well-flighted delivery from Dilshan. The ball went to Dilshan's right and the Sri Lankan opener picked up a superb catch.

It was then that a key change in strategy by the Indian team revealed itself. The whole crowd expected Yuvraj, the consensus player of the series, to come out. The in-form left-hander had scored 341 runs in the World Cup until then. But it was Dhoni, the Indian captain, who came out to bat instead at No. 5, with India still needing 161 runs. Yuvraj had struggled against the spin of Muralitharan quite often in his career. Dhoni, by contrast, had always handled him confidently.

With the score on 153, Dhoni hit a powerfully timed stroke through extra cover for four, off Muralitharan. As the innings went on, Dhoni stamped his dominance on the Sri Lankan spinners, with some bludgeoning strokes on the offside. He also played some powerful strokes off the seamers. The Indian captain brought up his half century in 52 balls. The Indian score was now 204/3. Just 71 runs were left between India and the World Cup, with 12 overs remaining and 7 wickets in hand.

The cheers from the crowd began to get louder and louder. The cauldron of the Wankhede had turned into a carnival. As Gambhir neared a hundred, Dhoni took the initiative to attack the Sri Lankan bowlers even more. A well-deserved hundred was alas not to be. With the Indian score on 223 and Gambhir on 97, the Indian No. 3 charged down the wicket at Perera but could only edge the ball on to the stumps.

M.S. Dhoni

It was perhaps fitting that Yuvraj was at the crease when the winning runs were hit. He looked in great form, getting his first runs with a pulled boundary in front of the wicket off Perera. Dhoni, on the other end, was in complete control. In the 48th over bowled by Malinga, Dhoni made an Indian victory appear a mere formality with two boundaries through square leg.

On 271/4, Nuwan Kulasekara ran in to bowl to Dhoni with India needing four runs off 11 deliveries. It was pitched on a length, and Dhoni launched into it with a mighty swing of his bat. The ball sailed over the mid-wicket boundary for six. Captain Cool twirled his bat on the follow-through and smiled. He was then enveloped in a hug by the Player of the Tournament, Yuvraj.

In the dressing room, Kirsten raised his arms in elation. The Wankhede Stadium erupted in joy, and the nation was engulfed in absolute delirium. For a generation of Indians, this was their most joyous moment in their years of watching the sport. In fact, it would not be unfair to say that for many of the Indian cricket followers, this was perhaps the happiest moment in their lives.

SCORECARD

Sri Lanka: 274/6 in 50 overs (Jayawardene-103, Sangakkara-48; Yuvraj-2/49, Zaheer-2/60)

India: 277/4 in 48.2 overs (Gambhir-97, Dhoni-91*; Malinga-2/42, Dilshan-1/27)

Result: India beat Sri Lanka by 6 wickets

40

FATHER TIME COMES KNOCKING

The Indian top-five that played all four Tests during the tour of Australia in 2011–12 made a whopping 50,730 runs and 136 centuries in their Test career. As many as 1,015 runs (0 centuries) were the combined statistics of the same top-five in the Border–Gavaskar Trophy played in Australia in 2011–12. To Indian fans who had seen the likes of Sehwag, Gambhir, Dravid, Tendulkar and Laxman conquer bowling attacks around the world and guide India to the No. 1 ranking in Tests, such a fall from grace was unimaginable. The No. 1 ranking was not just due to India's performance in home comforts, it was built on strong overseas performance—series wins in England (2007), the West Indies (2006 and 2011), New Zealand (2009) and a memorable series draw in South Africa (2010–11).

Even in Australia, India had performed creditably on their last two tours, drawing 1-1 in 2003–04 and losing a controversial and keenly contested series in 2007–08 with 1-2. In both those tours, the senior Indian batters had stood up and given some remarkable performances. The tours of England and Australia in the 2011–12 season were meant to underline India's pre-eminence in the world game, after they triumphed in the World Cup at home. Yet, those tours led to the disintegration of the greatest generation of batters our country has ever known. As they say, time and tide wait for none, not even legends.

India had a new coach post the elation of the 2011 World Cup victory, Duncan Fletcher. He was the man who had rejuvenated English cricket in the 2000s and guided England to the extraordinary Ashes series triumph in 2005. His first assignment was a tour to the West Indies for a T20I, five ODIs and three Tests. The T20 and the first three ODIs were won with ease under the captaincy of Suresh Raina who led virtually an A squad, with most of the big names missing. India's dominance prompted Fletcher to say, 'Indian cricket is in a very, very healthy state presently. I know five years in international cricket is a long time but unless some international teams suddenly come up big, I don't see it happening (India losing its grip).'[51]

Well, the grip loosened very soon. After a 3-2 limited-overs series win and a 1-0 Test series victory in the West Indies, India travelled to England to take on the very side he had a major hand in building in the first few years of this century. It turned out to be a tour of horrors for the Indian side as they failed to win a single international match, and were swept 4-0 in the Test series. The famed Indian batting line-up was ripped apart to shreds by the incisive England bowling, particularly the brilliant new ball pairing of Stuart Broad and James Anderson. However, amid the ruins of the England tour, one from the golden generation stood out. Rahul Dravid had an extraordinary Test series making 461 runs and three centuries. His performance, and the sheer weight of runs and victories that the golden generation had put together over

---

[51]Rao, K. Shriniwas, 'India Can Dominate World Cricket for Years: Duncan Fletcher', *The Times of India*, 13 June 2011, https://bit.ly/40jgPsJ. Accessed on 30 March 2023.

the past decade, convinced the selectors to stay with them, at least till the Australian series.

Before the Australian tour, India played the West Indies in a home series, hardly the ideal preparation for a tour Down Under. India disposed of the West Indies 2-0, with one of the matches being a thrilling draw in Mumbai.

Indians were determined to avoid a repeat of the England tour and that 0-4 debacle on their trip Down Under. They sent a group of players early to Australia to pre-condition and acclimatize with on-ground playing conditions. In the opinion of most experts, Australia was not nearly as formidable as England. Australia was a side in transition with an unstable top-order, an ageing and out of form Ponting in the middle-order, a bowling line-up yet to create a significant impact and a young man who had just started his captaincy career. It was on Clarke's shoulders that Australia once again rose to the top of world cricket, although not with the same degree of dominance.

The horrors of the England tour came back, as India were beaten convincingly in the first three Tests at the MCG, SCG and WACA. The Indian batters were left searching for answers against the quality of the Australian bowling. Even Dravid, who had had a stunning series in England, was made to look vulnerable against the incoming ball being bowled on multiple occasions. Laxman, once the scourge of Australian cricket, was not allowed to play any of his silken strokes. Tendulkar's batting exuded class and confidence, but he too failed to make the century that could rescue a side that was in free fall. Kohli provided some cheer to the Indian camp with a second-innings half century at the WACA but could not prevent an innings defeat. The bowling, too, appeared completely helpless against the Australian assault.

India vs Australia, 4th Test Match, Adelaide Oval, Adelaide, 24-28 January 2012

India arrived in Adelaide, 0-3 down in the series, looking to salvage some pride. Sehwag led India in the fourth Test at Adelaide. Dhoni, the regular captain, had received a one Test ban after the Perth Test, where India maintained an atrocious over rate. Under close to subcontinental conditions, Clarke won the toss and elected to bat first.

The Australian batters put on yet another sensational performance. Ponting, who was amid a resurgence in this series, made a superb 221, while Clarke (210) continued his imperious form with another double century. Together, they added 386 runs, their second epic stand in this series after their 288 run partnership at Sydney. Australia ended their innings on a massive 604/7 d.

In reply, the Indian top-five continued their miserable run, with even Tendulkar struggling to find his touch. Yet another incisive spell of bowling by Peter Siddle and Ben Hilfenhaus left India tottering on 111 for 5. Another humiliation was on the cards. That was until an audacious 23-year-old finally had his moment in the sun in Test cricket. Kohli had been in the eye of the storm during this Australian tour, receiving a heavy fine for making an obscene gesture at fans during the Test at Sydney. In fact, before the Perth Test, some experts wondered if Kohli should make way for the talented Rohit Sharma.

Kohli came in to bat in the first innings at Adelaide with the Indian score on 87 for 4. Soon, Laxman perished as well, and he was joined on the crease by Wriddhiman Saha. In the company of Saha, he began to unleash a series of stunning strokes. A superb pull with his score on 32, in front of square off Siddle underlined Kohli's confidence. He brought up his half century with a trademark shot through the onside off Hilfenhaus. This was followed by some spectacular shots off the spinners. As Kohli approached his hundred, he was subjected to an intense examination by Siddle. He played and missed a couple of times, with the ball just missing the edge of his bat. Finally, with the score on 239/8, he stroked a ball through the offside field and brought up a stunning hundred with two runs off Siddle.

Kohli celebrated in typical exuberant fashion. There was also a hint of anger in the celebration, as he mouthed a profanity on reaching the hundred. 'To give it back verbally and then score a hundred is even better,' he said as he reflected on his fantastic innings.[52] He was the last man to be dismissed, as the Indian innings ended on 272 all out, with Kohli top-scoring with a brilliant 116—a curtain raiser to his astonishing feats three year later on Australian soil.

Thanks to another quality innings by Ponting, Australia declared their innings on 167/5, leaving India an insurmountable target of 500 runs.

Sehwag then gave the Australian crowd a last glimpse of his phenomenal talent, with a blazing 62 off 53 balls. He was dismissed by Nathan Lyon, leaving the Indians on 80 for 2. However, Dravid (25), Tendulkar (13) and Laxman (35) could not make much of an impact on their last Test innings in Australia. For Dravid and Laxman, it turned out to be the last innings of their careers. Lyon took a haul of 4 for 63, and completed the last rites for the series with the wicket of Umesh. Australia won by 4-0. The toast of the cricketing world after their World Cup victory, India had succumbed to their second consecutive series whitewash overseas. Through

---

[52]'It Feels Great to Give it Back Verbally and Then Score Hundred', *The Indian Express*, 27 January 2012, https://bit.ly/3KiEdRr. Accessed on 30 March 2023.

this stretch, they had not only lost their No. 1 ranking in Tests but also the respect that they had earned through their resolute performances overseas, beginning from the days of Ganguly and Wright.

India failed to recognize the need to blood youngsters at the opportune moment. They resisted the need for change, whereas results dictated it. The golden generation could not produce remarkable feats for eternity, and it was to the misfortune of Indian cricket that their decline came all at the same time.

Dravid finally bid adieu to international cricket in a press conference on 8 March 2012. In Dravid's own words, 'It's the culmination of a lot of things. I don't think it's based on what happened in the last series. For each one it comes differently, for me it's come with a bit of contemplation, a bit of thought, with friends and family.'[53] His great batting partner Laxman soon followed with his retirement in August 2012. With a heavy heart, India said goodbye to two of her favourite sons and effectively bid farewell to an iconic era in Indian batting.

Amid the gloom, there was a glimmer of hope for the future. Kohli had finally shown the world that he could become a major force in the longer format of the game. He was soon entrusted with the task of rebuilding Indian cricket. Some of his sensational performances form the centrepieces of future chapters. For now, let us take a moment and applaud the extraordinary line-up of Indian batters that defined Indian Test cricket in the first decade of the new millennium—Gambhir, Sehwag, Dravid, Tendulkar, Laxman and Ganguly. Thank you for the memories.

---

[53]Ugra, Sharda, 'Dravid Walks Off, Sad but Proud', *ESPNcricinfo*, 9 March 2012, https://tinyurl.com/bdh3t8r2

SCORECARD

Australia: 604/7 declared (Ponting-221, Clarke-210; Ashwin-3/194, Zaheer-2/96) and 167/5 declared (Ponting-60, Clarke-57; Ashwin-2/73, Umesh-1/23)

India: 272 all out (Kohli-116, Saha-35; Siddle-5/49, Hilfenhaus-3/62) and 201 all out (Sehwag-62, Laxman-35; Lyon-4/63, Harris-3/41)

Result: Australia beat India by 298 runs and won the series 4-0

41

NEW INDIA, OLD CAPTAIN

Post the 2011 World Cup, Indian cricket was yet again haunted by the demons of the 1990s—'Tigers at home, lambs abroad'. Humiliating losses in both the Test and limited-overs format in England and Australia left the team's confidence in shambles, leaving the selectors and team management searching for answers. Was it time to look beyond the generation of Sehwag, Gambhir, Yuvraj, Zaheer and Harbhajan that formed the cornerstone of India's World Cup success? The final straw came during the India vs Pakistan series towards the end of 2012. Before the series even started, the entire nation was stunned by the sudden retirement of Tendulkar from the 50-overs format. A series defeat to the arch rivals followed, and the Indian selectors finally had to wake up to the grim reality of an ageing side with fading stars—a side desperate for an injection of freshness.

Champions Trophy 2013: Time for an Overhaul

The 2013 Champions Trophy happened when the selectors decided to pull the trigger and effect wholesale changes. Suddenly, there was an Indian squad going into a major tournament without any of the stalwarts mentioned in the previous paragraph. Only three remained from the XI that lifted the World Cup on that memorable night in 2011—the captain Mahendra Singh Dhoni, Virat Kohli and Suresh Raina. Even those who supported this bold move of the selectors regarded India's chances at the Champions Trophy with scepticism. Many expected an exit in the group stage itself. The sceptics, though, were in for a surprise.

The warm up matches brought fresh optimism into the Indian camp with a brilliant 300+ run chase against Sri Lanka and a massive win over Australia, where India bowled out the Kangaroos for just 65.

The confidence gained from the warm up matches in Cardiff was carried over to the first league encounter against one of the tournament favourites, South Africa, at the same venue. This match saw the debut of a new opening combination: Rohit Sharma and Shikhar Dhawan. The South African pace battery of Morne Morkel, Lonwabo Tsotsobe, Rory Kleinveldt and Ryan McLaren tried to intimidate the young Indian pair with a barrage of short-pitched bowling. However, the duo was up to the challenge, cutting and pulling with impunity. A 127-run opening partnership and a superb century by Dhawan set up a formidable total of 331. The Indians proceeded to defend the total successfully with an intensity rarely seen from the Indian teams.

Convincing victories over the West Indies and arch rivals Pakistan followed. Ravindra Jadeja and Ravichandran Ashwin emerged as a formidable combination in the middle overs, even under English conditions. The pace attack led by the swing of Bhuvneshwar Kumar also stepped up. The biggest star was Shikhar Dhawan, whose aggression brought back memories of his predecessor Virender Sehwag.

The semi-final against the familiar foes, Sri Lanka, turned out to be a cakewalk, as the Indian seam attack proved too strong for the Lankans under seamer-friendly conditions. Against all pre-tournament expectations, the young Indian team went through to the Champions Trophy finals with an ease and confidence beyond the wildest dreams of the Indian cricket fan. Lying in wait in the finals were the hosts, England.

For the majority of the day, the Champions Trophy final between India and England seemed to be headed for a no result. It seemed certain that India would have to be content with sharing the Champions Trophy for the second time (in 2002, they had shared the trophy with Sri Lanka, with the final being rained out). Destiny had other plans, and the skies cleared just in time for a 20-over match to be contested.

England vs India, ICC Champions Trophy, Final, Edgbaston Stadium, Birmingham, 23 June 2013

England won the toss and, as expected in a shortened match, chose to bowl first. The in-form Dhawan succumbed to a Ravi Bopara slower ball for a stroke-filled 31 off just 24 balls. Under typical English conditions, the middle-order also failed to contribute. Two of India's heroes of the Champions Trophy, Ravindra Jadeja and Kohli went about repairing the damage. Virat was in exhilarating form, playing some rousing strokes, including a six off Broad over mid-wicket. Ravindra Jadeja, at the other end, was also doing his best to up the scoring rate, with some punishing blows to the boundary. However, Kohli's well-made 43 and Jadeja's unbeaten 33 was only enough to guide India to a mediocre total of 129.

England's run chase did not begin well. Alastair Cook, Jonathan Trott, Joe Root and Ian Bell were all back in the pavilion, with the England score on just 46. Eoin Morgan, arguably the team's finest limited-overs batter, attempted to reverse the slide with some cracking boundaries on the offside. England's hero with the ball, Bopara, soon joined the party with a brilliant six off Ishant. There seemed to be a decisive shift in momentum towards the home side as Morgan reverse-swept Raina for a boundary. Now, 40 were needed from 25 balls. Bopara then hit a six off Jadeja in the very next over. With 28 needed off 17 balls, Morgan hit a six off Ishant and that put England firmly in the driver's seat. Then, the unthinkable happened: The much-criticized Ishant struck, not once but twice, dismissing the set batters Morgan and Bopara off successive deliveries. These dismissals seemed to trigger the panic button in the English camp. India's man of the match, Ravindra Jadeja, clean bowled the dangerous Jos Buttler, and soon Tim Bresnan followed, run out in the same over. England were left with an unenviable task of scoring 15 off the last over. Broad raised some hopes with a boundary, but it was too little too late as Ashwin stepped up to bowl the last delivery to James Tredwell, with an aim of getting 6. Tredwell missed, and the entire Indian team exulted with joy. The Indian captain seemed to be more expressive in his delight than on previous triumphs.

India won its third ICC limited-overs title under Dhoni—he became the first captain in history to win the ICC World T20, the ICC Champions Trophy and the ICC World Cup. This was a triumph for a new India, sans many of its stars. The next generation had stepped up and how. It was time for a new set of superstars to take centre stage. One enduring memory from the post-match celebrations was Kohli dancing to 'Gangnam style'. This team was more expressive than the previous generation, more enthusiastic and more athletic. They proved their mettle in alien conditions, in a global tournament where no one gave them a chance. They played with flair and convincingly beat all of their opponents, leading up to the finals. And when they were finally pushed, they emerged with all the right answers at the critical moments. India's future in coloured clothing appeared to be in safe hands for years to come.

> **SCORECARD**
>
> **India:** 129/7 in 20 overs (Kohli-43, Jadeja-33; Bopara-3/20; Anderson-1/24)
>
> **England:** 124/8 in 20 overs (Morgan-33, Bopara-30; Ashwin-2/15, Jadeja-2/24)
>
> **Result:** India beat England by 5 runs

42

'DO NOT GO GENTLE INTO THAT GOOD NIGHT'

When Virat Kohli said, 'He [Tendulkar] has carried the burden of the nation for 21 years. So it is time that we carried him,'[54] it was clear to everyone that no words could have better summed up the impact that Tendulkar has had on Indian cricket. He was the man who bore the burden of a whole nation on his broad shoulders for two decades, one whose every move was followed by a nation longing for a global sporting superstar since he was 16. The World Cup was the one jewel missing from his crown. On 2 April 2011, at his home ground, the Wankhede, that missing piece of the jigsaw too fell in place. Sachin Tendulkar could have bid an ideal farewell to cricket, after finally becoming a World Cup champion, having had a stellar tournament with the bat as well. The enduring image of him being lifted up by his teammates could have been his last hurrah. However, it was not to be. He loved the game of cricket too much and he was the man that cricket loved back. He could not imagine his life without the sport, so as long as his body

---

[54]Smith, Ed, 'Sachin Tendulkar: Indian Master Who Symbolised the Country's Rise', *BBC Sport*, 13 October 2013, https://bbc.in/3JYGxeX. Accessed on 30 March 2023.

and mind allowed him to go on, he did. There was one more landmark to be achieved, one that would perhaps never be reached again: 100 international hundreds, he was on 99 after the World Cup.

What seemed like a matter of mere formality became a laborious journey. In quest of the hundredth 100, Tendulkar resembled a mountaineer who had run out of breath in the final climb towards the summit. The journey towards the hundredth international hundred became a national obsession. This was accompanied by the humiliating series whitewashes in England and Australia. Amul summed up the situation perfectly in an advertisement with the headline 'Sau much pressure'.[55] The Asia Cup of 2012 brought an end to the wait for the hundredth 100. On 16 March 2012 at the Sher-e-Bangla Cricket Stadium against Bangladesh, Tendulkar scored his hundredth 100. The euphoria of the moment was dampened by India's eventual loss to Bangladesh, which ultimately led to India's exit from the tournament.

Arguably ODI cricket's greatest exponent, Tendulkar, said goodbye to the shorter format of the game just a few days before India's limited-overs series against Pakistan at home. We would see Tendulkar for some more time in the whites though.

A Shocking Announcement

At the beginning of the 2013–14 cricket season, it was assumed that Tendulkar would play his 200th Test match in South Africa. However, with Haroon Lorgat's ascension to the post of chief executive at Cricket South Africa, that tour ran into rough

---

[55]'Utterly Butterly Tondulkarlicious: 25 Amul Ads That Tell the Tendlya Story', *mxm*, 19 March 2012, https://bit.ly/3M312Kd. Accessed on 30 March 2023.

weather. In between, the BCCI announced a short series against the West Indies of two Tests and three ODIs to be played in November at home. However, it was an announcement that followed more than a month later which shook the cricketing globe. Sachin Ramesh Tendulkar had finally decided to bid farewell to the game he loved so much. His 200th Test match would also be his last. A chaotic contest of bidding for the final Test match ensued among the major cricketing venues in India and finally, and perhaps rightfully so, it was decided that the last act of Tendulkar's glittering career would be staged at his home ground, the Wankhede.

The West Indies' glory days were behind them a couple of decades ago, so a tour by them was almost dismissed as a non-event by the cricket viewing public. However, this was a tour with a difference—it was the last opportunity for Indian cricket fans to pay homage to 'God'. 'Cricket is our religion and Sachin is our God' was a sign that had been a permanent fixture of India matches for almost 20 years. Thousands thronged to the Eden Gardens in Kolkata for the first Test of the two Test match series, with the sole intention of catching one last glimpse of the Little Master. However, Shane Shillingford's accuracy and what some would say a 'howler' from Nigel Llong conspired to limit the great man's last innings at the Eden Gardens to just 10 runs.

India vs West Indies, 2nd Test, Wankhede Stadium, Mumbai, 14-16 November 2013

Despite Tendulkar's early dismissal, debutant Rohit Sharma and the all-rounder Ravichandran Ashwin managed to pull India out of trouble and post a formidable total. The bowlers, led by another debutant in Mohammad Shami, then put on a stupendous performance and propelled India to an innings victory.

Mumbai hosted the last act of this epic play. The stage was set for a grand farewell. The actors were in place and so was the audience. The royalty of the cricketing and the glamour world descended on the Wankhede. Lara and Warne came down to witness one final display of brilliance from their great rival. The best of Bollywood, including Hrithik Roshan and Aamir Khan, were present too. Also, for the first time in Tendulkar's career, his mother was there to see him play live. A special ramp was constructed to enable her to come up to the box to watch the match. The occasion rivalled the grandeur of the World Cup final two-and-a-half years back, yet it seemed that it was higher on emotion as a whole generation's life had run parallel Tendulkar's career. His rise coincided with the rise of India as an economic power and the rise of the ambition of the Indian youth.

The match was an unequal contest from the very start. India won the toss and chose to field—a rare occurrence in India. The tourists succumbed to 182 all out, with the last 9 wickets falling in just over 30 overs. Pragyan Ojha was the wrecker in chief, taking 5 wickets.

After a quick start by the Indian openers—77 in 13 overs—Shane Shillingford, the West Indies off-spinner, dismissed both the two Indian openers in the same over. Murali Vijay's dismissal was greeted with more applause than perhaps any dismissal in the history of cricket in Mumbai. The applause soon gave way to a collective chant, familiar to cricket lovers all around the world. The whole ground reverberated to the sound of 'Sachin Sachin' as the legend made his way to the pitch. Every step of his towards the hallowed 22 yards was an event in itself, the crowd's heartbeat rising as he made his way through a guard of honour made by the West Indies team. Tendulkar did not disappoint, stroking his way to 38 not out at the end of the day's play, displaying remarkable fluency.

The next morning, India came to a standstill. Employees did not have to make up an excuse to tell their superiors that they would be late to work—the reason was understood. Everyone in the nation was glued to their television set, hoping to revel in the last moments of the career of India's favourite son. With a marvellous straight drive off Tino Best, Tendulkar brought up his 119th score of 50 and above in Test cricket. The whole crowd stood up to applaud the great man and perhaps all the millions watching on the television screen rose up as well.

Anjali Tendulkar signalled from the audience, 'Stay there'. A few more memorable strokes followed and it seemed Tendulkar was coasting to his 52nd Test 100 and his 101st international 100. However, fate seemed to have a mind for symmetry. What the legend was destined to end with was 200 Test matches and 100 international hundreds. Narsingh Deonarine to Tendulkar. Tendulkar edged the ball to first slip. Darren Sammy took a superb catch. It was over. The crowd gasped. A stunned silence ensued. In a few seconds, the silence broke and the crowd rose; the eyes of each and every member of the audience was moist. They cheered their hero as he made his way back to the pavilion one last time. Gavaskar on commentary just said, 'Thank you, Thank you.'

The rest of the match is but a footnote in history. The home team continued their dominance as Cheteshwar Pujara waltzed his way to yet another 100. However, the most fluent innings of the match was played by Rohit, who played magnificently with the lower order yet again, scoring 111 off just 127 balls. India posted a formidable 495 in the first innings. The result was a foregone conclusion. The Indian spinners held sway again, picking 9 wickets between them in the second innings, Pragyan Ojha taking another 5-wicket haul. As Shami bowled Shannon Gabriel in the 47th over, Sachin Ramesh Tendulkar's international career finally came to an end.

The Indian team gave him a guard of honour with a difference, moving in formation on either side of him as he made his way back to the pavilion. However, the most soul-stirring moments of the final Test were yet to follow. After the formalities of the Man of the Match, the Man of the Series and the presentation of the trophy to the winning captain, Ravi Shastri handed over the microphone to the Little Master. What followed was an outpouring of emotion that not even the most diehard of Tendulkar's fans had expected. For perhaps the first time in his storied career, he laid his soul bare for all to see. The nation was teary eyed as he thanked all his companions through this wonderful journey, the ones there at the venue as well as the ones who had departed for their heavenly abodes. Fittingly, he ended his speech with a tribute to the cricket lovers who had showered him with so much affection over the years: 'I want to thank my fans from the bottom of my heart. "Sachin, Sachin" will reverberate in my ears till I stop breathing.'[56]

There was another moment that became etched in the memories of the cricket fanatic. Tendulkar made his way to the pitch one last time, and paid homage to the Wankhede ground. One could not escape the thought that we would never see him take centre stage on the 22 yards again. This moment was inevitable, maybe we should have prepared ourselves for

---

[56] Agrawal, Vandita, 'Sachin Tendulkar's Emotional Speech', *Indiatimes*, 16 November 2013, http://tinyurl.com/yepd6xxn. Accessed on 5 September 2023.

this long back, and maybe we should feel privileged that this legendary career stood the test of time, as long as it did. But there was still a sense of emptiness. As he bid his final goodbye, Dylan Thomas's lines echoed in one's heart:

> 'Do not go gentle into that good night,
> Old age should burn and rave at close of day;
> Rage, rage against the dying of the light.'

Aftermath: Later in the day, Tendulkar was announced as the first sportsperson to be nominated for the Bharat Ratna.

SCORECARD

West Indies: 182 all out (Powell-48, Bravo-29; Ojha-5/40, Ashwin-3/45) and 187 all out (Ramdin-53, Chanderpaul-41; Ojha-5/49, Ashwin-4/89)

India: 495 all out (Pujara-113, Rohit-111; Shillingford-5/179, Deonarine-2/45)

Result: India beat the West Indies by an innings and 126 runs

43

A NEW FACE OF INDIA TAKES CENTRE STAGE

In 2014, India toured England for the Pataudi Trophy. Unfortunately, after a promising start—drawing the first test, and winning the second—the Indian team crumbled to a 1-3 series defeat, with humiliating losses in the final two Test matches. The magnificence of Ajinkya Rahane's batting and the perseverance of Ishant Sharma at Lord's had been all but erased from public memory by the time India left the British Isles. What remained was now the age-old tag of 'Tigers at home, lambs abroad' and the recurrent visual of Indian batting's new talisman, Virat Kohli, taking the lonely walk back to the pavilion. After a degree of resurgence in the shorter formats, the Indian team stepped onto Australian shores with memories of the 0-4 whitewash in 2011–12 still haunting fans and experts alike. Doubts remained whether the new India can restore the pride in India's overseas performances, or will it suffer yet another crushing defeat?

The first Test match at Adelaide was played under the shadow of one of the great sporting tragedies of recent times. Philip Hughes, one of the brightest batting talents in Australia, died after suffering an on-field injury from a Sean Abbott delivery.[57] In a match full of brilliant batting performances and tributes from the Australian batters on reaching landmarks, the final act was the most exciting. On a remarkable final day, Virat, true to his name of being majestic and brave, put on an impressive performance of 115 runs. In what seemed an insurmountable run chase, he made the nation believe in him. Unfortunately, in the end, Australia's bowling attack held strong despite the Kohli onslaught and propelled the hosts to a well-deserved victory.

The second Test at Brisbane saw Australia's spearhead Mitchell Johnson breathe fire and destroy India with a scintillating burst of pace. Thus, India headed into the third Test at one of the great theatres of world cricket, the MCG, with 0-2 in the series. Another overseas series whitewash was very much a possibility.

3rd Test Match, India vs Australia, MCG, Melbourne, 26-30 December 2014

On Boxing Day, the young Australian captain Steven Smith won the toss and elected to bat. The wicket at the MCG looked barren and resembled a turf more likely to be found in Vidarbha than Victoria. Day 1 was arguably India's finest day with the red ball on the entire tour. The Indian bowlers picked up wickets at regular intervals to leave the game evenly poised at 259/5 at the end of the Day 1—one of the slower scoring days of the series. However, India's nemesis Smith was still holding fort at 72 not out and he had the dangerous Brad Haddin for company.

---

[57]Gibson, Owen, 'Phillip Hughes–'He Died Playing the Sport He Loved''', *The Guardian*, 27 November 2014, https://bit.ly/432ulm6. Accessed on 3 April 2023.

A New Face of India Takes Centre Stage 249

On Day 2, the Australian lower-order frustrated the Indians, while Smith kept piling on the runs at the other end with nonchalant ease. By the time Smith was the last batter dismissed for 192, Australia had amassed another 500 runs plus total. India had a decent start to their innings, and finished the day on 108/1.

The dismissals of Pujara and Vijay brought together two gentlemen of exceptional batting talent but with completely contrasting personalities. On the one hand, was the brash, some would even say cocky Delhi boy, whose in-your-face-aggression reminded many former Australian cricketers of cricketers from their own country. On the other hand was a shy, almost reticent, hardworking batter from Mumbai. From the start, the Indian vice-captain Kohli put on a remarkable display of controlled aggression, cutting, pulling and driving the ball through the covers. At the other end, Rahane was almost monk-like in his calmness, weaving his bat like a magic wand. What appeared like an inconspicuous punch raced through the covers, and not once did the Mumbai batter look like he was about to break a sweat. The Australian spearhead Mitchell Johnson tried his level best to dismantle the cocoon the Indian batters had built around themselves.

He almost succeeded. A poignant moment in the day's play was when Mitchell Johnson struck Kohli while trying to hit the stumps after fielding the ball off his own bowling. Johnson immediately apologized, but Kohli was not satisfied. He decided that it was time to repay the body blow with some more strikes to the boundary. He almost perished twice, with some tough catches dropped off him. However, he survived and carried on the assault, reaching his third century of the series. After the hundred, Kohli launched an awe-inspiring attack on all the Australian bowlers, signalling out Johnson for special

Virat Kohli

attention. After yet another punitive pull stroke, he blew a kiss to Johnson, mocking the world's most fearsome fast bowler. The most fluent innings of the day, however, was Rahane's—his poise at the crease almost a throwback to the days of old. Yet, he married that sense of control with aggression in his stroke play. The shot of the day was Rahane's pull for six off a Johnson delivery, which would have set the pulse of every Indian cricket fan racing. In nearly 58 overs, Kohli and Rahane had piled on 262 of the most beautiful runs ever put together by an Indian pair on foreign shores and made the Indian supporters believe that India may even push for an improbable win. Alas, that was not to be. After Rahane was LBW to Lyon, the Indian innings had a mini collapse and was wrapped up for 465.

In the Australian innings, Shaun Marsh led a recovery, after the hosts suffered some early setbacks. They ended Day 4 on 261/7. The beginning of Day 5 was almost inexplicable and very un-Australian. In 23 overs, Australia put on just 57 runs, and showed a surprising lack of purpose. India were set an improbable 384 to get in 70 overs. India's second innings began disastrously, with Shikhar Dhawan perishing for a duck and K.L. Rahul once again faced lapse of concentration. Murali Vijay was soon to follow and it was again left to the heroes of the first innings—Kohli and Rahane—to stage a rescue act.

Kohli after his first innings heroics had made some remarks that did not go down too well with the Australian cricket fraternity and the public at large. He said that he believed in giving respect to only those who respected him, and thus he did not see the need to treat the Australian cricketers with respect. Kohli was greeted with a hostile reception at the crease, both from the crowd and the Australian players. Kohli and Rahane followed by the resolute Cheteshwar Pujara stabilized the Indian innings. However, the Australian bowlers kept the pressure on and managed to keep chances of a victory alive. It was finally left to the Indian captain, Dhoni, and India's lead spinner R. Ashwin to play out 15 overs to restore India's pride and avoid any chances of another overseas whitewash. In a display of courage and calm, which has characterized the Indian captain's career, he battled it out for 11 overs with his comrade Ashwin, who displayed great technique. After 66 overs of the Indian innings, skipper Smith called the match to a close, the teams shook hands and Australia bagged the Border–Gavaskar Trophy.

Dhoni Bids Adieu to Test Cricket

The story of the third Test match of the Border–Gavaskar Trophy 2014–2015 did not end on the cricket pitch. Moments after the presentation ceremony, an announcement came from a BCCI official that shook Indian cricket to the core. Mahendra Singh Dhoni, the man who had led India to the No. 1 ranking in

Test cricket in 2009, the man who had been at the receiving end of two overseas series whitewashes in England and Australia, whose test captaincy was labelled stale and uninventive, had finally decided to bid Test cricket goodbye. He did it in his own fashion without any press conference, no fanfare, no farewell Test match. Perhaps, he felt that an act of defiance to save India a Test match at one of the iconic venues in cricket was an apt way to depart. It was time for India to awake to Test cricket under a new leader.

SCORECARD

Australia: 530 all out (Steve Smith-192, Harris-74; Shami-4/138, Umesh-3/130) and 318/9 declared (Shaun Marsh-99, Rogers-69; Ishant-2/49, Ashwin-2/75)

India: 465 all out (Kohli-169, Rahane-147; Harris-4/70, Johnson-3/135) and 174/6 (Kohli-54, Rahane-48; Harris-2/30, Johnson-2/38)

Result: Match drawn

44

MITHALI AND JHULAN

Unlike the 49 other matches in this book, the match we have picked here is perhaps not as distinctly significant as a match in itself. This chapter is a celebration of two of the greatest cricketers India has ever produced, and talks about the match where both of them were at their peak.

Mithali Raj, bookish and stoic, hails from Hyderabad. She is a woman who comes across as all focus and concentration in her interviews. She is also India's greatest woman batter and the highest run-scorer in women's ODIs. Like Gavaskar in the '70s and the '80s, Raj carried India's batting on her shoulders from the late 1990s as a 16-year-old, right up to late 2019. She had to cut down on her flowing, elegant stroke play often for the cause of the team. She was, for a while, the highest run-scorer in a single innings in women's Tests. She captained her team to two so-near-yet-so-far moments at the Women's World Cup, and has been the face of women's cricket right from the dawn of the millennium.

The story of Jhulan Goswami's life is scarcely believable. Girls from middle-class families in tiny Indian towns in the middle of nowhere do not become cricketers, let alone become legends of the game—it is completely unheard of. And of course, there is no chance that they become the highest wicket-takers of the women's game. Yet, it happened.

Mithali Raj and Jhulan Goswami

One of the most heart-warming cricket videos one can ever watch is a tiny three-minute section on the ICC channel, when Pakistan's quick bowler Kainat Imtiaz talks about how, as a ball-girl at the boundary-line, she was impressed by the Indian fast bowler and decided to take up quick bowling. This was Goswami, inspiring kids around the world to pick up quick bowling.

In 2022, biopics *Shabaash Mithu* and *Chakda 'Xpress* were released on these two biggest icons of the women's game and the pride of Indian cricket fans. Indian cricket will forever remain indebted to Mithali and Jhulan, for letting young girls know that cricket is not a game they can only cheer on from the stands, it is a game they can be excellent players of. They could be Mithali Raj and Jhulan Goswami.

Indian Women's Team Tour of England in 2014

While doing research for the match that we have written about in this chapter, we noted the articles about the lack of structure in the women's team game. This was mid-2014. The view has changed considerably for the better in the last few years of the 2010s. We cannot say that women's cricket is at par with men's cricket yet, but the stars of the modern game are household names, and women's cricket is a professional endeavour in India now. Its future is bright.

On to the match now. The limited-overs game is pre-eminent in women's cricket. Test matches are few and far between. Both Raj and Goswami have played only 10 Tests in their career (as of 2019), while they have played 232 and 204 ODIs, respectively. It is a bit of an anomaly, but they did get to play a fantastic advertisement for the game against England in August 2014. The match was held at Sir Paul Getty's Ground in Wormsley.

England were one of the best sides in women's cricket, and English women's cricket was already a professional set-up. India's was not, and barring Raj, Goswami and wicketkeeper Karuna Jain, none of the others in the team had played Test cricket earlier. This was a young team, bubbling with talent. Some stalwarts of Indian cricket were making their Test debut in this match. This was the first season as international players for Smriti Mandhana and Shikha Pandey, while Harmanpreet Kaur, Ekta Bisht, Punam Raut and Niranjana Nagarajan had established themselves in the one-day team already.

England had some of the most famous women cricketers in the world playing for them: the legendary Charlotte Edwards was winding down her career, and would captain England in this match. With Heather Knight, Tammy Baumont and

Natalie Sciver, this was perhaps the best batting line-up in the world. England had a four-pronged quick-bowling attack of experienced Jenny Gunn, with the youthful pace of Kate Cross, Sonia Odedra and the fastest of them all, Anya Shrubsole. And of course, there was Sarah Taylor, arguably the greatest wicketkeeper–batter the game has seen.

England vs India, Only Test, Sir Paul Getty's Ground, Wormsley, 13–16 August 2014

Raj won the toss against Edwards, and sent the English team to bat. The Indian seam bowlers were all over the English women soon after. This was the day of the lesser-heralded Nagarajan, who took four English scalps. Goswami and Pandey took a wicket each, both exploiting the conditions especially well. Taylor was the highest scorer for England with 30, before she was LBW to Goswami. England were all out for 92, and India had made a great start to the Test.

India, too, struggled in their first innings. All the English bowlers took wickets, but the most successful was veteran Gunn, who bowled a delightful spell of swing bowling to get 5 wickets. India crumbled to 114 all out. The 22-run lead could be seen as meagre, but in the context of the low-scoring game, the Indians were quite thankful for it. India's batting tail wagged, and that proved to be the difference between the two teams' scores. Goswami scored 17 and Nagarajan 27—these were important contributions from the lower-order.

In their second innings, England put up a more spirited display in very difficult conditions for batting. Opener Lauren Winfield scored 35, Taylor scored 40, but the big surprise was Gunn's 62 not out from No. 8. Goswami was at her absolute peak in this innings, and troubled every English batter. Four wickets did not flatter her. But perhaps a lead of 181 could be too much for the Indians?

India started very well in the second innings though. The openers, Thirush Kamini and Mandhana put up 76 runs, before both of them got dismissed in quick succession. This was the time for the captain to take centre stage. The English bowlers deployed all the tricks in their book but could not force Mithali into an error. She set up a 30-run partnership with Punam Raut, and then after 2 consecutive wickets—of Raut and Harmanpreet—she had another partnership with seam-bowling all-rounder Pandey. They got it in singles—as the phrase goes. In the context of the game, a 68-run partnership was invaluable, and captain Raj saw India home with a 50 not out.

Mithali Raj and Jhulan Goswami's amateur outfit had defeated the excellent professionals of the English team.

What started in 2014 continues in 2017 and in 2023. The women's U19 team is the U19 World Champions now. The Women's Premier League (WPL) has started, and is being played to packed audiences. What greater compliment can we give to the women's game except mentioning that of the last five matches in this book, three are women's matches.

SCORECARD

England: 92 all out (Taylor-30, Beaumont-12; Niranjana-4/19, Shubhlakshmi-2/12) and 202 all out (Gunn-62*, Taylor-40; Goswami-4/48, Shubhlakshmi-2/22)

India: 114 all out (Niranjana-27, Mandhana-22; Gunn-5/19, Cross-3/29) and 183/4 (Mandhana-51, Raj-50*; Cross-3/42, Knight-1/7)

Result: India beat England by 6 wickets

45

PERFORMANCE OF A LIFETIME

The current generation of Indian cricket truly emerged from the all-encompassing shadows of Sachin Tendulkar (and then M.S. Dhoni in 2014) at the MCG, through the mighty bat of Virat Kohli followed by creditable performance from the young brigade. The match we write about puts a rubber stamp on that claim.

England Tour of India, 2016-17

In 2016, England toured India to play five Tests, three ODIs and three T20s. For the Indian team, this English tour was nothing short of a revenge mission. This had to do with the fact that back in 2012–13, England had won the Test series in India on the back of momentous performances from Cook and Pietersen, and were able to out-spin the rather green Indian spinners, R. Ashwin, Pragyan Ojha and Ravindra Jadeja with their dual-spin attack of Swann and Panesar. In the interim, India had toured England in 2014, and lost rather comprehensively, 3-1 to them.

Back to English tour of India. The first Test was at Rajkot. The pitch had a little bit in it for both quick and slow bowlers, and while it was a long-drawn-out draw, it was quite a typical, slow-burning Test match. India won the second Test quite comprehensively by 246 runs, inaugurating the Y.S.R. Stadium in Visakhapatnam as a Test venue. Both of India's main batters, Kohli and Pujara, scored hundreds, and Ashwin and Ravindra Jadeja were both among the wickets.

The third Test at Mohali was a reasonably comfortable win for the Indians. Initially at a spot of bother at 204/6, replying to England's first innings total of 283, the lower-order of Ashwin, Ravindra Jadeja and off-spinner Jayant Yadav all contributed with the bat to take the match away from the English. Continuing the good run of form, India won the fourth Test by an innings on the back of a regal 235 by captain Virat Kohli, thereby completing the series win.

India vs England, 5th Test Match, M.A. Chidambaram Stadium, Chennai, 16-20 December 2016

The fifth Test was at the M.A. Chidambaram Stadium. Cook won the toss and elected to bat first. Cook and his opening partner Keaton Jennings were dismissed early, but England stabilized with a sparkling 146-run partnership between Joe Root and Moeen Ali. Root, one of the most promising batters among the new generation, departed at 88, for a disputed, DRS (decision review system)-referred dismissal, caught by keeper Parthiv Patel trying to play the sweep off Ravindra Jadeja. Jonny Bairstow, England's wicketkeeper–batter, came in next and continued playing confidently against India's spinners. Having hit three towering sixes, he departed playing a loose on-drive to Ravindra Jadeja, one short of his 50.

Ali was batting serenely from the other end, and completed his 100 in due course. After Ben Stokes' dismissal, there was a mini-collapse for England, as 3 wickets fell in quick succession. The English tailenders put up a fight though, and for the eighth wicket, there was a 108-run partnership between Liam Dawson and Adil Rashid. England eventually were all out for a competitive 477.

In reply, India put up a solid opening partnership for the first wicket. Parthiv Patel, the wicketkeeper, opened the batting along with the find of the series, K.L. Rahul. After a 152-run partnership in quick time, Patel got out to a beauty from Moeen Ali. The stalwarts of the Indian batting line-up, Kohli and Pujara, both fell cheaply and Karun Nair, compatriot of Rahul, joined him in the middle.

It was Nair's first international series. He had been brought into the team to replace the injured Ajinkya Rahane for the third Test. Initially, he batted steadily and let Rahul take the majority of the strike. Rahul was batting like a dream, and had already completed his century. Soon, Rahul's 150 came up and so did Nair's half century. Rahul was caressing the ball towards the boundary often, and sometimes over it. When the double century was a whisker away, Rahul threw it away by playing a rank poor shot at 199. At the end of Day 3, India was in a decent position—86 runs behind with 6 wickets in hand and Nair still at the crease with 71.

Day 4 was a Karun Nair show. He got to his first ton in Test cricket early in the morning and dominated the English bowlers all day, with Murali Vijay, then Ashwin and then Ravindra Jadeja for company. He got to his 150, and then steadied himself to not make the mistake Rahul had made earlier and got to the double. After that was carnage. Nair had got his 200 in 306 deliveries. In the next 75 deliveries, he went up to 300—only the second Indian after Sehwag to get to the triple-hundred. Off the last 75 deliveries faced, he hit 9 fours and 3 sixes. As soon as the 300 was completed, Kohli called his batters in and declared. India had scored a mammoth 759/7, with a lead of 282 runs.

With a series already lost and a pile of runs in deficit, a betting man would have perhaps gone for England to crumble. But behind the choirboy face and polite demeanour, Cook was hard as nails. He gritted it out against the onslaught of the Indian spinners, and guided his junior partner Jennings to a solid 100-run opening partnership. The Indian spinners kept on probing relentlessly, and eventually the floodgates opened after Cook was caught at leg slip off Jadeja. Jennings soon followed, and after that, India's master of the crumbling fifth-day track, Jadeja, ran through the England innings. He took 7, and England were all out for 207, falling for an innings-and-75-run defeat. England's 477 was the highest first innings score by a team which still lost a Test by an innings.

SCORECARD

England: 477 all out (Moeen Ali-146, Root-88; Jadeja-3/106, Ishant-2/42) and 207 all out (Jennings-54, Cook-49; Jadeja-7/48, Ishant-1/17)

India: 759/7 declared (Nair-303*, Rahul-199; Broad-2/80, Dawson-2/129)

Result: India beat England by an innings and 75 runs

46

A TRYST WITH DESTINY

The greatest limited-overs innings ever played by an Indian is by Harmanpreet Kaur, when she scored 171 not out against Australia in the semi-final of the Women's World Cup 2017.[58] No other innings comes close to Harmanpreet's innings when one looks at the context of the match, the opposition, the match situation and the impact it made. India has played more than 2,000 ODIs, and in terms of sheer impact, there is nothing beating Harman's monster.

Australia had dominated women's cricket through the last quarter of the last century, and they continue to dominate women's cricket even at present. Some of the greatest women cricketers of the game—Belinda Clark, Karen Rolton, Kathryn Fitzpatrick, Alex Blackwell, Lisa Sthalekar, Meg Lanning and Ellyse Perry are all Australian. Before the 2017 edition, Australia had won six of the ten previous Women's World Cups, England had won three[59] and it seemed inevitable that the two would meet in the finals again.

---

[58]Keshav, Karunya, 'Women's Innings of the Decade, No.1: Harmanpreet Touches Greatness', *Wisden India*, 6 December 2019, https://bit.ly/3KqeS8e. Accessed on 3 April 2023.

[59]Jolly, Laura, 'World Cup Winners Recognised in Brisbane', *cricket.com.au*, 3 June 2017, https://bit.ly/3ZBQC7t. Accessed on 3 April 2023

Making an Impression: ICC Women's World Cup 2017

India's journey in the World Cup started with a flourish. Aided by a stylish 90 by the elegant left-handed opener Smriti Mandhana, India got up to 281/3 against England in their first match, and defended it competently to win by 35 runs.

After confident wins against the West Indies, Pakistan and the emerging regional force Sri Lanka, the Indian women's team suffered a setback against South Africa, losing to a brilliant all-round performance by Dane van Niekerk. The next match was against Australia, and India was swept aside by the might of Lanning and Perry, two of the finest young cricketers in the world. The Indian team came back well from that chastening defeat, and defeated New Zealand in their final match of the group stage to book a place in the semi-final.

The signs were ominous though. England had managed to get an unlikely 3-run victory against Australia, but there was little doubt that the Australians were the team to beat. There were at least four Hall of Famers in the Australian team: Lanning, Blackwell, Perry and wicketkeeper–batter Alyssa Healy. Unfortunately, though India qualified third, since England had a better run-rate than Australia in qualifying and the same number of points, India had to face Australia, not England, in the semi-final.

India vs Australia, ICC Women's World Cup 2017, County Ground, Derby, 20 July 2017

In the first semi-final, England got the better of South Africa. India played Australia in the other semi-final, at the County Ground, Derby. The English weather intervened at the start of the match, restricting it to 42 overs-a-side. India won the toss and decided to bat first. However, by the very first over, Mandhana was dismissed by Megan Schutt. After the early debacle, experienced Raut and captain Raj set about building a platform for the team. In the 10th over though, Raut tried to up the tempo of the innings but managed only to hole out to deep mid-wicket. Enter Harmanpreet.

Harmanpreet had not been at top form in the tournament. India's batting was carried by Mandhana, Raj and Raut, with occasional contributions by Deepti Sharma. However, there was a feeling that Harmanpreet was a match-winner, and it made sense to persist with her. It is interesting to note that a little while before the series, Women's Big Bash League was held in Australia and Harmanpreet was one of the only two Indian players in that tournament. She had played well and her late-order big hits were appreciated by the crowds. What she had also gained was an understanding of the Australian players and their strengths. This came in handy for her in this match.

In the company of the legendary Raj, she went about pacing her innings. At the stroke of the 25th over, Raj was bowled by a skidder from leg spinner Kristen Beams. It was 101/3 now—was it time yet for the onslaught? The exact moment of this transformation was the 27th over by Beams. Harmanpreet was batting at 41 off 60 balls, and the time had come to move up a couple of gears. The fourth delivery by Beams slipped from her hand, and a free-hit was called by the umpire. She bowled the free-hit delivery on a length down the middle, and Harmanpreet smacked it sweetly over the long-on boundary and into the stands.

What followed was sublime savagery. A lovely flow of the bat, superb timing and the Australian bowlers were carted across the park. It wasn't just big hits, it was debilitating hits.

The bowlers lost their length. Jess Jonassen, the steadiest of left-arm orthodox bowlers, was bowling high full-tosses. Even the quick bowlers, Schutt and Perry, were biffed to the fence. And imagine how she celebrated getting to her 100? It was a risky 2, and Deepti hesitated on Harmanpreet's call. After a dive to the crease, Harmanpreet, livid, threw down her helmet, and roared at her partner. This was her match, this was her zone. She would not let her partners throw it away. Someone had to remind her that she had reached her 100.

Some more carnage followed. She had got to her 100 in 90 deliveries. What followed in the next 25 deliveries was mayhem. She added 71 runs in the next 25 she faced. The scorecard read: Harmanpreet Kaur 171* (115 balls, 20 fours, 7 sixes). India finished at 281/4 off their 42 overs.

The one trademark trait Australians have is that they do not lose a match before it is actually mathematically impossible to win. They went for it. However, India were not in the mood to let that happen. In the second over of the Australian innings, outswing bowler Shikha Pandey, the understudy and new-ball partner to Goswami, provided an absolute beauty and took the off-stump of Australian opener Beth Mooney. Inspired, the old warhorse Goswami provided a delivery, which could stand with any other in her illustrious career, to dismiss Australia's captain and best batter, Meg Lanning. A brave 100-run fourth-wicket partnership between Ellyse Perry and Elyse Villani, and a violent, back-to-the-wall knock from Blackwell made sure that the match was always competitive. But Blackwell eventually was the last to be dismissed for Australia, for a defiant 90 off 56 balls. Australia were then all out for 245.

The Indian women's team had done the impossible. The defending champions were out of the tournament, and India had reached the finals of the World Cup. It was all made possible by an innings for the Gods, Harmanpreet's 171—the greatest one-day innings played by an Indian.

It was so near, yet so far for India. They lost the finals by 7 runs, ambushed right at the death by supreme fast bowling from England's Anya Shrubsole. Mithali Raj and Jhulan Goswami's dream of lifting the World Cup remained unfulfilled.

> **SCORECARD**
>
> **India:** 281/4 in 42 overs (Harmanpreet-171*, Raj-36; Villani-1/19, Gardner-1/43)
>
> **Australia:** 245 all out in 40.1 overs (Blackwell-90, Villani-75; Deepti-3/58, Pandey-2/17)
>
> **Result:** India beat Australia by 36 runs

47

THE LAST FRONTIER

India had never won a Test series in Australia before 2018. As surprising as it might sound, there are valid reasons for that. The conditions in Australia and India are vastly different. Australian tracks are hard and the playing fields are large, quick bowlers hit the deck hard and spinners bowl with lots of revolutions on the ball. On the other hand, Indian tracks are slow and low. Playing fields are smaller. The batters deal in boundaries. Patience is a virtue, and so is waiting for the bad deliveries. The quick bowlers pitch up the new ball, and the old ball swings the other way. The wickets grip for the spinners, so side-spinners and top-spinners come into effect more.

In hindsight, when Steve Waugh said that India was the final frontier for him, it was not just because he had won everywhere else.[60] It was also because he understood that it was going to be the biggest challenge. And Laxman, Dravid and Harbhajan were on hand to prove him right.

---

[60] "Steve Was Adamant He Wanted to Win": Shane Warne Feels Waugh Missed a Trick During India–Australia 2001 Test', *Hindustan Times*, 23 August 2020, https://bit.ly/40VVLJ9. Accessed on 11 April 2023.

The Challenges Before India

Perhaps, India's greatest Test team, the vintage of early 2000s, drew a series against the mighty Australians of those times. In 1977–78, the Packer-Series-decimated Australians still managed to win 3-2. A raw, rebuilding Australian side managed to hold India to a 0-0 series draw in 1985–86. But there had been no win. The 2018–19 vintage wanted to change all that.

First of all, the Australian team was struggling in the aftermath of the 'Sandpaper gate' incident in South Africa, and three of their best batters, Steve Smith, David Warner and Cameron Bancroft were all banned for using a sandpaper to try to alter the shape of the ball in a test in South Africa.[61] India, on the other hand, was at full-strength, with almost all the key players in the team having had the experience of touring Australia previously.

Secondly, India perhaps had a quick bowling attack that was comparable with the Australians. It's not that India had never had good pace bowlers when they visited Australia. Kapil in 1981 had bowled right through the Australian team and got them all out for 83 in the fourth innings, winning a stirring Test for India. Srinath, Agarkar and others had individual performances worth remembering. But never had India had a group of fast bowlers who could sustain the pressure on the Australians. Bumrah, Shami and Ishant brought their distinct individual qualities and collective ability to make it a formidable attack. And to supplement that, there was quality spin from Ashwin and Jadeja. Do remember that while Australia's batting was decimated, their bowling was as strong as ever, with quick

---

[61] ANI, 'Cricket Australia Needed to Do More Thorough Investigation into "Sandpapergate", Feels Adam Gilchrist', *The Times of India*, 17 May 2021, https://bit.ly/3mtj8dV. Accessed on 11 April 2023.

bowlers like Mitchell Starc, Pat Cummins and Josh Hazlewood, and off-spinner Nathan Lyon, making it a bowling attack of quality and variety.

India were then the holders of the Border–Gavaskar Trophy, having won the Test series in India in 2017, thus they could retain the trophy if they just drew the series. The three-match T20 series was drawn, and the four-match Test series followed.

The Rising Star of Indian Cricket

An Indian player to come especially in focus in this series was Cheteshwar Pujara. A throwback to a different time and a different game, Pujara is that rare commodity of the modern game—the Test match specialist. With Test matches being sporadic over the year, the international cricket-watcher would get to see Pujara in patches. He would play the Test series and then disappear for a while during the ODI and T20 series. During the T20 leagues, he would play the English county season or in the Ranji Trophy for Saurashtra. Blessed with infinite reserves of patience and a stubborn refusal to give away his wicket, and with a limited repertoire of strokes in his command, especially at the start of his innings, he has been a bit of an anachronism in the modern world. But he has been invaluable to the cause of the Indian Test team, as he has provided cushioning to the batters around him in the line-up to express themselves.

Australia vs India, 3rd Test, MCG, Melbourne, 26-30 December 2018

The first Test was extremely competitive. On a green, juicy wicket, India batted first and scored 250, with Pujara scoring a hundred. Australia got near enough to India's target and the match effectively became a second-innings shootout. India won that shootout, marginally, as their 307—Pujara again scoring a 70—was slightly more than the 291 that Australia could muster. (In the first innings, Australia had made 235). The second test was all Australia. They came roaring back on the back of a fantastic bowling performance by Lyon. Indian captain Kohli's 123 in the first innings was in vain.

The third Test will be our themed match for this chapter. This was the Boxing Day Test of the season, played at the MCG. Kohli won the toss against Australian captain Tim Paine, and elected to bat first. Mayank Agarwal, playing his first Test, set up an excellent platform for the team with a brave 76. The gun batters for India—Kohli and Pujara—then continued their fine form and put up a solid 170-run partnership. They both got dismissed in quick succession—Kohli on 82, missing a well-deserved hundred, and Pujara with a phlegmatic 106. The lower-middle-order contributed to the cause, and Kohli declared the innings at 443/7.

Australia, batting second, were shaken by the fire and brimstone that Bumrah had to offer. A bowler with an awkward delivery action, but a wickedly quick arm, Bumrah has a lot of tricks up his sleeves and is a canny customer for most batters. He proved his qualities by running through a few of the batters with hostile pace, and making some play bad shots with short-pitched deliveries. Perhaps, the best of his dismissals was the one to Shaun Marsh. Playing a steady hand, Marsh was batting on 19 from 60 deliveries. When facing the last ball before tea, he was faced with an ultra-slow, gently-inswinging yorker. Marsh played his stroke way too early, and was LBW, plumb in front. Bumrah had a 6/33, Australia was all out for 151, and Kohli decided against a follow-on.

The Indians made a meal of their second innings. Neither could they accelerate the scoring rate nor could they stop the Australians from taking wickets. Cummins was bowling his heart out. The Indians could perhaps imagine what facing Bumrah could have been like for the Australians, for they were facing similar quality bowling from Cummins. Eventually Kohli decided that he had seen enough, and put a stop to the proceedings. India declared for the second time in the Test, at 106/8. Cummins had taken 6 wickets, his best haul in a single Test innings.

Australia's target was 399 runs; it was a tall order. They put up a brave front, as Australian teams are duty-bound to do, but wickets kept falling in regular intervals. Bumrah got a few, his strike partner Shami got a few, and Jadeja and Ishant chipped in with a few as well. A courageous lower-order innings was played by Australia's star with the ball, Cummins. Coming in at No. 8, he played some crisp strokes in between showing a good forward-defensive to score 63. Australia was all out in the early hours of the fifth day for 261. India had won by 137 runs and headed into the final Test at Sydney with a 2-1 series lead.

India went on to win the series 2-1, with the last two days of the fourth Test at Sydney being washed out. India were in a position to win this Test as well, having taken a commanding lead of 322 runs in the first innings. The two performances that stood out in the fourth Test were Pujara's 193 and young wicketkeeper Rishabh Pant's 159 not out.

India was nominally the best team in the world at the moment. They were not the dominant champions the way the West Indies and Australia teams of the past had been, but all things considered, this was the best team in the world at the moment. There is still time to consolidate their legacy, and that will happen in front of our eyes. I am sure you will be watching!

SCORECARD

India: 443/7 declared (Pujara-106, Kohli-82; Cummins-3/72, Starc-2/87) and 106/8 declared (Mayank-42, Pant-33; Cummins-6/27, Hazlewood-2/22)

Australia: 151 all out (Paine-22, Harris-22; Bumrah-6/33, Jadeja-2/45) and 261 all out (Cummins-63, Shaun Marsh-44; Bumrah-3/53, Ishant-2/40)

Result: India beat Australia by 137 runs

48

A NEW DECADE, A NEW ERA

In the last 47 chapters, we have covered matches that reflect Indian cricket's glorious past, the setbacks it faced and its vibrant present. Post the exploits of the Indian women's team in the 2017 World Cup, where Harmanpreet Kaur played that astonishing innings of 171, the attention of the media and the corporate world on the women's team has grown manifold. Players such as Mandhana and Harmanpreet can now be considered genuine superstars of Indian cricket. This has also coincided with the emergence of some precocious talent such as Shafali Verma.

The story of Verma travelling all the way to Lahli to watch Tendulkar bat in his last Ranji Trophy match has already been circulated widely on social media.[62] Just like her idol, at the age of 16, she became the cynosure of all eyes and the toast of a nation.

Shafali is one of the several young players who provide Indian cricket followers with hopes for a successful future. Jemimah Rodrigues, Radha Yadav, Taniya Bhatia and Deepti Sharma—all in their youth—have shown sparks of brilliance in their careers. We forget that India also possesses arguably the best woman batter in the world in Mandhana who is only

---

[62]Ghosh, Annesha, 'Shafali Verma: The Strong Girl Who's Batting Down Barriers', *ESPNCrickinfo*, 4 March 2020, https://es.pn/40Y0vxg. Accessed on 3 April 2023.

27. This group of youngsters, along with the experience and class of Harmanpreet Kaur, Poonam Yadav and Shikha Pandey have already made India one of the leading sides in the world game. Many of India's core line-up are not even near the peak, so it is natural to assume that several moments of glory await the women's cricket team in India.

Despite the plethora of talent in the women's team, one sensed that the country still did not openly support the idea of women playing in big tournaments. However, all that changed during the 2020 Women's T20 World Cup. Inspired by the brilliant performances of the team, the entire nation supported them fervently. The crowds in Australia also embraced the young Indian team, and every ground where India played featured a large Indian contingent in the stands. No match reflected the love that the Indian team received in Australia and the remarkable progress made by this young side than the very first match of the 2020 T20 World Cup against defending champions, Australia.

India had been part of a T20I Tri-Series tournament in Australia (England being the third team), immediately preceding the World Cup. An impressive performance by the team led them to the finals, wherein they lost to Australia in a tightly contested final. So, the team morale was high going into India's first encounter at the T20 World Cup at the Sydney Showground Stadium, against the defending champions Australia.

India vs Australia, 2020 ICC Women's T20 World Cup, Premier Match, Sydney Showground Stadium, Sydney, 21 February 2020

Australia won the toss and elected to field—a debatable decision considering the slow nature of the wicket. Verma soon announced herself on the World Cup stage, striking a boundary and an imperious six over long-on off the bowling of Molly Strano. In the next over, Verma went up another gear, hitting the No. 1 ranked T20I bowler in the world, Megan Schutt, for four boundaries shots both on the leg and the offside, all struck with scintillating power. In the next over bowled by India's nemesis Jess Jonassen, Mandhana (who had been watching Shafali's assault from the non-striker's end) missed a flat and straight delivery trying to sweep. To the disappointment of the huge contingent of Indian supporters at the Sydney Showground, Verma soon joined Mandhana in the pavilion, mistiming a lofted shot and holing out to mid-on off the bowling of Perry. Harmanpreet came in at No. 4 and was the next to depart, stumped by Healy off the bowling of Jonassen, who seemed to have a stranglehold over India. With the score on 47/3, Deepti came out to join the classy Rodrigues.

The two played resolutely and smartly, considering the sluggish nature of the pitch. They preferred to rotate the strike instead of going for big hits. In 9.2 overs, they put on an invaluable partnership of 53 runs, hitting only 1 boundary. In the last ball of the 16th over, Delissa Kimmince trapped Jemimah LBW for 26, with the Indian score on 100. With some timely hits towards the end by Deepti, India managed to edge their way to a respectable total of 132/4. As per many Indian supporters, India were at least 15 runs short, especially against the imposing Australian batting line-up. India did, of course, have an ally in the pitch, which was expected to aid spin further in the second innings.

For Australia, Healy got off to a confident start, hitting 10 runs off the first three deliveries bowled by the wily left-armer Rajeshwari Gayakwad. At the other end, Beth Mooney was struggling due to the accurate Indian bowling. She perished in the sixth over, caught at backward point off Pandey. Lanning, one of the best batter the world has ever seen, came out to join Healy who was in sparkling form. Off the first over bowled by Arundhati Reddy, Healy hit three powerfully struck boundaries. Then in the ninth over, Gayakwad struck a crucial blow, as Lanning misjudged a beautifully flighted delivery, only managing to edge it to the excellent Indian keeper Bhatia. Australia were 58/2 in nine overs, requiring 75 off 11 overs—a very achievable required run rate of 6.81.

Unveiling India's Trump Card

It was then that Harmanpreet unveiled her trump card, the diminutive leg-spinner Poonam Yadav, who had not played in the tri-series before the World Cup. Yadav struck gold almost instantly, getting the all-important wicket of Healy in her first over. A slow leg break bowled at just 63 kmph befuddled Healy and she got a leading edge, which floated straight to Yadav. Healy was out for 51, and Australia was at 67/3. Yadav is a classical leg spinner. Even a six by Healy, just the ball before she took a wicket, did not discourage her from floating the next ball up. In the 12th over, Poonam produced two moments of magic. On the third delivery, she flighted a googly that lured the left-hander Rachael Haynes out of her crease. The ball went past the outside edge and Bhatia effected a smart stumping. The next delivery to Perry was possibly the ball of the match. A loopy googly deceived Perry in the flight, as the great all-rounder stepped out and completely missed the ball. The ball went through the gate and hit the stumps. Poonam was on a hat-trick. She nearly achieved the mark, when Bhatia missed a tough chance off a Jonassen outside edge. Poonam, however, got Jonassen in her next over as Bhatia took a smart catch.

A New Decade, a New Era

Jemimah Rodrigues, Smriti Mandhana and Shafali Verma

At the fall of Jonassen's wicket, Australia was 82 for 6 in 13.5 overs. From then on, it was a struggle for the defending champions, as Pandey finished off a sterling Indian effort with the ball with some quality death bowling. Australia was all out for 115. India had beaten the defending champions in their own den in the first match of the World Cup by 17 runs.

This victory was achieved by cricketers who provided glimpses of the greats of Indian cricket history. If the explosive hitting and prodigious talent of Verma brought back memories of Sehwag and Tendulkar, the leg spin of Yadav reminded viewers of the great generation of spinners. Her tantalizing flight and powers of deception would have made Bedi, Prasanna or Chandrasekhar proud. India went on to the World Cup final, where they fell to the dominant Australian team.

India's unbeaten run to the finals and the extraordinary performances of the Indians forced the entire nation to rally behind them. Even after the defeat in the finals, there was an outpouring of praise on the Indian cricketers for their sensational game in the tournament. Visions of a stellar future for women's cricket in India abounded. The Indian women's cricket team, in many ways emblematic of the modern Indian woman, ensured that Indian cricket resounded with optimism as we began the new decade. Indian cricket is in good health, and we believe that in this new era, this nation of more than a billion would have plenty of reasons to shower their love on our cricketers, both men and women.

SCORECARD

India: 132/4 in 20 overs (Deepti-49, Shafali-29; Jonassen-2/24, Perry-1/15)

Australia: 115 all out in 19.5 overs (Healy-51, Gardner-34; Yadav-4/19, Pandey-3/14)

Result: India beat Australia by 17 runs

49

LAMBS TO THE SLAUGHTER, NO MORE

The Gabba! A word that evokes fear and trepidation in the minds of fans of many touring teams to Australia. The famous stadium also known as the 'Gabbatoir' (Gabba + abattoir) has often crushed the hopes of many teams who arrived in Australia with great expectations.

The Gabba provided the setting for the finale of the 2020–21 Border–Gavaskar Trophy. In the first Test in Adelaide, India crumbled to a historic low of 36 all out in the second innings, only to bounce back with a remarkable performance at the second Test match at Melbourne. Then came the astonishing final day rearguard at the SCG in the third Test. Ravichandran Ashwin, battling a back spasm, and Hanuma Vihari with a torn hamstring, soldiered on for almost 43 overs on the last day to hold out for a draw, which kept the series even. It was during this partnership that the Australian captain and wicketkeeper Tim Paine famously told Ashwin, 'Can't wait to get you to the Gabba.'[63]

---

[63]'"Want to Get You to India, May Be Your Last Series," Ashwin Claps Back at Paine', *The Week*, 11 January 2021, https://bit.ly/42ZJXa8. Accessed on 3 April 2023.

Australia vs India, 4th Test, Border-Gavaskar Series, Gabba, Brisbane, 2021

The Indian squad had been very unlucky in terms of injuries during the tour. The bowling attack that took the field at the Gabba bore no resemblance to the one that played the first Test at Adelaide. The makeshift Indian bowling line-up of Mohammad Siraj, T. Natarajan, Shardul Thakur, Navdeep Saini and Washington Sundar had played a grand total of four Tests before this game. India's batters had fought bravely without their talisman Kohli, but surely this was one bridge too far. What unfolded over the next five days became part of world cricketing folklore.

Australia won the toss and elected to bat. The new spearhead of the Indian attack, young Siraj, who had lost his father during the tour, bustled in. In the very first over, Siraj produced a brisk away-going delivery that caught Warner's edge. This was first blood to India. Fortunes ebbed and flowed the rest of the day, with the home team holding a slight edge, thanks to a brilliant 100 by Australia's new batting star, Marnus Labuschagne. The young Indian bowling line-up fought gamely, picking up wickets at crucial intervals and never allowing the home team to run away with proceedings. A 98-run partnership between Tim Paine and Cameron Green threatened to take Australia to a commanding total, but the Indian bowlers fought back. Debutants Sundar and Natarajan showed composure beyond their years, picking 3 wickets each as Australia's first innings finished at 369.

It was now time for the Indian batters to put up a solid effort. The rest of Day 2 was a start-stop affair due to rain, but before the day's play was called off, Australia struck a couple of crucial blows, dismissing Shubman Gill and Rohit Sharma.

Day 3 saw India looking towards its most experienced players, Pujara and Rahane to steady the ship. But instead, the star-studded Australian pace attack of Cummins, Hazlewood and Starc took control. Just like in the Australian first innings, the Indian middle-order were pegged back by regular breakthroughs. When Pant, who had played a dazzling knock of 97 in the second innings of the third Test, was dismissed for 23, the Indian innings was tottering at 186/6, still 183 runs behind the Australian total. With no reputation or experience at international level to speak of, even the most optimistic of Indian fans was probably having a sinking feeling. But the Sundar–Shardul show was about to begin.

That passage of play on Day 3 was remarkable. Sundar, the young off-spinner, and Thakur, the medium-pacer, showed their skills with the bat in a manner that could be best described as audacious. Thakur scored 67, even pulling the mighty Cummins for 6. Sundar played with classical elegance for 62. Their partnership of 123 set the stage for the rest of this Test match. India was finally bowled out for 336, a mere 33 runs behind the Australian total.

The injury curse struck again. Saini, the quickest bowler in the Indian line-up, suffered a groin strain in the first innings, and bowled only 12.5 overs in the entire match. In the second innings, the Australians seemed to have seized control of the match, as the openers put on 89 runs. But Thakur again provided the turning point, now with the ball, dismissing Marcus Harris with a well-directed short-pitched delivery. The rest of the Australian innings was a great tussle between the experienced Australian batters and the young Indian pace battery. The Aussies stitched together some crucial partnerships to set India a target of 328, with Steve Smith top scoring for the Australians with 55. The star for India was

Siraj—emblematic of India's new-found depth in fast bowling resources. Siraj ended up with a well-deserved 5-wicket haul, and Thakur picked up 4.

The target for India was 328, 92 more than the highest successful chase ever at the Gabba, against a bowling line-up comprising four of Australia's all-time greats. The Indian fans would probably have been happy even if the side held on for a draw on the final day. After all, there was a lot to be proud about the way they had fought back in this series, after the disaster at Adelaide. But moral victories could wait. New India dared to dream.

Australia drew first blood on Day 5. Rohit Sharma caught Paine-bowled Cummins. 18/1. And now, the battle-hardened Pujara joined the flamboyant Gill. Gill gave the Australian crowds a taste of his phenomenal talent—driving, cutting, hooking and pulling with elan. The phlegmatic Pujara, on the other end, fought on. Like a sponge, he absorbed blows on various parts of his body. Gill was stroking his way to what could have been a remarkable first century, but the wily Lyon had other plans. On 91, he edged to first slip. India were at 132/2. Gill's flamboyance had given India a glimmer of hope for victory, but surely India was aiming for a draw.

The captain, Rahane, had other ideas. He came in and played a swashbuckling cameo of 24 off just 22 balls—clearly signalling India's intentions. His next move was an emphatic statement of India's motive. At No. 5 came Pant. India were at 167/3. Pant showed maturity beyond his years in mixing caution with aggression. Pujara, at the other end, kept on taking the hardest blows from the Australian quicks, getting hit on the back of the helmet twice and being wrapped on the knuckles. Undeterred, he battled on to record his half century in 196 balls—his slowest in Test cricket.

The partnership guided India to 228/3 in 80 overs. Hundred runs were needed to win off 20 overs. It was now time for another major obstacle, the second new ball, in the hands of the world's No. 1 Test bowler—Pat Cummins. He delivered, ending Pujara's long vigil at 56. It was all up to Pant now. As Cummins increased his ferocity with the ball, so did Pant, unfurling his repertoire of spectacular strokeplay. A boundary was coming almost every over now. Cummins struck again, dismissing Agarwal. Sundar joined Pant at the crease, with 63 runs standing behind India and the most unbelievable of victories.

The first few overs of the partnership saw steady progress, but the required run rate was climbing. As Cummins bustled in for the 93rd over of India's innings, India needed 50 off 48 balls. It was Sundar once again who gave India the momentum with a spectacular hooked 6 off the fifth ball of Cummins's over. He flashed the next ball hard outside off stump, all the way to the boundary. There was no looking back now.

Pant played two spectacular shots off Lyon in the next over, one of them an audacious scoop over his shoulder. By the end of the 94th over, India needed 24 runs from 6 overs.

With some more audacious strokes, the two youngsters guided India to within 10 runs of the target, when Sundar was dismissed trying to reverse sweep Lyon. This did nothing to upset Pant's rhythm, as he pulled a Hazlewood short delivery for 4 runs in the next over. In a late twist, the next batter, Thakur, was dismissed with 3 runs to go. But it was Pant on strike now. For the final delivery of the 97th over, Hazlewood bowled a full delivery outside off stump, and with a mighty heave, Pant drove it to the long off boundary.

The series was won! 2-1 to India! Fortress Gabba was breached! Team India was now a force to reckon with at home and abroad.

SCORECARD

Australia: 369 all out (Labuschagne-108, Paine-50; Natarajan-3/78, Sundar-3/89) and 294 all out (Steve Smith-55, Warner-48; Siraj-5/73, Thakur-4/61)

India: 336 all out (Thakur-67, Sundar-62; Hazlewood-5/57, Starc-2/88) and 329/7 (Gill-91, Pant-89*; Cummins-4/55, Lyon-2/85)

Result: India beat Australia by 3 wickets and won the series 2-1

50
ONLY THE BEGINNING

On 13 February 2023, the day of the first WPL auction, a group of women sitting in South Africa had their eyes glued to the television. Mandhana became the first name to go under the hammer. As the bids kept flowing in, the cheers among this group of women, who happened to be the Indian women's team, then in South Africa, became louder. The smiles kept getting wider not only on Mandhana's face but all her teammates, as they realized this was a transformational moment. For a price of ₹3.4 crore, Mandhana would play for the RCB.[64] The genuine delight among every single person in that room was one of the most heart-warming pieces of cricket content that we, the authors of this book, have witnessed.

Sixteen years after the IPL had transformed the lives of so many male cricketers, it was time for women to have their moment in the sun. Indian women cricketers could now not only transform their lives but also the lives of their families through their cricketing excellence. The 20-year-old Richa Ghosh, who went to RCB for ₹1.9 crore[65], gushed about how she wanted to make her family happy and self-sufficient. Many

---

[64]Kishore, Shashank, 'Mandhana Gets the Biggest Bid at WPL Auction, Goes to RCB for INR 3.4 Crore', *ESPNcricinfo*, 13 February 2023, https://es.pn/3K7uqMT. Accessed on 4 April 2023.
[65]Ibid.

more women cricketers around the country could now dare to dream.

The revolution that began with Shantha Rangaswamy and Diana Edulji, and grew with Jhulan Goswami and Mithali Raj, had now attained a stage of maturity. The WPL became the stage for this brilliant generation of Indian cricketers—Smriti Mandhana, Harmanpreet Kaur, Shafali Verma, Jemimah Rodrigues, Richa Ghosh, Renuka Singh Thakur and many who had not even made it to the national side yet—to prove that a flourishing, stable career and stardom in cricket in India is no longer only reserved for male cricketers.

Let the Games Begin

After the dust settled following the life-changing auction for many players, it was time for the tournament to begin. A glittering opening ceremony was followed by the unveiling of the trophy by the five franchise captains: Beth Mooney (Gujarat Giants), Alyssa Healy (UP Warriorz), Meg Lanning (Delhi Capitals), Smriti Mandhana (RCB) and Harmanpreet Kaur (Mumbai Indians). The first edition of the WPL was played in two stadiums: the famed Brabourne Stadium and the D.Y. Patil Stadium between 4 March and 26 March. The words of the WPL anthem '*Ye to bas shuruaat hai* (This is only the beginning)' thundered and reverberated across the D.Y. Patil Stadium, leaving the excited fans stunned and awestruck.[66]

---

[66]"Ye Toh Bas Shuruat Hai:" Official WPL 2023 Anthem Leaves Fans in Awe', *News18*, 2 March 2023, https://bit.ly/3GfuTLJ. Accessed on 4 April 2023.

Mumbai Indians vs Gujarat Giants, Women's Premier League Match 1, D.Y. Patil Stadium, Navi Mumbai, 4 March 2023

Gujarat Giants and Mumbai Indians had the honour of being the first teams in history to play a WPL match. Packed stands greeted the two sets of players. Some of India's best players played that match: Harmanpreet and Pooja Vastrakar. Along with them were the superstars of the world game: Beth Mooney, Ashleigh Gardner and Natalie Sciver-Brunt.

Gujarat Giants won the toss and elected to bat first. The Mumbai opening partnership of Yastika Bhatia and the star West Indian all-rounder Hayley Matthews came out to a rapturous applause.

Bhatia faced the first delivery of the WPL from Gardner. However, it was Bhatia's partner Matthews who delivered the first big cheer of the encounter with a fierce pulled six of the bowling of Mansi Joshi. Bhatia was soon dismissed by Tanuja Kanwar, but that did not slow down Matthews. She displayed a sparkling array of strokes, the most glorious of which was a pick up shot on the onside off the bowling of Annabel Sutherland for 6. Sciver-Brunt, the reigning Rachael Heyhoe Flint Trophy winner (given to the women cricketer of the year), also put her stamp on the tournament with five boundaries. With the score on 69, Georgia Wareham dismissed Sciver-Brunt. This heralded the arrival of Mumbai Indians and the Indian national captain Harmanpreet to the crease. She had established a reputation of being a big match player with her stellar performance in the 2017 World Cup. It was only fitting then that she took the centre stage in this historic occasion.

After Matthews departed for an entertaining 47, Harmanpreet took control. If Matthews was all power,

Harmanpreet was elegance personified. She found gaps in the field with surgical precision, with some classical cover drives and her trademark sweep shot. The Gujarat Giants spinners were victim to some fierce sweeps and slog sweeps from her. She reached the first half century of the WPL in just 22 balls. She was eventually dismissed by Sneh Rana for a memorable 65 off 30 deliveries. Pooja Vastrakar and Amelia Kerr continued the momentum. Kerr displayed remarkable skill and placement, while Vastrakar struck some powerful blows. Issy Wong heaved the last delivery of the innings over deep mid-wicket for 6. Mumbai Indians finished with 207/5 in their 20 overs.

Disaster struck for the Gujarat Giants in the run chase, as captain Mooney suffered a calf injury, in the very first over, which ruled her out not just of the match but also the tournament. Harleen Deol was dismissed soon, top edging a delivery by Sciver-Brunt, caught at the boundary by Wong. Sciver-Brunt and Wong made further inroads into the Gujarat Giants top-order. Wong got the crucial wicket of Gardner who edged a short of a length delivery to Matthews at slip. In 2.3 overs, Gujarat Giants were left tottering at 5/3.

One of the key goals of the WPL was to give uncapped Indian talent a chance to shine at the global stage. In the very first encounter, it was the unheralded left-arm spinner, Saika Ishaque from West Bengal who stood tall. Bowling with guile, remarkable accuracy and clever changes of pace, Ishaque broke the Gujarat Giants middle-order, taking the wickets of Australian internationals Sutherland and Wareham. At the other end, the all-rounder Kerr displayed her crafty leg spin, dismissing Rana and Kanwar. The final word belonged to Ishaque, who first dismissed Mansi Joshi and then clean bowled Monica Patel, sealing victory for Mumbai Indians.

Mumbai Indians won the inaugural WPL match by 143 runs, with Gujarat Giants all out with 64.

Dawn of a New Era

As a contest, the inaugural WPL match was rather one-sided. However, this match went far beyond the numbers—it was the start of something revolutionary, something that will hopefully help transform India into leaders in women's cricket. One could argue that the Women's Premier League should have been started years ago, but let us rejoice that it is finally here, at a time when India have just won the U19 Women's T20 World Cup.

A new chapter in cricket was written on 4 March 2023. Fittingly, the talismanic Indian captain Harmanpreet Kaur emerged as the lead character. Keep watching. After all, this is only the beginning.

SCORECARD

Mumbai Indians: 207/5 in 20 overs (Harmanpreet-65, Matthews-47; Rana-2/43, Kanwar-1/12)

Gujarat Giants: 64 all out in 15.1 overs (Hemalatha-29, Patel-10; Ishaque-4/11, Sciver-Brunt-2/5)

Result: Mumbai Indians beat Gujarat Giants by 143 runs

AFTERWORD

We end our journey by indulging in perhaps the favourite pastime of all cricket lovers—creating Dream XIs. We would like to emphasize that this is a purely personal selection and is intended to spark debate. Feel free to write to us with your versions of dream teams to represent India, in case all our players had the gift of not ageing or did not have to face Asgard!

During this exercise, we felt that the purpose of this book might be defeated if we gave you just an overall all-time XI for each of the formats. Our endeavour has been to give you a glimpse of some of Indian cricket's most impactful moments and chronicle its progress throughout different eras. Hence, we have decided to put together five dream XIs for India in Test cricket (four featuring players from different eras and one combining all eras), three dream XIs in ODI cricket (two spread across different eras and one overall), an all-time Indian T20 XI and an all-time Indian women's XI.

For crafting the Test XIs, we took into consideration certain inflexion points in India's cricket history coinciding with the ascension to captaincy of three iconic cricketers: Mansoor Ali Khan Pataudi, Kapil Dev and Sourav Ganguly. Hence, our first dream XI features cricketers from 1932–62 (till Pataudi became captain); second one takes into consideration the years 1962–83 (from Pataudi's ascension till Kapil being given the captaincy); the third one takes into account 1983–2000 (till just before Ganguly was given the post of Indian captain);

and the fourth, of course, features performances from 2000–present. For ODI cricket, the division is far simpler. Our first XI takes into account performances from 1974–2000 (just before Ganguly became the captain) and the second XI features cricketers who played from 2000 till the present day.

So, here's to the joy of fantasy XIs.

India Test XI (1932-62)

1. Vijay Merchant
2. Pankaj Roy
3. Vijay Hazare
4. Polly Umrigar
5. C.K. Nayudu (captain)
6. Vijay Manjrekar (wicketkeeper)
7. Vinoo Mankad
8. Dattu Phadkar
9. Subhash Gupte
10. Mohammad Nissar
11. Amar Singh

India Test XI (1962-82)

1. Sunil Gavaskar
2. Farokh Engineer (wicketkeeper)
3. Mohinder Amarnath
4. Gundappa Viswanath
5. Nawab of Pataudi Jr (captain)
6. Dilip Sardesai
7. Kapil Dev
8. Karsan Ghavri
9. Erapalli Prasanna

10. Bishan Singh Bedi
11. B.S. Chandrasekhar

India Test XI (1982-2000)

1. Sunil Gavaskar
2. Navjot Singh Sidhu
3. Dilip Vengsarkar
4. Sachin Tendulkar
5. Mohammad Azharuddin
6. Ravi Shastri
7. Kapil Dev (captain)
8. Nayan Mongia (wicketkeeper)
9. Anil Kumble
10. Javagal Srinath
11. Venkatesh Prasad

India Test XI (2000-present)

1. Virender Sehwag
2. Gautam Gambhir
3. Rahul Dravid
4. Sachin Tendulkar
5. V.V.S. Laxman
6. M.S. Dhoni (captain and wicketkeeper)
7. Ravindra Jadeja
8. Ravichandran Ashwin
9. Anil Kumble
10. Zaheer Khan
11. Mohammad Shami

India Test XI (1932-present)

1. Sunil Gavaskar
2. Virender Sehwag
3. Rahul Dravid
4. Sachin Tendulkar
5. V.V.S. Laxman
6. Kapil Dev
7. M.S. Dhoni (captain and wicketkeeper)
8. Ravindra Jadeja
9. Ravichandran Ashwin
10. Zaheer Khan
11. Anil Kumble

India One Day International XI (1974-2000)

1. Sachin Tendulkar
2. Sourav Ganguly
3. Navjot Singh Sidhu
4. Mohammad Azharuddin
5. Ajay Jadeja
6. Ravi Shastri
7. Kapil Dev (captain)
8. Nayan Mongia (wicketkeeper)
9. Anil Kumble
10. Javagal Srinath
11. Venkatesh Prasad

India ODI XI (2000-present)

1. Sachin Tendulkar
2. Rohit Sharma

3. Sourav Ganguly
4. Virat Kohli
5. Rahul Dravid
6. Yuvraj Singh
7. M.S. Dhoni (captain and wicketkeeper)
8. Anil Kumble
9. Harbhajan Singh
10. Zaheer Khan
11. Jasprit Bumrah

India ODI XI (1974-present)

1. Sachin Tendulkar
2. Rohit Sharma
3. Sourav Ganguly
4. Virat Kohli
5. Yuvraj Singh
6. M.S. Dhoni (captain and wicketkeeper)
7. Kapil Dev
8. Anil Kumble
9. Harbhajan Singh
10. Zaheer Khan
11. Jasprit Bumrah

For the T20 XI, both IPL and international matches have been taken into account.

India T20 XI (2006-present)

1. Rohit Sharma
2. Virat Kohli
3. Suresh Raina

4. Suryakumar Yadav
5. Yuvraj Singh
6. M.S. Dhoni (captain and wicketkeeper)
7. Hardik Pandya
8. Bhuvneshwar Kumar
9. Harbhajan Singh
10. Yuzvendra Chahal
11. Jasprit Bumrah

For the Women's XI, we have considered all formats together since the number of Tests played by the Indian women's team in recent times have been minimal.

1. Smriti Mandhana
2. Sandhya Agarwal
3. Anjum Chopra
4. Mithali Raj (captain)
5. Harmanpreet Kaur
6. Anju Jain (wicketkeeper)
7. Shantha Rangaswamy
8. Shikha Pandey
9. Jhulan Goswami
10. Diana Edulji
11. Neetu David

So, here it is. Our selection of the 50 matches that defined Indian cricket and our selection of dream teams across eras, across formats. Hope you had as much fun reading the book as we had putting it together.

Now, let the debate begin!

Mail us at 50greatmatches@gmail.com, or tweet to us at @50greatmatches—we are here all day.

ACKNOWLEDGEMENTS

First and foremost, to Moti Nandi, for giving me sports.

To Baba and Ma, because eventually, one needs to be taught how to watch cricket.

To Apcar Garden, Asansol, because Asansol is love. And to Bangalore, for the coffee.

To Test matches at the Chinnaswamy, and Ranji games at the Gangotri Glades (i.e., the Srikantadatta Narasimharaja Raja Wadiyar) Grounds.

To Titash; this is a good team, perhaps even better than the one at quizzes.

To Tinka, because blood.

To R.K. Sarkar, my father-in-law, dearly departed, for telling us lovely stories.

To Bhumika Anand and Rheea Rodrigues Mukherjee, for the gift of writing. And the Yaks and Bodhi.

To Ramachandra Guha, Sujit Mukherjee and Vasant Raiji—success for us would be if a few who have read this would graduate to your books.

To Shehan Karunatilaka, because Pradeep Mathew exists.

To Arun Ramkumar who illustrated this book, his humour is visible.

To Roshni Mohapatra, in memory.

To *ESPNcricinfo*, a general thank you from all cricket fans. Shine on.

To Yamini, Sandhya and Sakschi, our editors at Rupa Publications, for being immensely patient with us amateurs.

To Suhas Cadambi, Blossom Book Stores and beer. That was an evening well spent.

To the sports quizzers—we are the splash of colour in between all the beige.

To Rashee, for instinctively knowing which matches require the big flatscreen TV (very few), and for which ones (most) the tiny one in the study would do just fine.

And to Diego. This is, of course, for you.

Soumyadipta (Shom)

࿋

To Baba and Ma, for the gifts of reading and creativity.

To Kaku and Kakima, for bringing fun and joy to our family even in the most tense moments.

To Tukush, Choto and Chhoton, for being the greatest brothers in the world.

To Debduti, my best friend for her constant care, support and encouragement.

To Berty, my first co-author.

To Kunal, for challenging me to be better at every moment.

To Aniket, Deepanjan and Prithwish, for the hours of discussion on sports.

To Sumantra, Nikhil, Sachin and all my teammates in sports quizzes over the years.

To Shom da, here's to more debates and more books on sports!

And to Thamma, the rock of my life, wherever you are, hope you are reading this!

Titash

www.ingramcontent.com/pod-product-compliance
Lightning Source LLC
Chambersburg PA
CBHW031422150426
43191CB00006B/357